Vampyre Hypothesis

Elizabeth Ramsey, MD
Series Book 1

Tammy Battaglia

This book is dedicated to my family and friends
who believed I could write it
and kept asking about it until I did.

CONTENTS

Chapter 1

LUCIANO

Pain. Searing and unrelenting. It was no longer a sensation; it was the sum of his existence, a red sea of flame that engulfed him and licked at his flesh. Perhaps after three hundred years, death would finally find him. Luciano welcomed it, prayed for it. Maybe it *had* found him already and this was the afterlife, the hell he deserved.

He was no longer aware of the motion of his limbs. His arms and legs continued on, slowly dragging him forward, leaving bits of burning flesh in his wake as the grass and rock clawed at what remained of his charred body. Then his hell became dim, a speckled haze of gray, before the blackness mercifully took him away.

CHAPTER 2

BETH

"ANYBODY HOME?" BETH SMILED at Aaron's greeting while she buzzed him into the morgue. He tried to be humorous. One of her all-time favorites was "Landshark!" bringing back memories of old *Saturday Night Live* episodes with Steve Martin and Dan Aykroyd. Those were, in her opinion, the best years.

Aaron pushed the gurney through the doors, a broad grin on his face. "Hi, Doc!" he said. He was nice-looking but not what one would call terribly handsome. His sandy-blond hair was always a bit shaggy, sometimes hanging nearly into his eyes. His jaw was overly square, the perfect model for a comic book thug, and it was usually covered with a bit of unshaven scruff. To Beth, Aaron's most pleasing feature was his eyes. No matter what he was saying, his pale blue, near-gray eyes always seemed to be smiling and would fill with light as he grinned. They were like clear glass, allowing Beth to see whatever crossed his mind. Smile lines already had begun to form at their corners, drawing even more attention to them.

And his eyes shone tonight as he told her, "I've got a crispy one for you! Found him at the scene of a fire close to the state line on 151st Street. He was lying in the yard next to the burnt house. Can't tell how he got free of the building, but I guess it didn't make much of a difference."

Aaron, an EMT, delivered the lion's share of the bodies she received these days. Unlike most of the EMTs she had worked with on night shift, Aaron was like her. He preferred the night shift and felt at his best in the wee hours of the morning.

"If you're ready for him, I'll help you get him on the table," he offered.

"Aaron, you're the best," Beth said, giving him a heartfelt thank-you smile.

Aaron was probably the closest thing Beth had to a good friend these days. He was young, twenty-five, but the seven or so years between them made little difference. He saw the world as she did, very black and white. Dealing with death and bodies never shook him, no matter how horrifying the cause of death. They both agreed corpses were just the shells that the souls left behind. Without the soul and mind to control the body, it was just tissue, left behind for Beth to examine, to unravel the mystery that caused the soul to leave the body.

It made her job easier to think of it that way.

The coroner and one of the officers from the scene weren't far behind and arrived just as Aaron and Beth finished settling Mr. Crisp on the autopsy table.

Dr. Zachariah Mishler was the coroner for Johnson County, Kansas. He looked about sixty, but Beth guessed he was younger. He was stout with a round face that was always a little flushed like he'd been running, which fit because he always seemed to be in a hurry to get on his way.

"We found this body about thirty feet from the fire," Dr. Mishler said. "The fire was in an old house that had been built on the property at least a hundred years ago. It was well-kept, though, and apparently owned by someone from out of town, but none of the neighbors have ever actually seen anyone live there. The police will try to track down the owner and see if they might know the victim."

The officer with Dr. Mishler was young, twenty-five at the most, and clean-shaven. Beth could tell he was trying to share information without breathing in through his nose. He didn't introduce himself, but the silver pin on his vest read "BUTLER."

"We arrived on the scene after a call from the neighbors several blocks over saying they smelled smoke. It had to have started around dark. From the closest houses you still couldn't see the fire because of the heavy trees, so it had been well on its way before the fire department got there," Butler said. "They managed to knock down the flames in about an hour and found what was left of this guy while they fought it."

Mishler chimed in, "He was lying face down on his stomach with one arm overhead and one leg bent at the knee, almost as if he had crawled free of the burning building. I could tell he was dead just by looking at him, but I checked for a pulse and breathing and found nothing. His liver temp was only eighty-nine degrees, though, which was weird. It's seventy tonight. Given the human body's normal temp of ninety-eight point six, and assuming roughly a drop of one and a half degrees per hour, give or take following death, the man would have to have been dead more than six hours. The fire wasn't out that long and its heat would have further slowed the cooling of the body. I checked it twice inside the liver in two different areas, though."

It *was* curious. Perhaps the corpse had been frozen in a block of ice before being tossed into the fire and burned to destroy the evidence. A mob hit, yes... that would add a little excitement to the usual mundane mix of traffic fatalities and natural-but-unobserved deaths.

Beth's imagination began to run wild envisioning Kansas City's own little version of the mob. *Why not*, she thought to herself. *It could happen.*

The group left her with the body about 2:45 a.m. The smell of burnt hair and flesh filled the morgue. It was a pungent and completely unique odor. For those who have smelled it, it is unforgettable. It's more than the smell of charred flesh, like meat at a barbecue left on the grill a little too long. There was something about human flesh burning that created a smell like no other. But while burnt flesh was awful, there were no smells on Earth worse than decaying flesh in water. "Floaters," as they were called behind closed doors. The stench was indescribable, turning the stomachs of those well-seasoned in dealing with other forms of decomposition.

Compared to water decomposition, skunk spray smelled like roses.

Beth organized her tools on the mayo stand, flipped on the overhead mic and performed an external exam.

"The victim is six feet one inch in height, one hundred seventy-two pounds. The corpse's skin is charred a deep brown-black over at least ninety percent of the body, see body surface area chart for reference." The skin was drawn and cracked like old leather. All of the hair had been singed away. "The corpse appears Caucasian from the small areas of remaining skin. Hair is absent, so hair color cannot be ascertained."

Certainly, the distortion of the skin made any facial features impossible to see. The jaw was tightly closed, as were the eyes. She would need to examine the mouth, throat and lungs. If she could find evidence that he had inhaled smoke from the fire, at least she would know he had been alive and breathing when it had occurred.

The fingertips were nearly burned to the bone. It looked like dental records might be the only option for identification. "Extensive burns to the fingertips make fingerprinting impossible. Dental films will be submitted for possible use in identification.

"A small scrap of what appears to be fabric, possibly tan cotton, is present, clinging to the top of one thigh." Beth gathered this into a small plastic bag. His leg must have been bent, or perhaps he was lying on this area when the fire engulfed him. It had somehow been protected.

"Portions of the sole of the shoe have melted to the bottom of the left foot with a small portion of the upper adhered to the heel, probably leather. There is a silver band on the third finger of his left hand which is kept for evidence." Perhaps it was a wedding ring, but there was no engraving on it to help with the mystery of his identity.

Beth removed it and placed it in a valuable's envelope.

That was pretty much it. No clues as to whom he might have been or to the kind of life he led. Mr. Crisp would officially remain John Doe 842 for a little while longer.

Beth took X-rays of the body, including the teeth, to look for any possible foreign material like bullets or other metal objects. Then she rolled the X-ray machine back to the corner of the autopsy suite while waiting for the films to develop.

The films from the chest and abdomen dropped first. Beth placed them on the light box and studied them.

Nothing. *Well, if he'd been shot prior to the fire, the bullet didn't stay within the body.*

She hoped the internal tissues would be intact enough to see a bullet track if one existed. That's when she decided to make the first incision.

Returning to the autopsy table, Beth gathered the scalpel into her hand, index finger on the back of the blade, and began making the typical Roux-en-Y incision as she always did, beginning at the right shoulder and extending down across the chest to mid-sternum.

That's when she thought she saw it. Beth thought... well, she thought she saw him bleed.

Chapter 3

BETH

BETH STOOD, MOTIONLESS, BLADE poised just above the incision, staring.

As bodies sit, the blood pools in the most dependent or lowest-lying areas. Blood could have pooled in the front of the body, as he was found face down, but it would at best "ooze" from the wound she had made, if it leaked from the burnt tissue at all. But she could have sworn the blood pulsed from the capillaries like she had made the incision through the skin of a live patient. But this corpse was not alive; he was most certainly dead.

Beth took a deep breath and decided she needed to pull herself together. "Ugh! Damned sleep deprivation!" she said, almost shouting.

What was she thinking taking on the extra shifts? *Day* shifts, no less. Now she was seeing things.

"Beth, take a break," she said aloud.

Fantastic, now she was even talking to herself. Not that anyone would have noticed. She had been alone in the morgue since just after the body was delivered. Even if the coroner or Aaron had overheard, it would merely be dismissed as an expected eccentricity of her profession. She was a pathologist after all. Most people who met her expected mismatched plaids, pocket protectors and tape on broken glasses, or maybe a hunchback like Igor in *Young Frankenstein*.

Mel Brooks, Marty Feldman and Gene Wilder together, now *that* was a classic.

The expected quirks and lack of social skills many of *her kind* exhibited was a real help to her at times. She had allowed the misconceptions to work in her favor when extracting herself from some of her less well-thought-out adventures. Much like the busty blond who lets a few crocodile tears fall from her cheeks and undoes the next button on her blouse before asking the officer for a warning instead of a traffic ticket. What was wrong with using what you had?

She tossed the scalpel back onto the mayo stand, shaking her head.

Well, quirky or not, she was certain she must be imagining things because otherwise this corpse had, well... *bled*. That was, of course, utterly impossible. No one could have survived the severity of these burns. Not to mention Dr. Mishler's recorded liver temperature of eighty-nine degrees, also incompatible with life.

Beth pulled off her gloves, thinking that perhaps a Diet Coke and a few bites of chocolate would give her enough of a caffeine and sugar rush to straighten out her thoughts and carry her through the rest of her shift. She always made sure to have plenty of plain M&M's and change for the Coke machine in her bag before leaving for work each day.

Beth glanced around the room as she headed for her desk. She liked the sterility of the morgue with its stainless steel countertops, sinks and cement floors. The autopsy tables matched with their shiny silver tops and sides. There were three in this room lined up in parallel lengthwise. At the end of her current patient's table was a glass-front cabinet containing knives of all sizes, scissors and forceps; any implement they might need to perform the autopsies. The Stryker saw that they used to cut through the ribs and skull to expose the organs beneath had already been pulled from the cabinet and placed on the mayo stand beside the body, cord dangling to floor.

Beth didn't drink coffee, never had. The scent and taste had never appealed to her. So she chose to get her caffeine in other, more enjoyable ways. And chocolate, producing a natural endorphin rush, was always pleasing, better than sex they said... but then, how would she know? It wasn't like she had a lot of social interaction, given the current state of things. Even if she knew *how* to get a date, she wasn't likely to find one with a lot of spunk here in the morgue. And, with all the extra hours she was putting in, she wasn't going out anytime soon, either.

Who was she kidding? Even with just her night shifts, she had never bothered to seek out companionship. The truth was, most of the time, Beth was perfectly happy alone, or at least mostly happy. Sharing her life meant sharing her space, and that was something she wasn't ready for.

Beth passed by the row of light boxes they used for viewing X-rays on her way to the double doors leading out of the autopsy suite. One had been left on, spilling a pale white pool of light onto the gray cement floor. Perhaps others would find it lonely, stark or somber, but to Beth it was a familiar comfort, softly lighting her way.

She pushed open the swinging double doors and crossed the open office area to her desk.

She sat down at her desk, identical to the four others in the space, all arranged with the fronts facing the middle of the room and the chairs to the wall. While the desks were identical, the items on the surfaces were not. Many were covered in stacks of haphazardly piled papers, reference books, coffee mugs and Styrofoam cups surrounding, and sometimes partially obscuring, their desktop monitors.

In contrast, Beth's desk contained a stackable file sorter on the lefthand side with new cases on the top, ones ready to be typed and then edited underneath and then those waiting for trial on the bottom. Front and center was a desk set with numerous small black plastic boxes for her supplies. All of the pens and pencils were in place, points down, and the paperclips sorted in smaller bins by size. On the right sat a flat-screen monitor which glowed a pale blue from the screensaver; a curving white line that wiggled and twisted across the screen. The rest of the area was clear with plenty of room to work. Beth's backpack sat beneath the desk, leaning against the CPU as always. She dug out M&M's from it and gathered change for the Coke machine.

Beth hated that the cafeteria was closed at night. Diet Coke from the fountain tasted so much better than cans or bottles.

She got up and walked slowly out the second set of double doors that marked the entrance to the morgue waiting area then through the locked perimeter doors to the hallway. The basement of the hospital was very still during the night shift. Though her rare visitors found it eerily quiet, for Beth, it was peaceful.

Occasionally, a member of the housekeeping staff would walk by pushing their cleaning cart and disturbing the near silence, wheels squeaking to announce their arrival before she could see them coming down the long hall.

The Coke machine was across from the stairs next to the maintenance room. As Beth rounded the corner, there was Dave, the night shift maintenance man, rummaging through the maintenance closet, a large plumbing wrench in one hand.

"Hello, Dave. How are you?"

"Great, Doc. Did you see the pre-season game scores last night?" he asked.

"No, I've been working these crazy double shifts and had to miss it. I haven't seen the scores yet. Did we win?"

"Yep, two-zero. The Royals are looking good this year. You missed a good one."

"Tonight's my last double and then I'm off on vacation. Hopefully I'll catch the next one."

Both paused, waiting; Beth shifted her weight to the opposite foot and smiled.

"Supposed to be nice tomorrow, I hear, but rainy next week. We could use it, I suppose," Dave offered.

"Yes, it has been dry. I'm sure the farmers would be thankful for it."

Silence again as Beth turned away to face the Coke machine. This was about all either of them had to add. After the recent sports scores and the weather, both were pretty much out of material. While she was willing to engage, Beth really didn't know what else to talk about. She had never been adept at conversation and guessed Dave wasn't either.

He returned to rummaging in the maintenance closet.

The sound of the aluminum can hitting the bottom of the machine echoed through the otherwise empty halls. Beth retrieved it, thankful the machine had been filled recently so she didn't have to make the trip upstairs to find another, and tapped the lid before opening it. The cold acidic taste was soothing, familiar, and she listened to the fizz as the bubbles from the carbonation broke and hissed, music to her ears with the promise of caffeine she so badly needed tonight.

"Have a great night, Dave," she said, turning back toward the morgue.

"You too, Doc."

Beth fumbled for the ID that hung from her neck as she reached the locked door to the morgue. The picture was humorous. She smirked as she saw her shoulder-length, dark brown hair, poker straight and far duller than she would have liked, hanging around her heart-shaped face. Her chin seemed too pointed, eyes too closely set. The fact that she had worn no makeup that day didn't help either. Beth looked very pale, almost ghostly, but her skin was clear. She remembered trying to smile pleasantly for the picture but it had ended up looking goofy and too wide. At least she hadn't closed her eyes. Everything about the image seemed awkward, which was exactly how she felt in front of a camera.

Beth waited for the green light after scanning her ID badge, then pushed the door open and returned to her comfortably tidy desk.

She ate her M&M's, choosing the brown ones first. She almost always ate them in order... brown, then orange, red, blue and then last, of course, green—just in case the urban myth about the green ones being an aphrodisiac were true.

Beth sighed. Wishful thinking.

As she sat and munched, her mind drifted back to the corpse.

Now, thinking back over those moments, Beth was certain it had just been her overworked eyes and sleep-deprived brain that had imagined the whole thing. Beth had been working double shifts about four days a week for the past three months, ever since Henry Adams, one of the day shift pathologists, had died suddenly. It was a freak accident, really. He'd been driving along Highway 32 about seven miles from the hospital when he had apparently lost control of his truck and struck a tree dead-on. The officers said he had to have been driving at least eighty-five miles per hour at the time. Odd for Henry; he was usually very careful.

Regardless, the cause of death was clear. The impact had collapsed the dash and steering wheel into his chest with so much force that he was completely crushed, every bone broken, lungs and heart burst from the impact. His spleen and liver were lacerated so badly the thin capsular membranes on the outside of the organs were impossible to piece together.

It was tough seeing him that way.

The accident had taken place just after his shift, as he was headed home for the evening. Lawrence Fluck on second shift had performed the autopsy. Beth knew it had been tough on him too; they all knew Henry.

Beth washed down the last orange M&M with another swig of Diet Coke and glanced up at the row of photographs of the partners on the back wall, her eyes settling on Henry. Heartland Forensic Specialists, which operated in rented basement space in Midwest University Hospital, was not a large enough group for all the pathologists not to know one another reasonably well.

After Henry's death, day shift had been woefully shorthanded. Beth had volunteered to cover several of his shifts until the group could find a replacement. She didn't need the money or the extra hours, but it seemed like the right thing to do. Of all of the pathologists, Beth was the only one with no family, not even a spouse or significant other... okay, not even a dog. So she had loaded up on the double shifts. Happily, however, this was the end.

Beth tossed the last of the green M&M's into her mouth, crumpling the wrapper in her hand.

The group had just signed their newest addition, Peter James. No one knew much about him, other than that he had trained at Creighton; certainly not a big-name program, but he had done a residency at LA County in California. He should have more than enough experience for their little operation. Lucky for Beth, the search and hire had taken only six weeks. According to the CEO, during their time of need, Peter had just "dropped out of the sky." Beth had met him briefly between shifts last week. One of her partners had introduced them.

"Beth, I would like you to meet Doctor Peter James."

Beth had offered her hand. He'd seemed eager, maybe a little too eager, shaking her hand vigorously. His green eyes were intense, no... *focused*, seeming to bore into her as though he were studying her for a test he would have to take later. This close she could see his light brown hair was thinning just slightly, making him look a little older than his thirty-three years.

"Pleased to meet you," Beth said. "We could certainly use the help."

His hand was slender but firm in hers. Beth, at five-foot-five and in tennis shoes, couldn't have been more than a couple of inches shorter than he was.

"Doctor Ramsey, I've heard a lot about you," Doctor James said. "It's a pleasure to finally put a face with a name. I'm excited to get started." His words were friendly, but his body looked tense, his muscles seeming to twitch with each movement under his shirt. His mouth was tightly drawn back from his perfectly straight white teeth in a rigid smile. Had his expression not looked so forced, he might have been attractive.

"Are there any questions I can answer for you?" Beth asked.

"You work the night shift, correct?"

Beth nodded.

"As I will be working day shift, is there anything I need to know about handing off or picking up cases when our shifts overlap?" They talked briefly about workload and the expectations that went with his day shift position, and then he was off to meet the evening crew.

Beth had been left feeling nervous and fidgety herself. It was as if the energy from this man had somehow rubbed off. Well, she would let the rest of his day shift coworkers worry about that.

Today was Tuesday, April first, Peter's first day on the job. She would leave for home at 6 a.m. to begin a two-week vacation and try to get back on schedule. The double shifts had severely disrupted Beth's sleeping cycle, and she hoped that meant her blissful days of effortless sleep would return quickly.

It was a good thing the extra hours were at an end, because she was apparently on the verge of a psychotic break. She was pretty sure hallucinations of bleeding corpses wouldn't look good on her performance evaluation.

She tossed the empty M&M's wrapper into the trash can, took another gulp of Diet Coke and headed for the autopsy suite.

CHAPTER 4

BETH

MR. CRISP, OF COURSE, hadn't moved.

Beth pulled on her gloves and tied the plastic apron around her waist.

"Shall we continue?" she said to Mr. Crisp, gathering the scalpel into her hand for the second time. Beth leaned over his chest, preparing to extend the original incision. The line from her first attempt was visible but hardly appeared deep enough to have bled as she'd imagined earlier. In fact, the marks seemed to barely extend into the thick charred skin.

Shaking her head, she began again at the lateral edge of the clavicle, slowly extending the incision toward the base of the sternum.

Beth stopped, staring motionless as blood pulsated in the wound. Disbelief washed over her, then lightheadedness as she watched the bleeding slow and the wound partially close.

That wasn't possible. Corpses didn't bleed and wounds didn't heal before your eyes.

Beth stumbled back from the table, scalpel still raised. She didn't know what she expected. Would he get up and seek revenge for the wounds she had inflicted? Was she dreaming, having dozed off in the office during her break?

Beth bit her lip, hard. She winced at the pain and tasted the small drop of blood with her tongue. She was awake. She might be insane, but she was awake.

She slowly lowered her hand and returned the scalpel to the mayo stand.

"Okay, get a grip." She had heard secondhand stories about a pathologist starting an autopsy on a living patient. Maybe there was some truth to those. Disregarding the apparent miraculous healing abilities, the possibility that a living patient could somehow have been so severely burned and left for dead while still living was the most logical explanation her mind could construct given the situation.

She took a deep breath and approached the table. Beth felt for the radial artery and carotid pulses in the wrist and neck... nothing. She watched his chest for a full minute in silence, waiting for any movement or sound that could suggest breathing.

Again, nothing.

He had to be dead, but there was absolutely no way she was cutting into this body for the third time without more reassurance.

Beth left the suite and went to the locker room. She fumbled with the lock on her locker, trying to remember the combination, so frazzled she hadn't even bothered to remove her gloves.

She had kept the stethoscope from her clinical days before residency, although she'd never really thought she would need it. But she was a doctor and it seemed appropriate to have it in case the situation ever arose for which she would be called upon to use it.

Well, the situation had arisen.

Beth jerked it from the locker shelf and hurried back to the autopsy suite, not bothering to close the locker door.

Shoving the ear pieces in, she placed the bell of the stethoscope gingerly on the left side of the chest. Then she listened in silence for what had to be two or three minutes.

There was no heartbeat.

He was indeed dead. Breathing a sigh, Beth decided she would have to mention the robust leaking or oozing (being careful to avoid the word *bleeding*) or whatever it was to the day shift and see if they had seen anything like that in a burn victim before. Maybe something the burnt flesh had been exposed to somehow made the tissue more readily adhere to itself, causing the appearance of healing.

There has to be an explanation, she assured herself.

But perhaps she should have another look at things before continuing.

Beth examined the body and remnants of clothing once more, looking for signs of chemical discoloration, trying to pick up on any odor she could have missed. She again looked over the chest and abdominal plain films, but there was nothing. She remembered the dental films and walked to the processor to pick them up.

She placed them on the light box and flipped it on.

Beth stared at the films open-mouthed. Another wave of disbelief passed over her. Was this a trick? Was someone playing games with her? None of this could possibly be happening.

In addition to a full set of teeth, an additional set of elongated, pointed canines were visible above and just medial to the usual set of canines.

Fangs. This corpse had fangs.

Beth decided enough was enough. She donned the lead shield, brought the portable X-ray machine over to the gurney and took another set of dental films. This time, she waited beside the processor, not even looking away, determined to see the process through. Someone had to have switched the films on her; a practical joke... very funny.

Beth jumped as the film fell into the tray. She picked it up gingerly and walked again to the light box. She raised her hands slowly to position the film, waiting for one of her day shift colleagues, or perhaps Aaron, to jump from the shadows of the next room laughing and congratulating themselves on a well-executed prank.

But there was no sound of laughter, only the sound of her quickly drawn breaths, her heart pounding in her ears.

Nothing had changed; the fangs were still there. Not caps, not fancy veneers like some of the overzealous Goth fans, but real fangs.

Beth turned slowly to the corpse.

"What the hell are you?"

He was dead; a very dead corpse that bled and healed and had fangs.

Beth had to see them for herself. She pulled back the leathery remains of his lips and, pressing with her fingertips, felt the extra teeth beneath the gums. She quickly drew back her hands and tried to think...*the ultrasound machine.*

She went to the equipment room and dragged the cart next to the gurney. Squeezing too hard in her nervousness, she squirted a large mound of gel onto his chest. Beth wasn't great at reading ultrasounds but knew enough to find the heart and lungs and perhaps see some of the organs without cutting into him.

She turned the probe, spreading the gel and angling toward the heart.

The heart moved!

Beth jumped backward, bumping into the mayo tray, rattling the instruments and dropping the probe. It banged loudly against the rolling cart, making her jump a second time. She stared, wide-eyed, at Mr. Crisp for a few long moments, then took a couple of slow steadying breaths.

She retrieved the dangling probe, placing it again on Mr. Crisp's chest with less-than-steady hands. To her amazement, the heart moved at a frenzied pace, the rate approaching 220 beats per minute, more than twice that of a normal resting heart rate. It was a regular, even rhythm. But there was still no sign of breathing.

She grabbed a glass flask from the counter and held it against his nose and lips. Nothing, no fogging to suggest shallow breathing. She found a flashlight in the equipment drawer and, with a deep breath, gently retracted his left eyelid and raised the light to his eyes.

The large round pupil in the center of the brown-black iris narrowed in response.

Beth leaped back, spinning away, chills running down her body. *Impossible!*

Closing her eyes tightly, she shook her head as if to clear the image from her own eyes, then took a deep breath. She walked back to the body and repeated the exposure. Again the pupil accommodated in response to light. The right eye had the same results.

She turned off the flashlight and held it to her chest.

Was this a human with mutations? Was it some other kind of humanoid being? A vampire, werewolf or something else? If it was, why was there no record of them? Whatever this thing was, it was alive. Beth didn't know *how* it could still be alive with its charred body and without breathing, but the heart still beat, even if it was silent, and at least some measure of the neurological system was intact. She was not hallucinating or going crazy. This corpse *was* alive.

What the hell was she going to do with him now?

CHAPTER 5

BETH

IT ALL CAME TO Beth with surprising ease from there on: acceptance that this creature was alive followed quickly by an acceptance of what he must be. As far-fetched as it sounded, it was a logical progression of thought. He had a decreased baseline core temperature that would explain the low liver temperature despite having prolonged exposure to the extreme heat from the fire. He appeared dead because he didn't breathe and because his beating heart was silent. He healed at a fast rate and had fangs—fangs so that he could drink blood.

This creature was a vampire.

This in itself didn't seem like such a far reach since she believed there were so many things yet to be discovered in this world. It seemed very egocentric to believe that life would be limited to what humankind knew on this one small planet and that life would be in a human form when found elsewhere. There was much humans understood here but also much they did not. Even with all of the advances in medicine, there were still large parts even of human physiology people didn't understand. The knowledge of the workings of the human brain alone was only the tip of the iceberg. So why should humans close their minds to other undiscovered possibilities here on Earth?

Beth leaned against the counter to steady herself and consider her next steps. If she called the burn unit to suggest admission, they would think she was insane. Beth could show them the ultrasound; she could prove his heart was beating. They would almost certainly explain away the lack of an audible heartbeat as something related to his injuries, some interference from the charred skin perhaps. The lack of breathing would be more difficult, but the fangs would be considered a genetic aberration.

The burn unit doctors would believe him to be a burn victim and would attempt to treat him as such. He would almost certainly be given plasma, but unless his hemoglobin (if he had normal hemoglobin) was low they wouldn't immediately give him blood, which was what Beth supposed he needed. How could she explain giving him blood? If she told them of her assessment, that she believed he was a vampire, they would send her to the psychiatric unit. Beth didn't know any of the surgeons on the burn unit well enough to convince them she should be treated otherwise.

If she carried the scenario to its conclusion, he would die—assuming he *could* die. If not, he would be in this horrible state for how long? Worse still, what if she could convince them it was true, that he was a vampire? He would become an object of interest, poked, prodded and experimented on with little concern for his life, like some new species of rat in a cage.

Beth shuddered. She didn't think she could live with that. Whatever he was, he was a living being. He didn't deserve to be treated that way. Whatever kind of life this creature had deserved more respect than that.

What if she was wrong? What if he was indeed human? What if there was some logical explanation for his apparent genetic mutation? If he were human, there would be no hope of survival. Burns to this degree were uniformly fatal. He would be heavily sedated, his burns dressed and debrided. If the fluid loss and imbalance didn't kill him, overwhelming infection would eventually take him. Admitting Mr. Crisp to the hospital would do him no good.

So, if Mr. Crisp couldn't be cared for here, then where? Beth could trust no one else with this secret. Who on Earth would believe her? She considered asking Aaron for help but decided against it. It could put him in danger, or at the very least put his job at risk, and she didn't want to put him in the position to choose between his livelihood and helping her. And as much as she liked her partners, the truth was they weren't close enough for her to know if she could trust them with this kind of secret. Plus, the choice would most certainly put their medical license at risk, and that was a favor too large to ask of any of them. She was a physician, and though she almost entirely cared for the dead, there was no way she could do nothing and allow a living patient to just die, no matter what he was.

The only answer was... home. She would take Mr. Crisp home and attempt to nurse him back to his usual state of life, or whatever passed for life for his kind.

The decision was made. She was really doing this.

The remainder of her shift was a mad dash to cover her tracks. Beth assigned Mr. Crisp a locker location which, of course, he would never occupy. She pulled the transfer log and marked it to indicate the examination was complete and that the body was released for cremation. She knew there would be hell to pay later to explain why an unidentified body was released so quickly, but she planned to feign exhaustion (which was not far from the truth) and an error of paperwork. Since the bodies were released for cremation over the night shift, she could reasonably hope to forge the log.

Back at her desk, Beth rushed to complete a death certificate indicating the cause of death to be extensive burns and proceeded to dictate the remainder of her bogus autopsy report, leaving out the extended canines, rapid healing and still-beating heart.

She went to the file room, lined with rows of metal slide and block cabinets housing all the slides and paraffin-embedded tissue blocks from past cases going back some twenty years. On the far side of the room were rows of large round plastic containers, called pots, filled with portions of organs from past cases. Beth submitted sections of a few organs from one of her recent cases.

Back in the morgue, she took a superficial biopsy from Mr. Crisp's skin (hoping he was beyond feeling the pain of it) and took photographs of his body to document the extent of the burns. She gathered all of the information into his file. It was a believable report. She would continue her forgery when she received the slides.

Beth paused for a moment, the full realization of what she was doing falling upon her. How many laws had she broken in the span of minutes? Any one of them would be enough to put her medical license in jeopardy. Did she really want to go through with this and submit the report? If this went poorly, it could be the end of her career. And if it went really badly, it could mean the end of her life as a meal for Mr. Crisp. But if she didn't, it almost certainly meant the end of his. She felt an intense need to save him, and her curiosity to discover what he was in a way that wouldn't bring him harm was too strong to deny. Her mind was made up.

The final obstacle for documentation was that of the dental records. Beth had been careful to document the complete lack of intact skin over all distal extremities to explain the lack of fingerprint data. She had submitted blood samples (praying nothing unusual would be found on the tox screen that she would be required to explain away later). DNA analyses were not commonly performed for identification unless a sample was submitted for comparison by a family member. Beth was counting on no family coming forward, leaving whatever abnormal DNA Mr. Crisp might have never to be identified.

The dental X-rays were different. They would certainly be submitted, and she couldn't risk the suspicions those long canines would arouse. The searchable database, though, contained only studies submitted for known missing persons and a few cataloged criminals. There were no clearly defining features on dental films to indicate the sex of a patient with certainty. Age, on the other hand, was at least partially predictable. With Mr. Crisp being so badly burned, his age wasn't clear. Certainly, examination of bony structures could give an age approximation, but after tonight, no body would be available to examine.

Beth supposed her dental films would be as good as any. There would be no reason to suspect she had used films of her own teeth, so there was no reason to think this could cause a problem in the future. If through some turn of events Beth someday needed identification by dental records, well, she didn't have any family to disappoint.

She took the films and placed them in a labeled folder along with the others from the evening. Mr. Crisp's real dental films she placed in her backpack to dispose of safely away from the hospital.

Now, how to manage the transport of Mr. Crisp?

CHAPTER 6

BETH

HER PATHFINDER WOULD HAVE plenty of room in the back to hold Mr. Crisp lying flat. It was the getting him to the car that would be tough.

She knew the covered drive that the mortuary used was monitored with a video camera. There was no chance that was going to work. And she couldn't use the emergency room ambulance bay; they were too likely to be seen and she certainly wasn't prepared for questions. And while there were no cameras on the morgue level apart from the exits, the lobby level was monitored.

Beth couldn't be seen removing a body, but what about helping a patient? It could work!

Beth grabbed a roll of gauze from the supply cabinet and began to gently wrap Mr. Crisp's head with it, then his hands, covering anything that would be exposed beyond normal clothing. She dressed him in scrubs from the locker room and added a hoodie from the hallway coatrack.

She would need a wheelchair to move him. She sprinted from the morgue and then up the stairs, taking two at a time to the lobby level. Pausing at the door, she smoothed her hair and calmed herself with a deep breath. Then she walked quickly toward the main entrance, reminding herself with every step to slow down. Like always, the wheelchairs were neatly parked next to the entrance, lined up and waiting for the next day's outpatients.

As Beth released the brakes on the closest chair and began to wheel it around, the main doors opened and the night security guard strolled through, talking to someone on his radio.

Beth's heart leaped into her throat. *Act normal*, she thought. There was no way he could know what she was up to. She was just another person in scrubs getting a wheelchair. It happened all the time.

The guard nodded in her direction and kept walking, listening to the reply over the radio. Beth nodded in return, trying to appear pleasant but feeling a bead of sweat beginning to trickle down her spine. Beth followed the guard, forcing herself to match his slow pace until they both reached the elevator.

He turned to face her. "Up or down?"

"Down, please." She was sure her voice waivered, but he didn't seem to notice, pushing the down arrow for her before continuing on his stroll down the hall.

When the doors opened and Beth was safely inside, she let out a shaky breath.

"You've got this," she reassured herself.

Returning to the morgue, Beth considered how to best get Mr. Crisp from the table to the chair. It was simple to slide a corpse from the slick metal table to a rolling gurney at the same height, but from this level to the chair without dropping and injuring him further was far more challenging. She decided feet-first and attempting to slide him carefully into the chair would be best.

She lowered the table as far as it would go. Then, with him still lying flat, she swung his legs over the side and lined them up with the front of the chair. She double-checked the brakes, making sure he wouldn't go rolling across the floor when she moved him. Beth held onto his forearms, hoping the gauze and hoodie would provide some cushioning, and pulled his torso up to slump slightly forward, leaning against her.

The weight of his torso was more than she expected, and she teetered on the verge of falling backward. Her calf muscles screamed in protest, but she slowly forced herself forward just enough to regain her balance. She placed her legs in front of his so they couldn't slide out beneath her, then pushed him by the hips to the very edge of the table. Bracing herself, Beth gave him a quick shove, and he landed heavily in the seat of the chair. She pushed him back as gently as she could and placed his arms and feet on the rests.

By the time he was decently seated, she was dripping with sweat. His 170 or so pounds of dead weight required every ounce of her strength. But sitting in the wheel chair, hoodie pulled forward over his forehead, he passed for a normal patient, bandaged, perhaps finally going home after a burn accident to finish his recuperation. The only missing piece was shoes.

Beth searched in the men's lockers since her autopsy shoes were far too small for him. She found a pair of beaten-up tennis shoes in one of the resident's lockers that looked like a good bet.

They fit loosely on his feet.

Beth wondered if he was in pain. She assumed he was comatose for now, unable to respond, and hoped that moving him wouldn't cause more damage to what remained of his tissues. She pondered a sedative or painkiller of some sort but had no idea how to obtain them on such short notice without arousing suspicion. She'd just have to pray he didn't wake up.

That was a train of thought she hadn't yet entertained. He was a vampire, and if he woke in her presence in such terrible shape, wouldn't he be thirsty? Beth would have to come up with a way to get blood, preferably not her own. But first things first.

Beth ran to the parking lot and pulled her Pathfinder around to the side patient entrance. It was by far the least traveled but still easily wheelchair accessible. She moved to the driver's side rear seat and laid it back as far as it would go.

Entering through the side door of the hospital, she ran the stairs to the basement and reentered the morgue.

Beth put on her jacket and pulled her hood over her head. If her colleagues saw her, they would surely think it odd, transporting a patient during her shift. But for anyone keeping watch on the video, Beth would just be another visitor, coming early before work to pick up a loved one from the hospital.

This was it.

She closed her eyes and took a deep calming breath. "In the through the nose, out through the mouth." She'd heard those words in a hundred step classes during cool down, and right now, she definitely needed to cool down. Her hands gripped the handles of the chair so tightly her knuckles shone white. Adrenaline pumped through every vein of her body.

She turned and wheeled Mr. Crisp out of the double doors and into the hallway.

Beth took the patient elevators, hoping only a precious few visitors would be on the elevators at this time in the morning. She breathed a sigh of relief as the doors opened to reveal an empty elevator. The lobby was quiet too, except for an elderly couple walking slowly toward patient registration. They both looked to be in their seventies, hair silver-gray. The man walked with feet wide, a shuffling gait. His wife held his arm, her arched back hinting at the osteoporosis she likely suffered from. It was hard to tell who was holding up who. Beth prayed neither fell or asked for help. Stopping to help them now would mean leaving Mr. Crisp unattended and they, or anyone else who happened by, would surely begin to wonder why he never moved.

Beth glanced quickly away, not wanting to take a chance on eye contact and a conversation.

She walked briskly across the inlaid wood floor. She had never noticed how very long a distance it was from the elevators to the front door. Until today, she had covered the span without a thought, but while pushing Mr. Crisp, drops of perspiration on her forehead and trickling down her back, it seemed endless.

Reaching the entrance, Beth pressed the automatic door button and the doors opened slowly in front of them. She wheeled Mr. Crisp around to the driver's side back door. With the cameras on the passenger side of the building, she hoped the SUV would shield her from their view while she hoisted Mr. Crisp into the back seat. Even though the Pathfinder wasn't as tall as some larger SUVs, Beth knew moving him into the seat was going to be ugly. There would be no other way than brute strength to get his body from the chair to the seat.

She laid the seat back as flat as it would go and snugged the wheelchair up against the side as tightly as possible, then locked the wheels. With that, she straddled the chair, bending at the knees so as to use her legs as much as possible, leaned him forward, arms around his chest, and lifted.

Grunting, she got his right hip to the arm of the chair and paused, leaning into his chest and pushing him against the seat to catch a breath. Her legs shook beneath her from the strain but held. With her left arm she lifted his right arm into the seat, then his left over his head so that the top half of his torso was leaning well into the seat. Then with one more grunting push, his entire torso was in the vehicle, legs dangling awkwardly out, Beth nearly falling on top of him.

Beth gave him a shove under the armpits to move him up on the seat. She had positioned her right foot between the footrests of the wheelchair, and when she spun his legs around and into the vehicle, her foot caught on the rest.

She stumbled back, falling none too gracefully into the wheelchair. She quickly jumped back up, wrenched the wheelchair free, and closed the door of the SUV, finally locking it with her automatic lock.

Beth parked the vehicle toward the back of the lot and hoped no one would wander by and notice a man lying so very still in the back of her vehicle. She wished she had thought to bring a blanket with her to cover him with. Well, too late now.

She returned the chair to the front lobby, jogging. Then she went back to the morgue as quickly as she could and finished cleaning up, checking over everything twice to be sure she had left nothing that would raise suspicion. It was 5:15 a.m.; forty-five minutes until shift change.

Beth returned to the locker and changed into her street clothes. She straightened her hair and splashed water on her face, hoping it would not only cool her skin but also clear her head.

Deep breaths, she reminded herself. *This is almost over.* But she couldn't help wondering, *What's the penalty for stealing a corpse these days?*

Chapter 7

Beth

The hands on the wall clock above the double doors to the morgue seemed to move in slow motion if at all. Finally, Beth heard a card key in the scan lock and footsteps as Phil Ellison, one of her day shift partners, entered from the hallway. She gathered her things and moved to greet him with the usual niceties.

"Good morning, Phil. How are you?"

"I'm good, but I bet you're better. Today is the last double shift, right?"

"Yes, it is... looking forward to getting some extra sleep." Beth tried to smile and hoped it looked more normal than her ID badge. "It was a slow night," she lied, thinking her voice was just a little too high. "Only one case, a burn victim."

"Oh, do you need me to finish it up for you?"

Beth's heart leaped into her throat at thinking of him reviewing the case and perhaps finding something she'd missed. "Oh, no, no, everything is wrapped up and I will review the transcription when I get back." She hoped she hadn't sounded overly defensive as she shook her head from side to side. She hurriedly said her goodbyes and waved across the room at Bob Riggens, their daytime diener who assisted with most of the cases, on her way toward the door.

Beth tried to act as naturally as possible but was certain her voice had been quivering. She had never been good at hiding her emotions, and she was certainly on edge now. Phil didn't seem to notice anything different. Perhaps he would blame any oddities in her behavior on her lack of sleep. The deep-brown-purple circles under her eyes were certainly a dead giveaway to her sleeping patterns of late.

She tried to walk nonchalantly on her way from the morgue to the elevator. Several hospital staff members exited the elevator but, to her relief, no one joined her on the elevator going up to the main level.

Beth half expected the cops to be waiting for her at the door to the parking lot when she stepped outside. Perhaps they would instead wait to see where she might be taking the body before arresting her? Could she really pull this off? She doubted the "eccentric pathologist" defense would get her out of this one.

But no one came. No one seemed to notice her hurried steps to her Pathfinder.

She climbed in, closed the door and turned the key nearly in one motion, breathing out as the engine roared to life. Despite the cool April morning air, sweat beaded on her forehead as she put the SUV in drive and headed for home.

The drive to her small house was only a few short minutes, but every stoplight seemed to take twice as long as usual. She glanced repeatedly in the rearview mirror, eyeing the disguised Mr. Crisp in her backseat as well as watching for police cars behind her.

As she waited on the third stoplight, the thought again entered her mind: *What will happen when he wakes up?* Assuming she did this right, he would eventually wake up, wouldn't he? And then would he see her as his caretaker or a handy snack? She would have to hope for the former.

She turned from Washington onto Strangline Road. While she had been amused with the name of the street when house-hunting several years ago, "Strang" just one vowel away from "Strange" which right now seemed to sum up the whole situation, she hoped that nothing else unexpected would follow her home. She approached the small two-bedroom house with the simple yard and, while it had felt like home from the moment she first saw it, today it felt like shelter in a storm.

Simple boxwoods and Knock Out roses added some color to the otherwise plain front of the house. Today they were not just decorative but hopefully concealing, a barrier between watching eyes and the secret she needed to keep hidden. Burgundy shutters which matched the front door added some interest to the dull brick. Until now, Beth hadn't noticed how close they were to the color of dried blood, reminding her of the dietary needs of her kidnapped patient.

The demographics of the neighborhood were one of those good news, bad news scenarios, with several elderly couples always watching the neighborhood and keeping crime to a minimum. But today, it meant curious eyes, making the transport of Mr. Crisp into the house unnoticed even more difficult.

Gene and Betty Raintree lived across the street. Betty seemed to time her visits to the curb to meet Beth's. She was always cheerful, up-to-date on the neighborhood gossip and very concerned about Beth's social life, or rather the lack thereof.

Beth pushed the button to open the garage as she approached the house and closed it again behind her after parking inside. It would rouse no suspicion; it was her usual pattern. She always entered the house through the garage; another means of avoiding passersby. The garage was slightly oversized for a one car, with ample room on the side furthest from the house for a mower, a small workbench and shelves.

Like the rest of the house, it was neat and well-organized, which would leave plenty of room for maneuvering Mr. Crisp from the Pathfinder to the house. But moving him from the morgue to her vehicle hadn't been easy even with the wheelchair. Hoisting him into the backseat had taken nearly all the strength she could muster. There was no way she could drag him into the guest bedroom without something to help.

She thought for a moment, then headed into the house to retrieve the rolling chair from her computer desk. It was black leather with high wooden arms on either side. Once she got him into it, they should help to keep him from falling off the sides of the chair. Beth also grabbed a couple of towels from the house and some bungee cords from the garage. She knew with Mr. Crisp's tender, or absent, skin, the friction of the bungee cords without some padding underneath could be very damaging and painful, if he was able to feel pain. He seemed completely unconscious... well, unconscious or dead. Without the ultrasound, she had no way of knowing if he still lived. For now, she would just have to take it on faith.

Beth placed two large boards that the previous owners had left behind in the garage over the two steps leading from the garage to the house to act as a ramp.

Just as she was considering the best way to move Mr. Crisp, there was a knock at the door. Beth froze and listened, hoping it was the mailman or a delivery person of some sort who would knock to let her know a package had arrived and then leave. But after a few seconds, the knock came again, louder this time and more insistent.

"Beth, it's Betty. Do you have a minute?"

Betty Raintree.

Beth closed her eyes and wished with all her might that Betty would suddenly disappear, but she knew better. Betty was nothing if not persistent. She had seen Beth come home and would not leave until she answered the door.

Beth reentered the house, closing the garage door behind her so that there would be no chance of Betty seeing Mr. Crisp. She smoothed her clothes and hair and went to the door.

Betty began talking as soon as the door was open.

"Hello, Beth, honey. I saw you pull in the driveway as I was out getting the paper and saw yours still at the end of the drive so I thought I would bring it to you and say hello. You haven't been around much lately and I wanted to be sure you were doing okay."

"Yes, I'm fine, thank you. I've just been picking up a lot of extra shifts at work and can't wait to crawl in bed and catch up on some sleep."

Beth hoped Betty would take the hint, but instead she continued on as if Beth hadn't even spoken. Beth struggled to focus on her words, all the while thinking of Mr. Crisp lying in the back seat of her Pathfinder.

"I know you don't date much but Susan, a woman I go to church with, has the sweetest, most handsome son about your age. She mentioned that he was single and not dating anyone right now and I thought that he might be just perfect for you."

Beth knew that Betty could not understand why an available young woman, a doctor even, would choose to spend her life living "as a hermit." She seemed to have an endless list of young eligible bachelors that would be "a great catch." But at Beth's age, most men interested in marriage had already taken the leap. Those left either had no intent to settle or had some major issues which made them less than desirable. So, if the single men Betty knew were still shopping, Beth was doubtful she would want to catch any of them. And with a burned vampire waiting in her garage, Beth really wasn't in the mood to talk about another blind date.

"Betty, I appreciate you thinking of me, but I really am exhausted. I'm just ready to close the curtains to block out the sunlight and crash. I promise to catch up with you soon, though."

"Oh, yes, dear, you do look tired. I've never seen such dark circles under your eyes. You rest and perhaps tomorrow I'll make you some tea that will perk you right up. You'll love it, it's a special blend I mix myself. Susan at church—"

"It sounds wonderful. I'll see you sometime tomorrow then," Beth said, already closing the door.

"Don't forget your paper," Betty said, hand sticking through the partly closed door.

"Thank you." Beth took the paper and finally closed the door. She headed immediately to the windows to pull the curtains closed, raising a hand to Betty who was waving as she backed down Beth's driveway.

The sun was just a faint glow in the morning sky. Beth was thankful that her nocturnal habits had moved her to add blackout curtains to most of the rooms. Sleeping with the midday sun shining through the windows was difficult. She didn't know if vampires really were harmed by sunlight, but she wasn't taking any chances with the early morning light.

Getting Mr. Crisp into the rolling chair wasn't as horrible as she had feared. She leaned him forward as far as she could with his head resting on the front seat, then turned his legs so that his feet nearly reached the ground. She braced herself and heaved him toward the chair.

He sort of half slid, half fell into it. He landed slouched since the chair had rolled back some as she'd moved him toward it. Beth hadn't considered the wheels, but thankfully the trash can beside the door had halted the chair's retreat.

She strapped him to the chair as best she could, placing the towels, folded, beneath each bungee cord to protect his charred skin.

It took nearly every ounce of remaining strength to push him up the makeshift ramp into the house, the wheels on the chair twisting unpredictably with his weight and the angle.

Once inside the doorway, Beth dropped to the floor of the kitchen, the cool tile of the floor soothing through her thin cotton shirt. She stayed there, panting, until she felt enough strength return to finish the trip to the guest room.

Moving Mr. Crisp to the guest bedroom was much easier. The wheels rolled smoothly over the ceramic tile which ran throughout the house. An area rug was in the center of the floor of the guest bedroom, a deep orange-red with a large yellow-gold leaf pattern. The remainder of the room mimicked the colors of the rug with the yellow of the walls a lighter complimentary shade. It made the room look cheerful and sunny, at least to Beth. The furnishings were simple, a deeply stained cherrywood sleigh bed with a matching clean-lined dresser. A low-backed armless chair was placed with a small round table in the corner of the room.

The only decorations were a simple reading lamp on a small bedside table, which matched the bedroom set, and black-and-white photographs, matted in red. They were photographs Beth had taken on walks in the park or trips to unfamiliar places for medical conferences. She knew they wouldn't impress a skilled eye, but they held pieces of her story. They showed the world as she saw it; beautiful but imperfect and often in black and white.

Beth wheeled Mr. Crisp to the edge of the bed and turned down the blankets. She made the bed with clean linens, placing an extra flat sheet—a draw sheet—across the bed with edges folded as they did in the hospital. The extra folded sheet came in very handy when moving or turning a patient who could assist you only marginally or not at all.

Beth carefully removed the bungee cords from Mr. Crisp's chest and stripped him from the waist up, removing the bandages from his face. She decided cleaning him would be much simpler if she completed the work from the waist up while he was seated and didn't have to worry about turning him.

She retrieved a pile of clean towels and wash cloths from the bathroom along with tweezers she sterilized with alcohol. She kept a bottle of sterile water and several packages of bandages in the house at all times. Beth lived alone and one never knew when an emergency might occur or what it might require.

She had a large tube of antibiotic ointment. It wasn't the Silvadene-impregnated bandages they used in the burn unit, but it would have to do. Beth began on his face and worked her way down to his waist, peeling and rubbing away the dead skin from the surface until the underlying intact capillaries oozed a mix of bright red blood and clear yellow plasma. This process was called debridement and was a procedure she had seen and assisted with numerous times in the burn unit. Only those patients were clearly human and heavily sedated. Beth hoped that Mr. Crisp's lack of consciousness shielded him from what she knew was a painful process. While she kept many medical supplies in the house, heavy duty painkillers were not among them.

The process was slow, but at least the oozing from the intact pink-red tissue was testament that he still lived.

The tissue of his hands was so badly charred that debridement was nearly impossible over several of his fingers. Had he been in the burn unit, the most severely charred would have been amputated. Since she had neither the tools to perform an amputation nor the knowledge of what his body was capable of healing, she merely cleaned the areas as best she could.

She covered all of the exposed tissue with antibiotic ointment and bandaged him loosely. She then removed his remaining clothing and lifted him as gently as possible into the bed. It wasn't a graceful move, but the bandages remained intact.

She repeated the process from the waist down. He must have crawled on his abdomen away from the flames, since the skin over the tops of his thighs, genitals and low abdomen were much less affected than that of his upper body and distal extremities.

When finished, Beth bandaged his lower body in the same way as his torso and covered him gently with the white flat sheet. The whole process had taken almost four hours.

Beth fell into the chair in the corner of the room, exhausted and spent. The physical and emotional strain of the day combined with the lack of sleep over the last few weeks had taken its toll. She had cared for Mr. Crisp as best she could. The only remaining hurdle to the care she would be able to provide was his nourishment. In the burn unit he would have been maintained with intravenous fluids and TPN, that milky lipid- and nutrient-rich IV cocktail that provided the calories and nourishment that a burn patient would need to rebuild lost tissue. Assuming she was right about Mr. Crisp's "special condition," she was pretty certain TPN would be of no help for him. Sure, you couldn't believe everything you saw in the movies or read in the books, but if vampires existed, and indeed Beth had now accepted that they did, then perhaps some of the other bits and pieces of vampire lore were also true.

It brought to mind her favorite Dracula quote: "Do you not think that there are things which you cannot understand, and yet which are, that some people see things that others cannot? It is the fault of our science that it wants to explain all; and if it explain not, then it says there is nothing to explain."

Mr. Crisp was a vampire, and Beth assumed that meant he needed blood to recover. How much he would need and how much she could get were uncertain. Beth wanted so badly to crawl into her own bed, to close the blackout curtains and sleep until her body woke on its own, rested. She was so very tired, there was little doubt that sleep would finally come. But Beth didn't know how long Mr. Crisp could go without blood. And if he awoke hungry, well, she would rather it wasn't her own he had for a snack.

Since she couldn't exactly run down to the local grocery store and order up a couple of units of O neg, where would she manage to get blood for Mr. Crisp? Beth supposed that as a vampire he preferred human blood, but she wasn't about to take one life to save another. The blood bank was the obvious answer, but the donated units were carefully inventoried and tracked from the time of collection until transfusion.

Of all areas of laboratory medicine, the blood bank was by far the most tightly regulated and staffed by the most detail-oriented of all techs. Units of blood had a limited shelf life and were given expiration dates. After the expiration date, or if units failed initial testing for infectious diseases, they were carefully logged and sent for incineration. And every day some units that remained in the blood bank just hadn't been a match to anyone needing blood at that time. When these units reached the end of their shelf life, beginning to break down and becoming unfit for transfusion, they had to be destroyed.

Maybe, with a little finesse, she could get her hands on some expired units.

Sherman Knudsen taught the resident blood bank course at

Midwest University and had for as long as anyone there now remembered. He and Beth had gotten along quite well. During many a conversation, they had discussed Sherman's interests in research. He had been involved in several projects across campus and Beth knew the expired units had occasionally been maintained for research purposes. She didn't know if a vampire would mind "stale" cells, but it was going to be the best she could hope to get her hands on.

She began practicing her speech for Sherman.

CHAPTER 8

LUCIANO

LIKE A KNIFE, JABS of pain tore through the oblivion of sleep, forcing him to be aware. The immensity of it held him motionless. A searing pain in his side, the sound of an engine. New pain trailed across his chest, stopped and began again. He gave himself over to the blackness when he could until new jolts of agony demanded awareness. A woman's voice, the sensation of movement all shrouded in waves of pain and darkness. But this new pain no longer burned. Large parts of his body no longer registered sensation at all; fingers and toes no longer existed. A relentless tugging and scraping that seemed to continue for ages finally gave way to a soothing but startling coolness. The woman's voice again, soft and gentle near his ear, before he again gave in to unconsciousness.

CHAPTER 9

BETH

WHEN SHERMAN ANSWERED THE phone, he seemed genuinely glad to hear from her. They discussed what had been going on in their equally predictable lives up to this point. After exchanging all of the niceties, Beth began to explain her fabricated research project while she tidied up the debridement supplies on top of the guestroom dresser.

"Sherman, I'm working on a new project. I want to place blood in numerous environments to study the damage to the red cells produced in different conditions in hopes that it could be applied to laboratory studies on the blood of victims dying in similar settings. Whole blood would certainly be ideal, but I would settle for packed red blood cells. I know fewer and fewer whole blood units are available these days. I'm on vacation for two weeks and thought now would be as good a time as any. You know how I hate to be still."

Beth expected Sherman to interrupt at any time to tell her that he didn't believe a word of it and ask what she was really planning to do with all of that blood. To her surprise, he didn't.

"Not a problem, Beth, I'll sign the units out to you for research. You still have your academic appointment. That should cover it. You can pick up whatever we have at the lab. We have two units that outdated today, if you're ready. Our storage space is pretty limited, so I don't know how many we could continue to hold. You should probably come by frequently to pick them up."

"I'll plan to come by daily," Beth said. "And since you have two expired units today, I will be by to get them in an hour or so."

"Perfect. I'll place a note to the other techs on the refrigerator doors to set aside the expired units for you."

"I'll be sure to bring my university ID along for the newer techs," Beth said. "Thank you very much, Sherman. I can't tell you how much I appreciate it." *As though a life depended on it*, she thought to herself.

"It's been good talking to you, Beth. Don't be a stranger." And with that, Mr. Crisp's ready-made meals were arranged.

After a quick shower, Beth donned a pair of her old university scrubs and a clean white lab coat. She knew she would need infusion supplies and thought the clothing might help her to blend in with the current residents. Perhaps she could slip in and out without being noticed.

Beth checked in quickly on Mr. Crisp. He lay exactly where she had left him, in exactly the same position. As before, she would just have to assume he was still with her. Beth hoped at some point he would awaken, grateful. And that if her caretaking was successful, he would heal. The stories of vampires were all so different, ranging from bloodthirsty monsters with no remnants of humanity to creatures that revered humanity and chose to abstain from drinking human blood, preying only on animals. Beth had no idea what camp Mr. Crisp would fall into, but she certainly hoped it would be the latter.

Knowing there was nothing else she could do for him, she locked the house and headed to the drug store.

Seeing the pile of bandages she was buying, the cashier said,

"Goodness, are you making a mummy? It's not even Halloween."

Beth smiled. "You just never know what you might need. Better to be prepared and not need it than to need it and not have it."

She had tried to think ahead and gather anything she thought might be useful, so she had quite an assortment of supplies including several tubes of antibiotic ointment, six gallons of sterile water and normal saline, twelve packages of gauze 4 x 4s, a case of regular sterile gauze bandages, five rolls of paper tape, five boxes of clear adhesive bandages, a large package of plastic-lined chux pads and three bottles of rubbing alcohol. Beth even threw in ten bottles of liquid Tylenol. It wouldn't be of much comfort in the face of Mr. Crisp's extensive burns, but there was really no other painkiller she could easily get and administer without arousing suspicion.

She saw the cashier raise her eyebrows as she scanned all the bottles of Tylenol, so Beth added, "I've never liked taking pills and the liquid tastes so much better than the ground-up tablets."

The cashier lowered her eyebrows and accepted her explanation. Beth seemed to already be getting better and better at making up these little cover stories. She wasn't one for lying, remembering the old saying about the truth being much easier than trying to remember all of the lies. But considering that the truth at this point would likely provide her with a one-way ticket to either the psych unit or jail, she figured she'd learn to take notes if it became necessary. She also decided it would be best to gather supplies more frequently and to use various stores to better avoid suspicion and blamed it on her exhaustion for not thinking of it sooner.

From here it was on to the university for one last crime for the day. After parking the Pathfinder in the visitors' lot, she took the collapsible cooler she'd brought along from home with her. By the time she reached the blood bank, Sherman had left for the day but a very friendly second shift tech named Barry knew all about it. He quickly retrieved the units for her, and she placed them in the cooler along with the cold packs she'd purchased. She knew it wasn't the ideal transport environment for the blood, but considering what she was planning to do with it, she thought it should suffice.

From the blood bank, Beth walked directly to the day surgery floor. She was counting on the unit being nearly abandoned at that time of day. It was a very busy place from about 7 a.m. to 2 p.m. since the majority of the day shift nursing personnel left at 3 p.m. In the holding room, patients waited behind curtained partitions for their turn to go back to the surgery suites. It was there they first met the anesthetist, or at least the resident on for the day, and an IV was started.

All of the IV supplies were in bins in the back of the holding area. With only the ward clerk currently there, Beth walked purposefully to the back of the room and began to gather supplies as if she belonged there. She hoped the scrubs and long white coat would make her nearly invisible given the setting.

With her back to the ward clerk, she positioned herself directly in front of the bins she was working in just in case someone entered from the door to the surgery core behind her. She gathered several handfuls of 18-gauge needles and as many packages of IV tubing as she could fit into the cooler. Assuming a couple of units a day, she had enough to last until she could order more from the internet.

An amazing thing, internet shopping. It allowed some privacy and access to all sorts of things that weren't readily available in your corner drugstore. Sure, Beth supposed the government would monitor certain supplies or searches, but certainly they would primarily pertain to controlled substances, wouldn't they? Why would the government care if she was stockpiling IV tubing and 18-gauge needles? In any case, a box of medical supplies delivered to her front door would go unnoticed in comparison to stealing what Mr. Crisp needed from the university.

As a last passing thought, she grabbed several blood collection tubes and a vacutainer. Her objectives met, she closed the lid on the cooler and quietly walked out the same door she'd entered.

Beth hadn't realized how quickly her heart was beating until she was seated safely in the front seat of the Pathfinder. She let her head fall forward and rest against the steering wheel. Her hands were shaking, a fine sweat sparkling on her forehead, mind swimming with thoughts of all she had done since meeting Mr. Crisp for the first time last night.

When she had regained control of herself, she began the drive home for the second time that day. This one was less stressful, but Beth did worry what a policeman might think about her transporting two units of blood and piles of IV tubing in a personal cooler. She was guessing it would be easier to explain than a bandaged corpse in her guestroom. She decided watching the speed limit signs and traffic lights closely was the best approach until she made it safely home to her garage.

Beth assembled the IV tubing and placed one of the units in her refrigerator. She considered warming the unit. It wasn't the way units were administered in the hospital for the most part. Blood warmers were used for trauma patients mostly, or patients in surgery. Occasionally a patient with a cold autoantibody—an antibody a patient's body made against their own cells that only caused problems when the blood temperature dropped—would require prewarmed blood, but most patients just received the unit as is.

Mr. Crisp would be used to the blood being warm, though, wouldn't he? But of course he probably wouldn't be used to getting it through an IV either.

Ultimately Beth decided that getting him the blood he needed was probably more important that having it be at his preferred temperature.

Placing a chux pad under his arm, Beth spiked the unit and began to search for a vein. His left antecubital space, the bend in the arm opposite the elbow, was in better shape than the right, so she decided to start there.

She used a large rubber band from the kitchen junk drawer—one she kept for opening jars with tight lids—as a tourniquet. While she'd never imagined needing it for this purpose, it served well enough. The five stolen vacutainer blood tubes were laid out neatly on the bed beside Mr. Crisp's forearm. After floating the 18-gauge catheter, Beth drew a rainbow, which meant collecting tubes of all types with different colored lids signifying the chemicals in each. Though she wasn't sure what she was going to do with them just yet, having some of Mr. Crisp's undiluted blood could be interesting and perhaps give her a little more insight into his physiology.

After filling and inverting the tubes to mix them, Beth connected the IV tubing. Not having an IV pole handy, she suspended the unit as high as possible using her entryway coatrack. She assumed that gravity would be enough to infuse the blood, but wasn't sure how fast to run it. Most units were given over two to four hours, but an infusion pump was used so one could enter the volume, divide by the number of hours over which it was to be given and program the infusion rate. In the absence of an infusion pump, she opened the line until it seemed to be dripping briskly but not too quickly. She would watch it and slow it down if needed.

With the catheter in place and both it and the tubing safely secured with paper tape, she settled into the corner chair to rest for a moment. Beth had purchased the chair almost two years ago but had never actually sat in it for any length of time. The modern, high-backed armless design was attractive but not terribly comfortable. As tired as she was, though, she dozed.

Beth woke to the sound of dripping. Her eyes opened lazily, thinking it was probably time for a new washer in the bathroom faucet. What she saw, though, had her on her feet in half a second. The IV had come free from Mr. Crisp's vein, and blood was slowly dripping from his resting arm, over the soaked chux pad and onto the floor where a puddle about eighteen inches in diameter had formed. It was a mess but certainly not what it could have been had she not awakened when she did. Her first thought was to stop the bleeding from his vein.

She closed the flow valve and wiped at his arm with the 4 x 4s on the bedside table that she'd made into a sterile work surface of sorts, holding all of her needed supplies. The tape she had used to carefully secure the IV and tubing were still in place. But the IV needle was lying on top of the skin and the puncture site wasn't bleeding. Not only was it not bleeding, the puncture site was hardly visible. It had already healed.

She looked to the hanging unit of blood and saw that about half of it had been infused, even accounting for the amount on the floor and soaked into the chux pad. The bedside clock said 5:07 p.m., so she had been asleep in the chair for almost thirty minutes. She hadn't considered the fact that he could heal so quickly and might extrude and seal off the IV site. Not having a better idea, she inserted another

18-gauge needle at the same site and restarted the blood.

While the rest of the unit infused, she changed the chux pad, thankful that her compulsiveness had saved a changing of the sheets. She didn't think she had the energy for that again today. The blood didn't seem to want to come out of the grout as she mopped, so Beth grabbed a bottle of bleach and a cleaning brush from under the kitchen sink and scrubbed it free. A few tiny droplets had splattered from the floor onto the bottom edge of the fitted sheet and bed frame, but it was a small enough amount that the sheets could wait. Thankfully, the whole mess hadn't made it as far as the rug.

Cleaning the floor was one thing, but a floor rug would have been another.

After that, Beth checked the IV site frequently and increased the flow rate of the blood. She managed to get the remainder of the unit into Mr. Crisp before his body again rejected the needle. Beth infused the second unit uneventfully, but it required constant monitoring and periodic repositioning of the needle to keep it in place. Even so, she had to use two additional needles to get the job done.

She would have to be certain to order extra needles. At this rate, she'd need about thirty a week.

Even though it was just the needle site, it showed he was healing, and this was a very good thing. It was at the same time comforting and unsettling to know that he was indeed still alive. All in all, Beth felt pretty good about her efforts for the day.

With a final check on Mr. Crisp, Beth walked to her room. She knew Mr. Crisp could awaken while she slept and decide she was a quick meal, but apart from kitchen knives, she had no weapons to defend herself and no knowledge of fighting. What use would they be? His fast healing would likely make whatever wounds she could inflict insufficient to keep him away.

She walked to the window nearest the bed and opened the curtains, spilling sunlight across the room. The light wouldn't last for long, but perhaps it would keep him away if he did awaken, assuming sunlight even worked on vampires. Beth was certain she was too exhausted for the light to keep her awake, so it couldn't hurt.

She crawled under the sheets, not even bothering to remove her clothes or brush her teeth. In seconds, her breathing slowed to the gentle rhythm of sleep.

CHAPTER 10

LUCIANO

HIS NEXT MOMENT OF awareness was one of warmth. A rush of energy swam through his veins... Blood. The sensation began in his left arm and radiated through his body. It was odd, coming from his arm. When he fed, the tickle of warmth began in his mouth and moved from there through his core to his limbs.

Someone was giving him blood.

Thoughts of who that someone might be and the realization that they must know what he was were pushed aside as he focused on the small bit of healing and comfort the blood allowed. It pushed back against the pain, only slightly, but he held to it and prayed more would follow.

CHAPTER II

BETH

WHEN BETH AWOKE, THE clock said 12:14 p.m. She blinked a few times, clearing away the last of the haze of sleep. For a moment, she thought it was the middle of the night, but then the "p.m." sunk in. She had slept for over sixteen hours! Beth couldn't remember sleeping that long in her lifetime but felt wonderful. She stretched her arms and legs, reveling in the warmth of the bed, and felt the tenderness in the muscles of her limbs. For a short moment Beth was confused, not remembering what she had done to make her sore.

Mr. Crisp!

She sat upright in bed and was on her feet almost instantly. She nearly ran into the next room. He was there, undisturbed, in the same position she had left him.

Breathing a sigh of relief, she walked to the side of the bed and once again listened in vain for breathing and felt for a pulse that was nowhere to be found. Gently raising his lids, she saw the eyes fixed in a forward stare.

"I don't know if you can hear me, but good morning."

Of course, there was no response. Shaking her head, she grabbed the folded sheet and shifted him slightly in the bed. She didn't know if vampires could get pressure sores, but figured it didn't hurt to take precautions. She pulled back the covers and placed a second pillow beneath his feet before covering him back up.

Feeling confident then that all was indeed still well, she continued on with her usual routine. She brushed her teeth and pulled her hair back into a messy ponytail. She changed into her jogging shorts, sports bra and tank and pulled on her running shoes. As she tugged the laces tight on the right shoe, she noticed the frayed ends of the shoestrings and told herself it really was time for a new pair. She'd been jogging two to three miles a day for years now. It was great for her body, helping to keep her lean and toned, but it was very rough on shoes. It also helped Beth separate from and process whatever was going on in her life. When she ran, her body took over and her brain took a back seat. It was the most mentally relaxing part of her day.

Beth walked to the combination office/gym at the end of the hall and flipped on the wall-mounted TV. She surfed until she found an old James Bond movie before starting the treadmill. This one had a young Sean Connery as Bond. *Yum!* If he would have turned that brown-eyed sultry stare in her direction, she'd have swooned just like the Bond girls in the movies.

Of course, in reality, Bond would probably be receiving about his tenth round of antibiotics for gonorrhea, chlamydia or trichomonas infections. Heck, maybe all three; the guy got around. But the platinum blond with the generous bust and curvy silhouette didn't seem to mind.

It would be nice, Beth thought, to have those days back; the days when the most attractive women weren't stick figures. Having some soft flesh over the bones and fullness in their faces instead of the gaunt, sunken cheeks of today's stars were things of beauty. It made the women look soft, seductive and, well... feminine. The women in popular magazines these days just didn't look real. And with rampant plastic surgery, many weren't. Beth always found it amusing to see a size 0 model wearing a 32DD bra. Yeah, like those didn't come out of a box! It wasn't that they wanted to improve their appearance that made her question their choice to modify their bodies, only that the changes made didn't in any way look natural.

She lost herself in Bond's seductive brown eyes again and finished off her three miles. After her cool down, James and his leading lady sailed away into the sunset in a small lifeboat with a quick-witted one-liner and a very suggestive embrace and kiss. Beth sighed wistfully.

She returned slowly to her room, shed her damp clothes quickly, tossing them in the closet hamper, and stepped into the shower. A good night's rest had been refreshing beyond description. The hot water felt so soothing on her skin, like tiny massaging fingertips. It was as if each drop washed away a small bit of the stress of the past weeks and of the ordeal that was yesterday. She had made it home with a corpse along with misappropriated blood and supplies from the university hospital. Surely by now, if Mr. Crisp had been missed, the hospital would have called trying to sort out the discrepancy or, more likely, the cops would have knocked down her front door. If she played her cards right from here on out, she might just stay out of prison after all.

Still reveling in the heat and steam of the shower, she took the time to shave her legs and actually let the conditioner set in her hair for a few minutes before rinsing it out and reluctantly turning off the water. She toweled off and began to brush through her hair. Despite leaving the door open, as she always did to dissipate the steam, the mirrors were completely fogged. She reached out with her towel to rub the mist from the center of the mirror when she had an overwhelming sensation that she was not alone. She hurriedly wrapped the towel around herself and peered out into the bedroom.

Stupidly, she called to the empty room, "Hello? Anyone there?"

If someone *was* there, did she really want to meet them in a towel?

But, of course, there was no one. Beth walked to the hallway and checked on Mr. Crisp, just to be certain she hadn't been discovered and his body revealed, cops at the ready with cuffs just her size. But there he was, once again lying in the same position in which she had left him. Of course, she was a fool, probably still a little jumpy from yesterday's antics.

She walked back to the steamy bathroom, dropped the towel to the floor and continued getting ready for the day. Beth always got ready in the nude. It was just so much simpler. She was more than a little accident prone at times, and dropping a large blob of toothpaste on her chest was much easier to wipe away from bare skin. For her, wearing clothing while getting ready was sort of like a bad golfer near a water hazard. Try as she might to avoid the inevitable drip or spill, she always ended up in the middle of the pond and taking the extra stroke.

Beth dried her hair, using the round brush to flip the ends. It felt good to let it hang loose rather than in the ponytail she always sported at work. But, let's face it, with her job, having hair falling into her eyes and worse, into her work, was just not an option.

She finished her routine and left the bathroom. Even though she would be going by the university today, it was on unofficial business, which meant her usual faded jeans and comfy long-sleeve cotton KU T-shirt would do. She pulled the clothing on over her pink-striped cotton bikini briefs and hot-pink cotton bra.

She preferred the feel of cotton against her skin.

After dressing, she walked to Mr. Crisp's room, still thinking about the clothing.

"There's just no way to mimic the natural, breathable softness of cotton, Mr. Crisp," she said and smiled, thinking she sounded like a commercial. "Jeans are always such a treat. Mid-rise Levi's are my favorite, you know. They give in all the right places." The hugging and caressing on her legs and hips as she moved was just heavenly. "Since I know you won't tell anyone, I'll let you in on a little secret of mine. There's another reason I'm so fond of my Levi's. The seams are in all the right places. Sometimes the vibration from riding in a car while wearing them can be very... stimulating."

With this she laughed, thinking how ridiculous she must look talking away to what looked, for all intents and purposes, like a corpse. Assuming he was still alive, Beth guessed he would technically be in a coma. Didn't some people say they could hear the voices of their loved ones while in a coma but just couldn't respond? Of course, there were also those that swore they had out-of-body experiences, floating above themselves, or that they saw relatives, long passed, that steered them away from the light.

Well, whether he could hear her or not, talking to him seemed comfortable. If she was going to be caring for his every need until he recovered, if he recovered, where was the harm in getting acquainted?

"Well, I suppose you would probably like to eat today, which means I should head to the university to see what they might have for you after rotating their stock. Sit tight and I'll be back as soon as I can."

With that she crawled into her Pathfinder and shut the door before pushing the remote button. There was no use opening the garage before she was ready to pull out and take the chance of getting cornered again by Betty before she could escape. She'd been fortunate enough not to be caught on her second trip in and out the day before.

She turned the key just as the door started to lift and backed out as soon as the door was fully open. It was a good call. There was Betty out sweeping her steps and looking ready to pounce. Beth waved at her as she quickly pressed the remote to close the garage door, hoping to evade her. But Betty was already on the move, and as Beth entered the street, Betty was approaching her door.

Knowing she was caught, Beth put the Pathfinder in park and rolled down her window. She left the car running, hoping this would let Betty know she was in a hurry.

"Good afternoon, Beth, dear. I am so glad I caught you. Oh my, you do look so much better today. Not that you looked horrible yesterday, just oh so tired. I'm assuming you were able to get a few hours of sleep?"

Beth nodded, knowing a response wasn't really necessary.

"I made up that special tea this morning, but your curtains were still drawn so I decided to take it over to Mrs. Porter instead. You know, her husband died last summer after fifty-two years of marriage. She said it was very fast after a major heart attack. They tried to do bypass surgery but just too much of his heart muscle had been damaged for him to pull through. Mrs. Porter has seemed a little lost since he passed, so I try to check on her every few days."

Unlike Beth, having chosen solitude, Mrs. Porter had been used to sharing her space and her thoughts with someone else. Beth could understand the loss, she supposed, even though she had no real point of reference in her own life.

"Gene and I were high school sweethearts; did you know that? He asked me to the high school prom. I was shocked since he'd always been so quiet, but I said yes and we've been together ever since. I just can't imagine what it must be like for her. I've never seen any family visit and don't think she had any children."

Beth could relate to that much, having no remaining family of her own. Her mother had died in childbirth. From what she could piece together from the layman's account her father provided, she had begun bleeding heavily as soon as she went into labor. Her obstetrician had performed an emergency cesarean section to save Beth's life, but hadn't been able to control the bleeding fast enough to save her mother's. From the sound of it, she probably suffered from placenta previa, a condition where the placenta that nourished Beth had grown across the opening of her cervix. When her cervix began to dilate, the fragile vessels had torn, leaving both of them in danger. The tragedy had left her hardworking father heartbroken with a newborn infant daughter to support on his machine worker's salary. Then, sixteen years later, Beth had lost him too.

"But speaking of sweethearts, I was telling Susan from church about you this morning and she said you should come over for dinner and meet Ronald. Did I tell you her son's name was Ronald? He's an accountant and works for a big firm downtown—"

"Mrs. Raintree, I am so sorry to rush off but I was heading to the university and need to get there before the lab tech leaves for the day," Beth cut in.

"Oh, yes, dear. You are just so busy and hard to catch. But I'll watch for you later and we can talk some more."

Beth smiled and told Betty to give her regards to her husband before escaping. She would have to remember to look for Betty through the curtains before heading out next time.

Pulling into the university parking lot brought her thoughts back to the task at hand. Grabbing the cooler from the back seat, she headed into the blood bank. Beth was pleased to find four units waiting for her. Showing her badge to the young brown-haired tech with very alluring hazel eyes, she introduced herself. His smile was just as warm and inviting as his eyes as he told her his name was Scott. Scott with the big hazel eyes also had a big gold band on his left ring finger; another human who had chosen not to spend his life alone.

CHAPTER 12

BETH

IT HAD BEEN ALMOST a year since Beth had last seen Lu, but he greeted her warmly with proper English and a still-obvious Chinese accent, "Beth, so good to see you. What brings you to visit us lab wats?"

"You mean besides your smiling face, Lu?" Lu was his last name. He was unfortunate enough to have a first name that no one raised to speak English could properly pronounce. Beth, who'd spent time in his lab during medical school and residency, had tried to pronounce it once but ended up settling on "Lu" like everyone else.

Beth held up her hand, waggling Mr. Crisp's tubes of blood.

"What have you brought me?" Lu asked.

"Samples from one of my patients. I'm working on a paper and wanted to get some baseline values from some of my autopsy patients for comparison. I was hoping you wouldn't mind me running them through your chemistry and hematology instruments."

Lu had come to the states from Beijing, where he'd finished medical school and residency and practiced neurology for three years before deciding to try his hand in the US medical field. Having always had a propensity for research, Lu chose to take a position in a lab at the university. He'd worked his way through a PhD program and had received grants to run his very own lab.

"Sho. Sho. No problem. You're welcome to them. They were

serviced about a month ago and calibrated. They should be accurate. Knock yourself out, and let me know if you need help."

"Thanks, Lu. I'm sure I can manage." Beth didn't know what she might find and was certainly happy to get the results without Lu hovering.

She had no centrifuge at home and knew some of the values might be affected by the specimen not being spun down quickly, but it was the best she could do. Beth dropped the green top in the centrifuge along with a balancing blank and set it in motion. The purple top she placed on the vortex to mix before running. She watched as Lu sat down at a microscope at the next bench.

"How have things been going with your research?" Beth asked.

"The research has gone well, but the university hired another new dean last summer. As usual, he is cleaning house and replacing everyone high up with people he knows while the rest of us wait to see if we will still have jobs when he is finished," Lu said. "And all the while, we are all still competing for less and less grant money. It is hard to know whose butt to kiss." With this he looked up from the scope and puckered his lips.

Beth chuckled. She understood the university politics and didn't envy Lu having to continually wade through them. "How's your wife?"

"Now that is happier topic. We just celebrated our tenth anniversary in Antigua. What about you? Dating anyone?" Lu said, turning again to bury his face in his scope and avoid eye contact.

Beth gave him the glare he'd anticipated even though he wasn't looking. "Lu, you know I'm perfectly happy on my own. Besides, my career doesn't exactly expose me to a lot of eligible bachelors." *Perfectly happy* was probably a stretch. Beth was fine on her own. She had accepted that she and the life she'd chosen were a lot for others to deal with. While a relationship was something she secretly did wish for, she was resigned to the fact that it was unlikely to happen for her.

"I know a few grad students that would be very interested in meeting a beautiful young career woman."

"Thanks, but no thanks. Now stop it with the matchmaking. I think your romantic getaway has gone to your head."

"Okay, okay, just worried about you. A young woman like you should have someone to go home to at night."

They left it at that. Beth knew Lu meant what he said. She didn't think he was meddling, and believed he was truly concerned for her happiness. But she had met some of his awkward, geeky grad students in the past and friendly hellos in the lab were enough for her.

Beth loaded the specimen on the hematology analyzer and stood by to receive the results. While some of the chemistries had an on-board time of fifteen to twenty minutes after centrifuging, complete blood counts were whole blood tests, so after five minutes the results began printing. The first thing she noticed were all of the flags suggesting the specimen was hemolyzed, meaning the blood cells had been broken apart. The hemoglobin, the measurement of the oxygen-carrying red cells in the blood, was remarkably low, as was the white blood cell count, the cells that helped human bodies fight off infection.

Since Beth knew the sample had been collected properly with no risk for cell lysis, she again inverted the tube, checked for clotting, and loaded a second sample. With no clot and good collection, she could only hope that adequate mixing would give better results. The first results didn't make sense. Mr. Crisp seemed to be improving with the blood she was giving him.

She made peripheral smears from the sample and set them aside to dry before staining. The printer again began to produce results that looked exactly the same as the first. Frustrated now and thinking that her samples from Mr. Crisp might be useless, she turned and began tapping her fingers on the console of the chemistry analyzer, hoping those results would fare better. The centrifuge finished its loud whirring and she popped open the door to inspect the sample.

As she feared, the plasma was bright red. This sample was also hemolyzed. Her hopes fell, but she decided to run the sample anyway and loaded it on the chemistry analyzer.

The blood smear slides were still not dry enough to stain, so Beth began pondering the possible causes for such overt hemolysis in a fresh specimen. She had already excluded collection error. She had used a needle that was large bore, so the cells couldn't have been broken by trauma from collection. Other causes could include some kind of antibody-mediated process. In this case, the body would produce antibodies against its own cells that would help in breaking the cells apart, causing hemolysis within the patient. But Mr. Crisp showed none of the obvious signs. Beth supposed it could be masked in the most severely burned areas. But the sclerae, the white parts of the eye, were almost always affected first, and his were clear, not yellow.

There were occasional patients that developed antibodies that only caused hemolysis when the samples cooled to below normal body temperature. Prosthetic, man-made heart valves could also hemolyze cells, but again Beth should see some signs in Mr. Crisp if it was that severe. And she was doubtful, given his healing abilities, that he would ever have needed or had access to a heart valve replacement.

In any good differential, the last line should always be "other," and "other" in this case was a category she favored. With Mr. Crisp, who knew? Beth was in uncharted territory.

The one thought that lingered was concern for a blood type mismatch. Everyone, well, every human, had a blood type. Human bodies recognized things that weren't their own and could produce antibodies to fight against them, just like building immunity to a virus by taking a vaccine. Blood was no different.

Beth assumed vampires would drink from all types, but she wasn't giving Mr. Crisp the blood to eat, she was transfusing him. Perhaps he did have a blood type. She would have to find out. The usual symptoms of hemolysis would be jaundice over time, but more immediately blood in the urine, possibly fever and chills, pain and low blood pressure... none of which she could assess in Mr. Crisp. His tissues and rare bits of skin felt cool to the touch, but that was likely owing to his lower core body temperature and lack of an intact body surface to retain heat. Remarkably, he'd passed no urine or feces, so looking for blood wasn't an option.

Realistically, she had nothing else to give him. Beth had to serve up the blood bank's "soup de jour." With a sigh, she returned to work.

The chemistries showed a markedly elevated potassium level. It was the highest Beth had seen and not compatible with normal human life. Red cells contained high levels of potassium and their breakage as they hemolyzed would certainly allow that potassium to leak into the blood, raising the level, but she hadn't observed levels this high even in patients with ongoing hemolysis in residency. The sodium was near normal for human values, but glucose, the blood sugar, was quite low at 40. Beth had assumed with Mr. Crisp's regeneration that blood was all he required, that she was meeting his needs, but perhaps she was missing something. Was he hypoglycemic, having a low blood sugar, and needed some IV supplementation? Did his body need food too?

She stained the smears manually. Not the best staining she had seen, but adequate. The blood had smeared like red Kool-Aid, much thinner in consistency than typical blood specimens, which had a thickness closer to that of whole milk.

Beth placed a slide on the microscope with a drop of oil on it then settled in the desk chair to look it over. As she should have expected, there were very few intact red cells. They must have all broken down. Something she had done in collection or something inherent to his physiology had left her almost nothing to review. The few cells that remained where swollen and round, called spherocytes—changes often seen with hemolysis.

"Three strikes and you're out," Beth said aloud.

After all this, Beth knew almost nothing more about Mr. Crisp than when she started. Disheartened, she gathered the reports and remaining samples and said her thank-yous and goodbyes to Lu.

CHAPTER 13

BETH

BACK HOME, BETH TOSSED three of the units she'd retrieved from the blood bank into the refrigerator and hung the fourth on the coatrack while she prepared an IV. Beth let the blood run at a quick pace, knowing it wouldn't be long before the needle would be extruded by Mr. Crisp's rapidly healing flesh.

While the unit dripped into Mr. Crisp, she dragged her wheeled desk chair into the room along with her laptop. She propped her feet on the end of the bed and opened a new Word file.

"Assuming that you are what I think you are and that we'll be spending quite a bit of time with one another until you're healed, I hope you won't mind me jotting down a few notes about our adventures. While I have no intention of turning you over to the scientific community to be studied and exploited, I wouldn't be a good scientist if I didn't at least try to unravel a few of your secrets." Beth paused as if waiting for him to object.

"For starters, I should record my observations during our first meeting." As she spoke, Beth began typing out the details of that first examination. She also included his height and weight and created a table to record the blood she had and would infuse during his recuperation. Beth downloaded a body surface area burn chart from the internet to use to document his injuries graphically and to chart the improvement she hoped very much that she would soon see.

Beth carefully photographed Mr. Crisp's extensive injuries and uploaded the pictures, renaming and dating them as she went. Lastly, she began to describe her actions from the day. Beth finished by password-protecting her work. Should her computer ever fall into the wrong hands, at least they wouldn't have access to her findings. She copied the files to her primary flash drive as well as a backup and stood to check on Mr. Crisp.

How had the world functioned before computers? She was first exposed in early high school and embraced them immediately. She entered a workforce where they had already become the norm in business management. By undergraduate college, many of her assignments were completed using Lotus Notes or Microsoft Works.

She found the predictability of computers comforting. The computer was given rules to follow, and short of a power outage or operator error, it followed those rules indiscriminately. As processor speed and storage capabilities improved, the possibilities quickly became nearly limitless; from computers the size of a house used to complete the functions of a small calculator of today, to holding a device capable of storing many gigabytes in the palm of her hand. Beth thought it was amazing. If humans were capable of that in such a short span of years, what would they produce next?

Science fiction had become reality in so many ways. The internet and email connected humanity like never before. Information could be shared and sought out without ever leaving home. Beth's computer had, in so many ways, become her portal to the world. She could manage it in a way that suited even her reclusive nature.

As she checked on the IV, Beth wondered if Mr. Crisp could be the biologic version of the next leap, a first peek at the possibilities untapped in every person.

The first change she noticed in him took her by surprise. She was turning his left hand over to reposition his arm for yet another new IV. As she did, being careful to apply only gentle pressure, his index finger came off in her hand. No snap, no tearing, just one second it was attached and the next it was sitting in the palm of her hand quite separate from the rest of him.

Beth stared at it blankly, comically to be sure. Like a child wondering where to hide her mother's broken vase, the thoughts of what might be the next step flashed through her mind. Realizing, however, that he was not in pain and quite obviously, and thankfully, unaware of his loss, she relaxed a bit and felt her heart begin a more regular rhythm.

Beth had known his hands were terribly damaged, hadn't she? A normal burn unit would surely have amputated them immediately. This was just simpler, right? An "autoamputation."

She set the finger aside on the bedside table and knelt next to the bed to more closely examine the amputation site. Beth gently pulled away the remaining fragments of dead tissue only to feel her heart race yet again. There at the base of the detached digit was a pink-red nub of tissue. The surface was completely covered in new skin. It was smooth and soft like a baby's. The little nub extended about three-quarters of an inch from the knuckle. The finger was regrowing!

She quickly began to examine the other severely damaged fingers and found that some of them also broke free from the limb with her touch.

She sat down firmly on the end of the bed. What was this guy, part lizard? Since when did vampires regrow extremities? How would she know anyway?

It was then that Beth really committed to studying Mr. Crisp, but only in ways that caused him no harm. She had been fascinated with him before, sure, but at that moment it occurred to her what harnessing some of his abilities could do for patients. Imagine regrowing limbs for amputees or children with congenital deformities, not to mention those with spinal cord injuries. Yes, harnessing the rapid healing would be a boon to almost everyone, and probably put everyone in the medical field out of work. But imagine the benefits for the human race! Sure, people regrew portions of their livers, and skin grew back, though scarred when deeply damaged. It was nothing compared to this. Regrowing organs after trauma or surgery might be possible too.

But Beth was not so blinded by the possibilities that she didn't realize it could also mean a very prolonged life span, a population explosion from longevity, not births.

She also realized what this could mean to the military. Imagine soldiers that healed rapidly, regrowing damaged appendages and organs. It could create a nearly indestructible force for the country that commanded it—or the insane terrorists bright enough to steal it, pervert it, and use it against others. Weren't there similar arguments about stem cell research and cloning? How could one ignore the potential good in fear of the possible exploitation? Science was not meant to be judgmental. It was purely discovery and understanding. It was, at its heart, amoral. It was those who applied it which made it ethical or unethical in its use.

Beth rose from the bed with a purpose. She would study and learn whatever she could from Mr. Crisp. She would discover whatever it was that made him what he was and find a way to harness it to improve the human race. Lofty, yes, but how could she not try?

It had been thirty-six hours since she'd brought him home and about twenty-four hours since she had placed his bandages. Beth decided with the rapid growth of his hands that she should examine the rest of his body as well.

So, after hanging a second unit of blood, Beth began cutting away the bandages over his head and neck. The changes were breathtaking. Using the same gentle debriding techniques she had after his arrival in her guestroom, she smoothed away bits of dead flesh to find areas of new baby-soft skin in areas that had been less damaged. In areas of deep tissue burns, the underlying soft tissues showed a beefy red granulation-tissue-like growth. Areas over the neck muscles of the left side looked fuller and more robust, giving his neck a more normal contour, rather than the skeletonized, dried and dehydrated appearance he initially had. While she still couldn't define any facial features to speak of, the tissue of the lips had begun to regrow. The tip of his nose was lost with debridement, but a fresh mound of healthy pink-red tissue waited beneath. Beth continued her inspection and debridement over the rest of his body, making notes to refer to later and measuring the regrowing digits to establish a rate of growth.

Several of the toes were also lost, but happily the penis was intact, being only superficially burned. The trauma of holding a charred finger in hand Beth could handle; a penis may have been harder to get over. Although, the thought of being able to regenerate genital tissues as well opened a whole new realm of possible uses for Mr. Crisp's unique abilities. *Forget Viagra and Extenze, there's a new treatment in town! We'll grow you a new one with healthy vasculature, Mr. Johnson, how long would you like that?*

She had to chuckle aloud at that one. Beth was once again pleased that Mr. Crisp was unconscious, at least at this moment. She would imagine that even badly burned, having a woman laughing while examining your genitalia would be quite damaging for an ego.

Nonetheless, she decided to explain herself.

"You'll forgive me, I hope, Mr. Crisp. I am not at all laughing at the appearance of your... genitals. They are quite... adequate"—and that was not giving him the credit he deserved—"but I was just reflecting on your regeneration and its obvious possibilities."

Even speaking the words to herself aloud brought a warmth to her cheeks which she knew meant a nice red flush had blossomed. After all she had seen in her years as a physician, you would have thought the reflex would have waned.

Beth finished her examination and debridement, turning him as gently as possible, replacing his draw sheet and applying a fresh layer of ointment and bandages to all the affected areas. She saw no signs to suggest a developing infection. This would have been a major concern in any human burn patient, but she supposed there must also be some upregulation of the immune system along with his regenerative ability. Even with grafting and the best surgical care, there would have been almost no healing on a human patient after such a short period.

Though Beth did not yet understand his physiology, she could assume she was on the right track. Evidently the blood she was supplying was meeting his needs, and her concerns of blood incompatibility lessened. His regenerative abilities seemed to be improved even, requiring three separate IVs to complete the infusion of a single unit of cells. A single line lasted only about an hour before his tissues forced it out, like a festering splinter from a human.

Having finished caring for him, Beth moved to reclaim the fingers, toes and various other lost tissues from the bedside table which had become her makeshift mayo stand. She intended to keep them for further study. They were badly charred, but surely some residual DNA would be lurking deep within the bones.

Barely touching the first, though, it disintegrated before her eyes, almost instantly becoming nothing but ash. As she was deciding how to approach the remaining fragments, they too began to fall apart until nothing remained.

Beth looked from the table to Mr. Crisp. "No wonder no one knows anything about you. You certainly don't leave anything behind."

She decided to save the ash anyway, placing it in a Ziploc bag labeled with the tissues it represented and the dates collected. As she began planning to take small, additional living tissue samples that she now knew would quickly regenerate, she began to wonder if they too would turn to ash before they could be analyzed or if removing living tissue would buy a little time. Perhaps placing them in cell culture media would preserve them long enough to get them to a lab. Could something similar have happened in the blood samples she'd drawn? They hadn't become ash, but the cells had disintegrated. Of course, Beth couldn't process the tissue sample at just any lab. She would have to be certain any information they revealed would be either discounted or overlooked entirely.

Once again, her thoughts turned to the university, specifically its cytogenetics lab. Her continued academic appointment and association with the university was turning out to be worth its weight in gold.

Chapter 14

LUCIANO

HE COULD TELL IT was dusk; an uncanny awareness of the day's end that all of his kind shared. Sure, he could make himself awaken before sunset, but during daylight hours he was sluggish, fatigued, weak. The night gave him strength and energy.

He lay comfortable in the converted wardrobe, an early wedding gift from his grandmother. Made of solid oak by his grandfather before he was born, its thick and sturdy walls were stained a beautiful glowing golden brown. Hand-carved vines spanned the length of both doors, the intricate pattern of leaves a near perfect mirror image. It was one of the only items he'd managed to keep from his first home.

He didn't need to rest inside the oak box, but its familiar smell, smooth walls and tight-fitted doors were a comfort to him and completely held out the glow of the daylight hours.

The smell of the oak reminded him of Nonna, his grandmother. His own mother had died giving birth to him. Already a widow at that time, Nonna had come to live with his father to help care for him. A tiny woman, even amongst Italians of that age, Nonna ran the house. Her white hair, always tightly back in a bun, was all that hinted at her years. It was Nonna who patted him on the head and kissed his cheek each night before he closed his eyes. It was why the oak wardrobe had been so precious a gift and made it such a comfort to him now.

The years rolled by, the world moved on, the faces and fashions changed as time dragged past. But the old oak wardrobe tied him to the memories of his past. He had removed the high shelf and the hooks that once held Nonna's few dresses and coat and added metal claw feet to the back, laying it horizontal on the floor rather than standing it up vertically. New hinges prevented the doors from hitting the floor when they opened. It had the look of an enormous long sofa table. He raised his hand and brushed his fingers against the lock on the inside, added for a small additional amount of security while he slept. It was still latched. Not that his strength wasn't formidable, even during daylight hours, but one could never be too careful, especially with the one who called himself "Master" always on his trail.

He preferred to call him "il Diavolo," meaning "the devil" in Italian; the evil, vengeful vampire who had turned him so long ago. Il Diavolo had turned him out of spite. Turned him only so he could watch him take the life of his beloved bride. It was payback for interfering with il Diavolo's plans to rape and kill her many months before.

But night was upon him and he would not allow il Diavolo to occupy another moment of his thoughts.

He unlocked the heavy metal lock and pushed the doors upward as he had every night for countless nights. But on this night the doors did not move. Confused at first, he pushed harder on the heavy oak doors, but they moved barely a quarter inch. That was when he heard the laughter.

It was nervous laughter, with rapid heartbeats revealing their anxiety. These were humans. He should have heard the heartbeats sooner, but he had dozed, enjoying the slow setting of the sun.

As he rattled the doors with his continued efforts to open them, he heard the metallic clinking of chains.

These humans had managed to chain him into the wardrobe.

As he struggled and his focus increased, he could also smell fresh pine outside the familiar old oak of the wardrobe. The laughter subsided, and the human men began to talk. Their voices were muffled, but with his enhanced hearing he could easily make out: "We have him now" and "Master will be pleased."

Master. With the single word the blood in his veins heated. He felt the familiar hatred tighten in his chest followed by fear; not fear of this devil but fear over what he now had planned for him. After so many years of successful avoidance, il Diavolo had found him and sent his human pets, drudges, to kill him.

Minutes passed, and the humans spoke of mundane things—sports scores, politics, movies, but still nothing happened. No movement, no threats, no gloating. It was infuriating and unnerving being trapped and at their mercy.

Just as he could feel the sun beginning to set, he heard the humans start to move about and smelled the distinctive odor of gasoline. The understanding of their intentions soon spread over him. They intended to burn him!

The scent of smoke began to filter through the planks and crevices of the wardrobe. It first was mildly uncomfortable and then quickly became stifling. Even for one who no longer breathed, the smoke was irritating and burning his eyes, causing him to squint. Shouts came from the human voices and then the sound of their feet running as they climbed the basement stairs and crossed the floor overhead.

The heat began to build; first warm but suffocating, slowly escalating to intolerable. The walls of the wardrobe became so hot any touch burned even though the flames had not yet reached him.

He began to lose reason, fear overtaking him. He thrashed around inside this bed that had become an oven, hitting the walls with his fists.

His closed fist burst through the right side of the wardrobe—

And he awoke panting.

His mind swam with the panic of the dream and the pain that the movement of his body caused him. It took several seconds for him to realize he was awake. His eyes opened and his heart began to assume its more normal rhythm.

The room was not familiar. He had no idea where he was or how he'd come to be here. He was disoriented and moved his head from side to side, trying to bring sense to it all. Light spilled into the darkened room from outside the doorway, the brightness hurting his eyes and making it more difficult to evaluate his surroundings. His night vision, usually excellent, seemed polluted by the nearby light.

He was lying in a full-sized bed, covered by a clean white sheet. His whole body screamed in agony with even the smallest movement. A pole stood at his side with an emptied blood bag hanging from it, a coatrack it seemed, now serving as a makeshift IV pole. The room was small with a nightstand beside the bed holding a lamp and an alarm clock which read 9:36 p.m. He knew it was night but had no idea what day it was. How long had he slept?

The pain in his body drew his attention. He was covered in bandages, clean, with the smell of ointment and blood and serous fluid that oozed into them from his exposed flesh. The reality of the dream sank in. He had been set on fire by il Diavolo and left for dead. Who had saved him and who had brought him here? The bag of blood was clearly meant for him. He remembered vaguely the sensation of the infusion. Whoever brought him here seemed to be trying to help him, but who was it and why?

He heard footsteps approaching from outside the room and closed his eyes. He lay perfectly still, feigning sleep, and waited.

CHAPTER 15

PETER

PETER WAS ANXIOUS TO get on with it. Waiting for the approval of his medical privileges had been painful. Master had not been pleased with the delay. Now that he was finally here on the job, he could begin to investigate what had happened to the vampire Luciano's body; a tedious matter. He was supposed to have been consumed in the fire.

Master was not pleased to hear a body had been found at the scene and transported to the morgue. It was messy, very messy. Master had called him careless, useless and unworthy. And oh, how he longed to be worthy. For when Master decided he was worthy, the gift would be his to control, no doors would be closed to him. Master could be cruel, but he had promised to change him when he had earned it. He recalled the night he had pledged his loyalty to the Master:

"Get back here you stupid, snot-nosed brat!" his father slurred, lunging and nearly falling over the threadbare and sweat-stained lounge chair.

"No!" snarled Peter, a defiant glare thrown over his narrow shoulders as he ran for the porch.

"When I get ma' hands on you, I'm gonna make you sorry you ran," he spat, slapping at the screen door as it squealed away from him.

Peter stopped at the Master's side, just inside the rickety gate on what remained of a cracked and grass-covered sidewalk.

"Who the hell are you?" the man bellowed, waving his bottle of Jack and wrenching up his sagging belt with his other hand.

"I'm a friend of Peter's."

"The goddamn kid ain't got no friends. They don't want him anymore than I do! His own mamma couldn't stand the sight of him and left him here with me."

"I've come to make sure you never harm him again."

"Oh yeah? Just how you plan on doin' that? This is my house and as worthless as he is, he belongs to me. What I do in my house ain't nobody's business but my own. Now get the hell off my prop'ty and stay away from my boy."

The Master was at his side before he could blink his glazed eyes.

"How the hell did you..." he said as the bottle slid from his hand and smashed on the wooden porch, glass and sweet-smelling liquor bursting out around the impact site in a wet star. The Master's hand was over his mouth, fangs in his beard-stubbled, sweaty neck before his drunken brain thought to fight back. When he did, the struggle was brief, his sluggish punches to the Master's arms useless.

When Peter's father was drained, the Master dropped his body unceremoniously to the floor. It landed with a muted thud.

As the Master turned to Peter, he said, "Follow me, and no one will ever harm you again."

Peter's heart hammered in his chest, his breath quick and ragged. His eyes were wet, but he held the Master's gaze, closed his gaping mouth and gave a short nod.

Over the years, Peter had risen through the ranks and now answered only to the Master. The time for him to be turned had to be close.

Right now, however, Peter had to be patient, biding his time until he could get access to the transport records without causing suspicion. The body had indeed arrived at the morgue. The EMS records indicated the coroner had pronounced the body dead at 9:16 p.m. He noted the body was severely burned. Elizabeth Ramsey had been the pathologist on duty to receive him.

Amongst the crowd of other pathologists, dieners and administrators he had met on his visits, Beth Ramsey stood out. She was average height, but that was where "average" stopped. Her dark brown hair had been pulled back into a ponytail that had likely begun neat and tidy, but unruly small locks had fallen from the band and hung loosely, framing her face. Her skin was pale and made the pink of her cheeks and lips more noticeable. Even though he knew how many hours she had been working lately, her eyes were alert and intelligent. She seemed to scan him while they spoke. She had a sexy athletic build along with a tight little runner's ass that he followed with his eyes as she walked away.

This was the kind of woman who would not be swayed by handsome but shallow men. This was a woman that would demand intelligence, who would demand respect. This was the kind of woman he wanted and deserved; the kind of woman that he would have when the Master gave him the gift. The Master had kept him busy since the death of his father and sex had consisted of one-night stands and prostitutes. But Peter liked strong, lean women, and particularly liked dominating them, and he imagined bringing Beth to her knees in front of him with his hand wrapped tightly around her teasing ponytail or perhaps her arm wrenched in the middle of her back as he bent her forward over his desk.

He pulled his thoughts from what she would look like beneath those loose-fitting scrubs and focused on the task at hand.

It took some doing to get access to Beth's autopsy record. She had dictated the case and sent it on to transcription. Transcription, knowing she was taking vacation, had placed it at the end of the queue, which meant it wasn't typed until late Thursday. He didn't know what he really expected to find. If Beth had performed the autopsy on Luciano, she would have either seen the altered canines or the rapidly beating heart upon opening the body, which she certainly would have noted as unusual and transferred the "patient" to the floor. Instead, she found a severely burned corpse and finished the autopsy, complete with dental records.

It couldn't have been Luciano; it must have been a human passerby, caught somehow in the blaze and burned. The only point of concern was the coroner's recorded liver temp, which would indicate the human died far earlier or, of course, the corpse was no longer human at all. Being a John Doe, the body was placed in a cooler to await possible identification before being released for burial. He had tried to view the body but found the assigned locker empty.

A completed mortuary release form was found in the file. This was clearly against protocol. A call to the mortuary to return the body revealed no record of the body having ever been received. He would call Beth and ask what had happened to the body. Why would she release it early? Could it have been a misstep or did she know what he was? Could she possibly be a drudge, pledged to Luciano as he was to Master? It did not fit with what he knew of Luciano, and Master would surely have told him to find and kill her if he was aware. She could not have completed the autopsy without removing the heart and killing him, unless she had falsified the report entirely. Could Luciano have awakened and managed, even in his severely compromised state, to place another charred body where his should have been? But then, what had happened to that body?

Beth's record was impeccable. Coworkers told stories of her willfulness and ability to think about cases "outside of the box." Lawrence Fluck had told him of a case in which an anesthesiologist's wife had been found and presumed drowned after her car left the road and crashed into a local creek. Beth had found the lungs to be free of water, no frothy liquid typical of a drowning victim present, and refused to believe she had drowned. She scoured the body and found a needle mark between the great and second toes of the right foot. There was no other evidence of injuries unrelated to the crash and no tissue bleeding from the wounds present.

Knowing the patient's husband was an anesthesiologist with access to numerous drugs, Beth sent the blood for evaluation for common paralytic agents and their metabolites. It came back positive for rocuronium, a surgical anesthetic. The investigation showed the husband had injected the wife with rocuronium, paralyzing her completely, and causing her to suffocate since the muscles that controlled breathing were affected. He then put her in the car, drove to the creek and wedged her foot against the gas pedal to send her over the bridge and into the creek below. They said Beth had been tenacious, refusing to accept drowning as the obvious cause of death.

That didn't sound like a woman who was lazy enough to falsify a record just to get rid of the case and certainly not one to miss a beating heart or fangs.

The dental films from the burn victim had been sent through the database but, of course, the database only held copies of films from missing persons and some criminals, neither of which would include a record of Luciano. And again, a set of elongated canines would have been a quick red flag. So, he was left with three possibilities: one, the corpse was a passerby and Luciano had burned in the blaze; two,

Luciano, badly burned, had managed to switch out another charred body for his own and escape; three, Beth was a drudge and had falsified the record to save him.

Given the little he knew about Beth, the latter seemed unlikely. The woman he investigated didn't seem to thrive on power. The stories showed her to be more interested in truth and justice than glory. But the promise of immortality was intoxicating and had been too much for even him to resist.

The second possibility also seemed unlikely. The men Peter hired had been there until the whole basement of the house had gone up in flames, the old wood perfect kindling. They left only when first responders began to flood the area. Luciano could not have escaped without being severely burned. It would take time and a great deal of blood for him to regenerate if he had survived. That amount would have resulted in several new corpses, and there was no increase in suspected homicides or unobserved deaths in the last few days.

Luciano was a loner from the Master's description of him. It seemed unlikely he had the friends to nurse him through such a crisis. His severe burns would also make it unbearably painful to move about, not to mention being more than a little conspicuous.

So the first possibility seemed far more likely. Luciano had perished in the fire and the corpse Beth had examined belonged to some unlucky soul caught in the flames.

But Master insisted Luciano had survived. He said he could sense Luciano and that Peter had failed him... miserably. So, to please Master and regain his favor, Peter would continue to investigate. He had to admit the missing corpse was quite odd. The mental lapse for Beth, releasing the body too early, the lack of a body at the funeral home, it was all very suspicious.

He would get to the bottom of this. If Luciano lived, Peter would find him and kill him while he was still weak and Master... Master would be pleased.

Chapter 16

BETH

THE CALL CAME EARLY the following morning, just after day shift would have arrived. She knew it wouldn't take long. The missing body wasn't likely to go unnoticed. It was Peter James, the new guy.

"Hello, Beth, this is Peter at the lab. Sorry to disturb you on your time off, but we have a little dilemma here. I noticed the body from your last case, the John Doe burn victim, was released early on the morning of the first. I'm sure you know that protocol dictates the body be kept for a period of thirty days before release if the subject is unidentified."

Though the call had her heart racing, Beth was prepared for the conversation.

"I'm aware of the protocol. I was exhausted, though, as you know, picking up all of Henry's shifts. I apologize for the error. Please contact the funeral home and explain the error, or I can call if you like. They shouldn't have issue with returning the body. With no ID and no family to notify, they wouldn't have disposed of the body this rapidly."

"Tried that; they have no record of the pick-up and no body," he said.

"What? He can't have just disappeared!" Beth hoped the fabricated surprise and dismay in her voice sounded genuine. "Have you checked the coolers? Perhaps the body was moved or mislabeled."

"Yes, yes, I checked the coolers before calling you, of course," Peter said, sounding a bit annoyed.

"Well, bodies don't just get up and walk away after an autopsy, or disappear into thin air—"

Interrupting, "No, Beth, they don't, not without help."

"Shall I come in and help you look for him?"

"No, I'm sure he will turn up soon enough."

The call ended with a *click*, no "goodbye," no "thank you, ma'am," just *click*. It was abrupt, but her only other interaction with Peter had also been intense. She was guilty, but her record was excellent and there would be no reason for him to suspect her part in anything as unusual as an abduction of a corpse. The conversation had gone as well as she could have expected.

As she fed and re-examined Mr. Crisp, Beth relayed the conversation and described Dr. James.

"It was pretty surprising that we were able to hire someone with experience so quickly. It was as if he were just waiting for the position. That's ridiculous, though. There is no way he could have predicted Henry's death.

"Oh well, on to more important things. Your finger buds are a full quarter inch longer today than yesterday. I see new growth of the muscles and tissue membranes of your arms and legs, as well as your neck, and you are growing new skin over your lower abdomen and central face. That's quite a lot of progress in such a short time. It must certainly be the quality of care I'm providing." Beth chuckled.

"Perhaps it's my sparkling personality and wonderful bedside manner. Yeah, that's the response I usually get. Look at me, a few days with you and I've become Chatty Cathy. In the presence of a new complete stranger, I'm usually much more reserved. Truth is, I'm just terrible at starting conversations. Most of what I'm comfortable talking about is work related and hardly material for casual dinner conversation. The few times I have shared those thoughts, I've been met with complete repulsion or utter fascination; there's no middle ground." She sighed deeply before continuing.

"Shortly after I entered practice, I broke my own 'no blind dates' rule and went out with the friend of a friend. During dinner, consisting of pasta with marinara, he asked me about my work and what I had encountered that day. I started to explain the gunshot wound to the head from a male suicide victim. I was just explaining the differences between an exit and entry wound when he vomited all over the table. I guess the marinara reminded him a little too much of blood, but it looks quite different to me. And, of course, there is the difference in smell as well. Anyway, that effectively ended the date and my attempts at sharing my work."

She paused for a moment, cocking her head and looking at his bandaged face. "I'm guessing, given your condition, blood doesn't bother you much. It's really rather fascinating. It is the life force of the body; our tissues bathe in it. It's beautiful in its makeup and functionality, such a perfect media for life. Of course, I've never considered it until now as a sole source of nourishment, or even a beverage. I've tasted it enough times from mouth injuries, bloody noses or a paper cut on a finger I then stuck in my mouth.

"It really doesn't taste that bad; thick, minimally salty, but otherwise not a lot of flavor. But of course we all interpret taste a little differently, smells as well. I, for one, hate the bitter, strong smell of coffee, but I'm a minority. Perhaps for you blood is what I would interpret as chocolate milk or sweet tea."

She exhaled again loudly, shaking her head. "There are so many things I would like to ask you. In the vampire movies, the vampires live on for centuries, never aging. It makes me wonder what you've seen in this lifetime. If you have centuries of stories to tell or if you were recently made and still learning the ropes. How was it you came to lie on my autopsy table appearing near death—assuming you can die. And, if not this, what on earth would kill you? I would like to know how it is you came to be a vampire and what other abilities, besides the power to regenerate, the change has afforded you. I'm curious to know how much you understand about your condition from a medical standpoint. Is it possible that you were born to this rather than made as I assume? And, at this point, I'm still wondering what you might look like. I would also very much like to know if you'll kill me when you awaken." With this Beth let out a weak and nervous attempt at a chuckle.

He had already shown remarkable healing since she began giving him blood. What she had only suspected of him at first was now supported by her findings. It was a sobering thought, but she must consider that she might be nursing her future murderer.

Mr. Crisp had been wearing clothing before receiving his burns so he was at least that civilized, but what else did she really know? Her views were so influenced by the vampire lore and romanticized horror films she had seen. But could he be just a killing machine, following animal instincts to seek prey and kill? He had to have some higher functioning, didn't he? How would vampires manage to conceal their existence if they were merely instinctive predators?

Beth also remembered removing his personal items which included a ring. She supposed it could just be part of the camouflage, but it certainly suggested more. As for being his first snack upon waking, there was really no good way to protect herself. Fire worked against him, but she couldn't exactly keep an open flame with her at all times. In the movies it was sunlight, garlic and all things holy. She supposed she could gather some holy water and crosses, but she had no way of knowing if they would work without trying them on him and risking injuring him further. If she could figure out a way to get a tissue sample to survive detached from his body, maybe she could test it.

And then the idea hit her. Mr. Crisp's entire existence, at least as far as she knew, was centered on the intake of blood. Perhaps a tissue sample, bathed in blood as support media, would survive.

Beth had been to the blood bank shortly after 8 a.m. and had pulled in quite a haul with three units of O positive and one of A positive. Not having any sterile containers lying around, she boiled a small plastic bowl and lid to collect the sample. She filled the bowl with about five cc of O positive blood and removed a small piece of granulation tissue from Mr. Crisp's healing abdomen. She placed it quickly into the blood and waited.

The tissue seemed to expand slightly but kept its pink color.

She placed a second small fragment of granulation tissue on the lid of the container but offered it no blood. In seconds, the tissue on the lid began to discolor from red-pink to tan-gray, finally becoming dry and dark gray-black before turning into tiny ash-like flakes.

"One mystery solved," Beth said aloud, feeling quite proud of herself.

As she later sat, entering her thoughts and findings into the computer log, waiting for Mr. Crisp to extrude his third IV needle, she kept an eye on the small tissue culture of sorts that she had started on Mr. Crisp. Rather than clotting, drying and becoming a reddish-brown paste, the blood surrounding Mr. Crisp's tissue became noticeably thinner, looking more like cherry Kool-Aid, like the plasma from a patient who had hemolyzed. The tissue itself still looked the same: no discoloration.

The failed complete blood count studies to check his hemoglobin for anemia and the chemistry studies from the previous day came to mind. They, too, had shown findings that would suggest hemolysis, even though Beth knew she had collected the sample properly. She used a clean needle to place a drop of blood from the plastic bowl on a glass slide and made a smear. She would take it by Lu's lab or hematology tomorrow to stain and examine. She also decided to draw a new sample from Mr. Crisp in the morning before heading to the lab so it would be as fresh as possible before she ran it.

Two of the four units had been infused by 1 p.m. There really was no way of knowing at this point how much he really needed. With the hemolyzed sample she had run, the hemoglobin would be inaccurate, so she couldn't tell if he needed more or if she was overloading him. But if his body was somehow lysing the cells, perhaps it was impossible to overload him. And then there was always that lingering doubt that he did need type specific red blood cells and this was a transfusion-related hemolytic process. His continued healing, visible even over the course of the transfusion of today's three units, suggested otherwise. If she truly had induced that kind of trauma to his system, he should be doing poorly, not healing before her eyes. And again, the frustration was there as she knew regardless of whether or not he needed type specific blood, she had to take what she was given.

With that, Beth decided the fresher the cells the better and planned to give the remaining units as soon as she awoke that evening, and headed to bed.

CHAPTER 17

MASTER

VENICE, ITALY 1722

In the warm night air, the smell of blood hung heavily on the skin of those around him. The dilated vessels, open wide to release the heat that seemed to emanate from every human he passed. He could smell the sweat that clung to them. It wafted to him in rhythm with the fans the ladies waved in an attempt to create a cooling breeze in the stagnant air.

He had been looking to feed and saw a beautiful woman hurrying from the steps of an old stone building into the street. She was clothed in the dress of the times with her long, flowing skirts, cinched waist and open bodice showing the pale pink swells of her bosom beneath the lace trim. Her hair was piled atop her head, curls trailing from the high knot. The heat had freed a few unruly curls from near her temples and at the nape of her neck that clung to her damp skin. Her hair, the color of honey, her skin such a soft pale cream; he ached to taste it.

He spoke to her in perfect Italian. *"Buonasera, signorina."*

With this she turned to meet his eyes, and he hypnotized her into walking with him on his arm into a nearby narrow alleyway. It was there he faced her and drank in the water-clear blue eyes that held such tenderness, such innocence.

He cupped her breasts in his hands and, regaining some of her faculties, she protested, pushing back at him. But, of course, he was far stronger and even her best attempts to hit him were mere caresses against his cold skin.

He tore open the bodice of her dress and suckled her right nipple as she screamed in fear, crying out for God to save her. He would not hypnotize her into silence or submission now. He enjoyed the terror that filled her face, the desperation he saw in her eyes as she realized there was no escape.

It was in that moment, as he nipped at her breast, that Luciano rounded the corner and entered the alley, leading a group of eight men who had responded to the woman's cries. He had thought them far enough from the main corridors not to be disturbed. The men smelled of liquor and pipe smoke, likely having come from a nearby tavern.

Seeing him, the men froze, sensing he was not merely a mortal man and seeing the monster as he wished them to. But Luciano, unwavering, continued forward, pulling a pistol from his belt.

"*Liberala, mostro!*" Luciano yelled, demanding her release.

Luciano's show of courage motivated the rest of the men to follow suit. Healing from bullet wounds was not something the Master would enjoy, and he decided to leave the woman for another night. He would find her again easily enough and finish what he had begun.

He moved so quickly the men were left staring open-mouthed at the woman, now alone. Luciano hurried to her, covering her exposed breasts with his shirt. The Master watched from the rooftop as Luciano soothed the woman and gently led her away.

He returned to the area after nightfall the next evening. Knowing her scent, he followed it easily and was both surprised and irritated to find Luciano already in the woman's company. His anger grew as he watched him flattering and doting on the woman.

And as he planned to enter and kill them both, a better plan began to form. He was immortal, he could afford patience.

He fed on another woman that night and for many nights thereafter, always returning to watch Luciano and his lost kill. The two were soon engaged and the wedding set for the coming spring.

He waited patiently until dusk the day of the wedding and found them easily. He entered their bedroom silently, listening with a mixture of revulsion and amusement to their declarations of love. He had learned long ago: love was a fleeting and wasteful emotion. It left you weak and vulnerable, neither of which he desired.

As Luciano entered his new wife for the first time, the Master lunged in and pulled him naked to his knees in front of her on the bed, sinking his fangs deeply into his neck. He fed sloppily from him, allowing the blood to splash onto his wife's naked skin beneath him. She screamed in terror as he drained Luciano nearly to the point of death.

Then he opened a gash in his own wrist with his teeth and forced it into Luciano's mouth.

Weak and unable to fight back, Luciano struggled only meagerly before swallowing the offered blood. It was then that he dropped Luciano's limp body to the bed, half atop his terror-stricken wife. He left the room and proceeded to nail heavy planks over the closed door and outside the only window to the room. And then, he waited.

He listened and relished in the woman's sorrow as she tried to wake Luciano, who was likely already warm with fever. He heard her attempt to reassure him that he would be alright. She occasionally cried out for someone to help them, beating at the door with her fists, calling out to God in fervent prayer and even praying the Rosary.

Luciano was strong and lasted most of the following day as Master hid from the sun in the shadows just outside the door to the room, waiting for the inevitable. Had he not been able to hear Luciano's beating heart slow and finally stop, he still would have known the time of his passing from the inconsolable sobs of the woman. He relished in them, her misery abating some of his anger over having his kill interrupted.

He was anxious now, nearly giddy like a child waiting for a gift on Christmas morning. He heard the woman gasp and say Luciano's name and knew he was rising. She called to God, thanking him for returning her beloved husband to her. But her cries of joy soon turned to questioning.

"*Luciano? Luciano, che cosa e sbagliato? Che cosa fai?*" his wife asked, confusion and fear clear in her voice.

It was followed once again by screams of terror, the sound of running feet and then screams again which began to soften to whimpers and then finally to silence. Soon after, he heard sobs of grief, now in the baritone voice of a man.

"*Cosa havel fatto?*" the man cried in anguish.

Master felt a sense of satisfaction and laughed aloud. He had won.

In a fit of rage, Luciano burst through the barricaded door, and seeing his wife's old attacker, lunged at him. The two fought and he continued to laugh at Luciano, taunting him.

"*Mostro!*" Luciano screamed at the Master.

The Master smiled back. Luciano had denied him release, and now he had taken the same from Luciano.

"*Mostro! Demone!*" Luciano yelled at him, but he also looked at himself, seeing the blood of his wife on his own hands.

And so, he had made Luciano immortal. Many newborn vampires didn't survive their first year. Some died out of sheer stupidity, failing to find shelter from the sun, impinging on the territory of another and being killed, or in some cases, killed by humans when careless about feeding. Vampires also policed their own, killing those who were not discrete, to preserve the secrecy of their existence. Still more, with their lingering humanity, could not bear to kill even to survive, and slowly starved or sought the light, willingly exposing themselves to the sun to die and end their suffering. The Master expected Luciano to fall into this last category, the guilt of killing his own new bride becoming too much for him to bear.

But he had been wrong.

For Luciano's first century, the new vampire had followed him. It was entertaining at first. He could sense Luciano's presence and would often make his feedings even more dramatic and brutal than he had intended. For months Luciano watched in silence. But one night just as he got his beautiful plaything alone, Luciano stepped in, yelling to draw attention and fighting him off the girl long enough for men to hear and run to investigate. He was forced to forego his feeding and flee. This went on for several nights, and he became nearly frantic with thirst; Luciano, tracking him until just before dawn.

Finally, in an act of desperation, he attacked a shop owner near his home and drained the man swiftly before hurrying home to rest in the darkness of his cellar.

He had been so ravenous and absorbed in the feeding he'd failed to notice the shop owner's daughter hiding beneath the stairs to the apartments over the shop. She had later fled, called law enforcement and pointed them toward his home. Hearing the story of a monster ripping at the throat of his victim and draining him of blood, they surrounded the house with torches in hand. If it were not for his carefully planned escape route, a tunnel to the cellar of a neighboring home, he would have been burned to death.

He waited until dusk there, furious that Luciano had driven him to a point of such carelessness and fearful the townspeople would discover his secret and find him before the safety of darkness could free him.

But they did not find him, and as dusk fell, he left the cellar to survey his still-smoldering house. Enraged, he left to feed and to find Luciano. He would once again have his revenge.

But Luciano was nowhere to be found. After hours of searching and nearly destroying Luciano's home, he was forced to flee the city to find shelter in a crypt in the cemetery outside town. Living for centuries was useful in obtaining property and investments, and he had many homes throughout Italy. But to lose one, and be forced from the city by his own creation, was intolerable.

CHAPTER 18

LUCIANO

A HUMAN ENTERED THE room. He could smell her scent and hear the wet beating of her heart as the blood pumped in her veins. He felt his extra set of canines begin to elongate. The smell of her blood was so intoxicating.

She spoke, "Hello, Mr. Crisp," as she entered and turned on the nearly blinding overhead light. Even through the filter of his lids, it took effort not to flinch and remain still. He heard her motion as she removed the empty bag from the makeshift IV pole and hung a new one. She swabbed his left arm with something cold and damp... alcohol... and then he felt a small pinch of pain, a needle, followed quickly by the intoxicating warmth of blood as it began to flow again from his arm to his chest and then throughout his body. He felt his tissues begin to heal.

The woman began to speak about a phone call from a Dr. James at the lab looking for him, or his body anyway. He realized that they were already growing suspicious of this woman caretaker, which meant she would be in danger and he would soon have to leave. He tried to focus, to come up with a better plan, but her words were overshadowed by the soothing healing the blood allowed, and he realized how exhausted he really was. Safe or not, he didn't have the strength to help himself and gave in to the relentless pull of sleep.

Chapter 19

Beth

Beth couldn't turn away from the handsome man with shoulder-length, dark mahogany-brown hair. It hung, all one length, in loose curls, framing his deep-olive-skinned face. His eyes were a soft brown, the color of semisweet chocolate. He stared at her through long black lashes, gentle but intense. His lips were full and deep red, the color of blood. As he looked at her, Beth realized it *was* blood and knew instantly that it was hers. Her fingers flew to her neck and were covered in the same thick red liquid.

Beth looked up to meet his eyes and saw the slow leering smile spread across his lips, revealing his elongated canines, and felt the world slip away into shadow.

Beth awoke to twilight, breathing heavily, her skin clammy, hair sticking to the back of her neck. The bedside clock flashed 8:12 p.m.

Having no desire to return to the dream, she pushed aside the linens and sat on the side of the bed, flipping on the bedside lamp. Of course, it was the same bedroom she had fallen asleep in, no monsters lurking in the corners waiting to pounce. The haze of the dream slowly began to slip away, and she decided to check on Mr. Crisp. Her waking thoughts were filled with him; Beth supposed it should come as no surprise that the same thoughts would begin to spill over into sleep.

Though she had only slept a few hours, the change in Mr. Crisp was remarkable. Skin had begun to cover the areas of his face that were still pink-red. She couldn't tell clearly what his coloring might eventually be. The growth of his regenerating nose was remarkable, and even before measuring it she could tell it was at least quarter inch longer than the day before. Granulation tissue and small patches of skin had begun to form over the badly damaged areas of his neck.

His healing seemed to accelerate with each unit she infused, and she wondered how long it would have taken him to regenerate with a constant infusion of blood products. Surely vampires had been injured before. Did they find their own blood sources? Perhaps there was some vampire clinic with a constant blood bath? Surely being unconscious would have hindered his recovery. Beth had so many questions for Mr. Crisp about himself and wondered if she would ever have a chance to ask, to have even a few answers to her growing list of unknowns. What if being so horribly burned had affected his brain somehow? What if he fully regenerated, only never to awaken? How long could she continue to care for him like this? And if she decided that he would never awaken, that she should let him die, if he even could die, then what? It wasn't like she could just throw a body out with the garbage. And what if someone else found him and realized what he was? What then?

Well, for now, he was healing, getting better. She would focus on that and worry about the rest if the time came.

Beth continued with her examination. Just above the base of Mr. Crisp's neck, in one of the skin-covered patches, short, fine brown hair like peach fuzz had begun to grow. Though still short and thin enough to see his scalp through, the hairs looked deep brown, nearly black.

"A brunette then," Beth said. "I'm told blonds have more fun. Perhaps bleaching your hair would have kept you out of this mess!"

There was a time in high school when it seemed most everyone was bleaching their hair and tanning. Beth had tried tanning once and ended up burning herself in areas that were never meant to see the sun in the first place. She never went back, which in the end was a good thing; much less sun damage. With her sleeping during the daylight hours, sun exposure was pretty limited. So she should still have young-looking skin when her contemporaries were covered in wrinkles.

"I suppose if Bram Stoker was right, your sun exposure should be limited too! Hmm, that's one theory I might actually be able to test. But don't worry, I'm not planning to roll you into the sun when we've only just begun to get you healed."

Since darkness had already fallen for the day, this experiment would be put on hold until morning. Beth sat at Mr. Crisp's bedside and recorded her findings, then waited as the files copied to her backup flash drive.

When she was a teenager in foster care, Beth was almost always the oldest of four or five kids in a one-bathroom house. Any journal she attempted to keep hidden was always found by the younger kids, who would read it and mock her incessantly. Her foster family had a computer, an ancient thing that took ten minutes to boot up but could still manage to run a word processing program, so she started keeping her journal digitally, keeping it password-protected and backed up on a floppy disc. But where to hide the disc?

On a day when the young boys at the house were being particularly pest-like, she ran to the bathroom and slammed the door, hoping for at least a few minutes of privacy. Beth closed the toilet seat and plopped down, cradling her head in her hands.

Frustrated, tears began to fill her eyes and she tore off a few squares of toilet paper to blot at her eyes. Squashing the toilet paper into a ball, Beth tossed it in the trash can next to the sink and missed. It landed at the base of the can, and she leaned over to pick it up. That's when she realized what a perfect hiding place it would be. So, when no one was watching, Beth closed herself inside the bathroom and taped a half-sheet of paper to the bottom of the can, leaving an opening just big enough for her disc.

In the fourteen months she lived in that house before aging out of the foster care system, no one ever found it. It had been her chosen hiding place ever since.

She ejected the drive from the laptop and returned it to her simple gray plastic can. It now held her secret securely duct-taped to its base.

CHAPTER 20

MASTER

HE COULD FEEL HER warmth around him as he thrust into her, his climax building. She struggled to keep pace. His stomach knotted and he plunged his fangs into her neck, piercing the artery and drawing deeply. The arousal combined with the overwhelming rush of warm blood into his mouth was too much. He came violently, thrusting deeply with each gulp of delicious warm blood. He felt her going slack in his arms but continued to drink until her heart, strong and steady moments ago, slowed and beat its last. He had intended on keeping this one for a while. Her white-blond hair and generous curves had pleased him.

Of course, she was not meant for changing. She was far too insignificant for that, but she would have amused him for some time. She hadn't minded being bitten. But there was always the risk she might turn by accident, and he had no need for a stupid big-breasted blond. And so it was with sex and humans. They were fragile and his self-control wasn't always the best. As a vampire, all pleasures were related to blood. Sex with another vampire was exquisite, biting at will and tasting the blood of their most recent kill. The abandon of any concern for the partner's survival to complete the act and the ability of the vampire to keep pace with his needs were powerful draws. But the blood did so quickly lose its warmth.

The fiery heat of the blood fresh from a human during sex could not be paralleled. Sometimes he enjoyed a willing human donor, their recklessness with their fragile lives intriguing, but the conquest of an unwilling human donor was intoxicating. There was excitement in the struggle, the fear adding an extra edge to the blood. And the final moment when the realization reached their eyes that he would take not only their body but also their life was a rush that he could not deprive himself of for long.

He rolled off the blond, her eyes already dull with death. Sated, at least for now, he rose to dress and turned his thoughts toward business. The body he believed to be Luciano's was missing. There was no proof of his death. The knowledge that his careful plan had possibly been thwarted was infuriating. Luciano's fate should have been sealed. He had planned the fire for weeks after discovering Luciano's involvement with the local blood collection centers.

His human drudges kept tabs on the area vampires according to his wishes. While checking in on one of them, the Master's human had seen bags of blood in his home. The Master had demanded an audience with the vampire and discovered that he had been feeding on blood collected from one of the local research centers. After questioning him, he discovered that the center, and many others like it in the region, were owned by Luciano.

His distaste for Luciano had been established long ago, but this new development was intolerable. Vampires were meant to feed on humans. The Vampyre name must remain synonymous with evil and death and should inspire fear and hatred for what they had done. He had dedicated his life to this and would not allow Luciano to subvert all he had worked for.

The Master stationed drudges at all of the area collection sites until

Luciano made an appearance and tracked him from there to his home in the outskirts of Overland Park.

His men had waited all day in Luciano's home and, just as dusk had fallen, had set ablaze his resting place, leaving him encased in the heavy layers of oak planks he had chosen himself. Luciano had, of course, awakened with the setting sun and realized he was trapped, the heavy oak and metal chains resistant to his efforts to break free. The dry old oak would have burned hot. It should have left him a pile of ash, but somehow, he believed Luciano had freed himself from the burning wood. Firefighters, responding to the blaze, had found a charred body only feet away. They had presumed him dead. There was no way to identify him, but he knew—*he knew*—it was Luciano once again surviving his attempts to end him. The body had been taken to the university hospital for autopsy and identification.

For months now he had planned in order to place, without suspicion, an ambitious new pathologist, Peter James, in just the right place. He was an annoying and tedious man but hungry for power and advancement. He met him about fifteen years ago but had seen the boy several times before. That night he had heard him whimpering like a wounded animal. He'd been crouched leaning against the side of a ruin of a house with a broken down once-white picket fence. The gate, open and askew, was overgrown with weeds blocking its swing. The gray paint peeled in large gaping strips, and the smell of the garbage, heaped in the dented can, reeked.

Feigning interest, the Master had asked, "You alright?"

"No! Leave me alone!" he'd answered.

His bruised face and arms had been visible even in the dim glow from the neighbor's yellow porch light. His dusty face was tear-streaked.

"Peter!" a man screamed from inside the house.

"Your dad do that?" the Master asked.

"What do you care?" the boy said, wiping at his eyes.

"What are you, fourteen? Fifteen?"

"Fifteen," he breathed, as though it had been forever.

"Almost a man. I wouldn't treat a son of mine like that," he said, seeing an opportunity.

The Master began to walk away, deciding there may be more than an easy meal here.

He heard him call after him, "Hey, mister, what's your name?"

"They call me the Master."

He had soon after killed Peter's father and raised the boy, freeing him from his father's abuse and guaranteeing his devotion. The lure of immortality, which he would never give him, was enough to ensure his loyalty and keep him as obedient as a dog on a leash. Tedious, but he was ruthless and carried out orders efficiently, so the Master had given him more and more responsibility through the years so that now Peter reported only to him and commanded his other servants at his behest.

He had intended on sending him into the morgue the week prior, having arranged the death of another physician some weeks earlier to ensure an opening would be available. Controlling the city was sometimes a messy business. Having a drudge in the local morgue to cover his various indiscretions was not just convenient but a necessity. Dr. James could have been very useful in this situation, but Luciano was never intended to leave that box, let alone be delivered to a morgue. The Master's men, and therefore Peter, had failed him.

An error by a Dr. Elizabeth Ramsey had allowed the body to be released early for cremation. While it would have amused the Master to have Luciano burned by cremation after having survived the house fire, charred but alive, the autopsy record showed a normal human body had been released. And moreover, the transport service had no record of moving the body.

Clearly something was amiss, but how had Luciano arranged to cover his tracks and make his way from the morgue? With the degree of damage to his body indicated in the autopsy report, Luciano would have been unable to feed quickly. Even with a river of blood, he could not have healed in time to have saved himself. Someone clearly had helped him, but who he had on the inside was unclear. So, the Master was pushing Peter into the situation to investigate and find Luciano before he could fully regenerate.

Luciano was a special kind of trouble, a thorn in his side.

He had obsessed over him for nearly three centuries after turning him, always keeping his eyes and ears open for sightings of Luciano with revenge heavy on his mind.

And finally, he had heard a story of Luciano having traveled to the New World.

So, he had left his home and traveled to the United States. Though he spoke fluent English, adjusting to the US was still difficult. The Americans were wealthy people but overly confident, arrogant and uncultured. They exercised their freedoms recklessly and often to a point of ridiculousness. Still, the liberal attitudes and morals made his life easy. His eccentricities were tolerated almost without notice. This society was so bold. Luring young women back to his home where he could do with them what he would was almost too easy. The promise of sex or drugs was all the enticement he needed.

Though, early on, he had been careful not to kill them, for fear of raising suspicion. He had quickly learned that he could easily go unnoticed in the crowds, and the hiding places for a body in the city were endless. Now he hardly needed to make an effort to hide his tracks. Since he had placed Peter in the forensics office, any "messes" could easily be covered up. But he hadn't been in place in time to intervene with Luciano. His idiot underlings had bungled even the most perfect of plans.

But wherever Luciano was, he had to be near death and near crazy with pain and thirst. Even if he was able to feed at will, the healing process would take time. He was vulnerable, and if the Master could find him once again, he could finish him and rid himself of this nuisance forever.

As dawn approached, he called his drudge to take the girl's naked body and readied himself for rest.

Chapter 21

BETH

BETH STARTED UNIT THREE running after placing a few drops of blood in another small plastic bowl. She used a pair of tweezers cleansed in alcohol to pluck another small fragment of tissue from Mr. Crisp's healing wounds and placed it in the small blood-filled plastic bowl. The blackout curtains were drawn through most of the house, as she didn't want to risk exposing Mr. Crisp to sunlight. So there was no risk to the tissue as she headed for the kitchen, but on the way she grabbed a towel from the bathroom rack and wrapped the specimen in it just in case.

Morning sunlight poured in through the open window in the kitchen onto the counter. Out of the direct light and a few feet from the counter, Beth removed the towel and watched the tissue. It remained pink and viable with no outward signs of change. Two steps forward and the tissue was in full sunlight. It immediately began to sizzle, sounding like a steak on a grill. Beth could see small bubbles rise and break on its surface.

And then with a sound like a gas-powered stove coming alight, the tissue burst into blue flame.

Startled, she let out a muffled shout and tossed the bowl to the sink, pushing up the faucet handle in nearly the same motion. But the flame continued despite the water until the tissue was reduced to a tiny fragment of gray-black ash, the blood around it dried a dark red-brown, singed into the base of the plastic bowl. The smell of burnt flesh filled her nostrils, and she reached for the can of air freshener she kept beneath the counter. A few sprays covered the scent a bit but didn't get rid of it entirely.

So, Bram Stoker was clearly not kidding about a vampire's sensitivity to sunlight. If anything, his writings had minimized it. Beth had never seen anything like it. There were reports of sun sensitivity in otherwise healthy individuals. Certain medications could induce some sensitivity as well. There were also reports of patients with severe forms of porphyria whose skin severely blistered and sloughed with only the smallest amounts of exposure to direct sunlight. But, even in its worst forms, the patients didn't spontaneously combust into blue flame and burn to ash before your eyes.

One more curiosity to add to the ever-growing list; another question answered that created countless more.

Over the course of the day, Beth tested more "folklore" vampire defenses. She placed crosses and garlic against Mr. Crisp's skin with no effect whatsoever. She stopped by St. Michael's Catholic Church on her way to the university for blood and filled a small container with holy water which, when she dripped it on his skin, only made him wet.

Silver, however, did illicit an allergic-type response. It was nothing like the reaction to sunlight, having no visible effect on a small fragment of granulation tissue. On Mr. Crisp's skin directly, however, it created a papular rash with small raised pink lesions forming wherever the metal touched. The response developed about two to three minutes after exposure and was slow to resolve, even after cleansing the skin in that area and with his remarkable healing. It was hard to know what to make of this. It appeared to be more of an allergic response like that many people exhibited to soaps or fragrances. Metal allergies weren't terribly common in normal adults but certainly well documented. Given the slowness of the response and mild nature, it certainly couldn't be useful in deterring him in an attack.

She really should try to repeat the lab work with fresh samples to see if she could learn more, perhaps even take a tissue sample this time, bathing it in blood to keep it from turning to ash.

The light was going to be a problem though. His cells may not tolerate the bright light of the microscope. Even a dissecting scope might be too much. Mr. Crisp tolerated the bedside lamp and even the overhead light, though dim. Perhaps as long as it wasn't direct UV light, this tissue would survive. Beth was also not certain if the tissue, taken from the blood pool, would survive in a fixative like formalin to be processed. She decided to bring home a couple of formalin-filled vials from her next trip to the hospital. Given the robust response of his tissue to daylight, it would be best to try the microscope exposure with her scope at home first.

With unit three still infusing, Beth heated up some leftovers and sat at her kitchen table to think. The only remaining methods to deter a vampire that Beth could find mentioned in popular literature were a stake through the heart, decapitation or not inviting them into your home. Since she had willingly allowed Mr. Crisp into her home and wasn't about to drag him around to other houses to test the theory, and stabbing him or removing his head were certainly contrary to her efforts to save him, she would just have to live with not knowing. She did know that his heart still beat, even though it wasn't palpable or audible. Driving a stake through a beating heart would logically be an effective way of ending his life. But would it heal if removed?

So, given her small size and the closeness of combat required for a stake to be effective, sunlight was really her only mechanism of defense. So, how could she weaponize sunlight to use in the middle of the night? Beth couldn't be sure what wavelength of light was affecting him or if it was something about the sun itself. But she did know UVA/UVB lights were made for therapy. Some skin diseases responded nicely to treatment with artificially made sunlight lamps, and they were also used for patients with seasonal depression. So, she decided to get a lamp with UVA/UVB bulbs, a small portable battery-powered unit, to test. If it worked, being battery powered meant she wouldn't be bound to an outlet, which seemed like a great idea.

Finished with her supper, Beth removed the completed blood unit and made a quick run to Home Depot, gathering a full-spectrum grow light and a battery-powered shop light before returning home.

Not wanting to chance harming Mr. Crisp without good reason, she removed yet another small fragment of granulation tissue, placed it in a sterile container and headed to the bathroom. She placed the container in the center of the shower and, thinking of the first attempt with real sunlight, retrieved a flame-resistant hot pad to put beneath the container. Having prepared as best she could for a violent combustion, she turned on the lamp and trained the beam directly on the tissue.

The response was again immediate and intense, the same blue flame leaping from the tissue before turning it to ash.

Finally, she had a weapon. She hoped Mr. Crisp would awaken grateful for her efforts, but at least she was prepared for the alternative.

She cleaned up the mess and placed the lamp on the bedside table. She would sleep a little more easily tonight.

Chapter 22

BETH

After hanging Mr. Crisp's breakfast, Beth began her next round of experiments. Placing a tissue fragment in a small pool of blood, she carried the sample to her office. She placed it on the microscope and turned the LED light on at the lowest setting.

Nothing. The tissue appeared unchanged.

Beth increased the light source until she could see the tissue as she looked through the objectives. It was difficult, as this scope was not made for dissecting, but she could at least see the contours and vascularity of the tissue. It looked normal.

What made it react like a porphyria patient on steroids with sunlight, then?

With the jar of formalin open and immediately next to the tissue, Beth grabbed the fragment with forceps and dropped it into the clear liquid. She held the vial at arm's length, eyes squinted and head turned, not sure what to expect.

A minute passed and still nothing.

She warily brought the vial closer to examine it. It remained intact. Finally, success!

She entered the spare room and began babbling happily to Mr. Crisp. "Your tissues aren't affected by LED light, Mr. Crisp. That means I will be able to take a look at your cells under a microscope. And because they don't turn to ash in formalin, I should be able to process them and get an ever better look with properly made slides. Beyond that, if I can see what's inside your cells with the electron microscope, maybe I can figure out what machinery your cells have that humans' don't. It could be a key to your rapid regeneration and to harnessing it for humans with spinal cord injuries or those who need new limbs. It is beyond exciting."

She began photographing his progress.

"I suppose you probably won't share my excitement about being able to look at your tissue with a microscope. Perhaps I should explain. When I was twelve and in the seventh grade, my science teacher, Mrs. Pernot, brought in some blank slides and water from a pond near her house. She also had onions, potatoes and a couple of butterfly wings. She let our class make wet mounts of them with a drop of water along with small scrapings of the plant material, cells scraped from inside of our cheeks and even hairs plucked from our own heads.

"We put the slides on the old microscopes, and it was as if a whole new world sprung to life before my eyes—like learning of a world of fairies that you never imagined existed. I saw small organisms that wiggled and danced as they swam through the pond water, the rigid cell walls of the onion, the huge oddly shaped squamous cells from inside my cheek. I was hooked. I found there were microscopic building blocks making up everything in and around us."

She paused from picture-taking and stood. Her voice became lower and wavered when she spoke again. "My dad saw how much I loved looking in the microscope and he saved up enough money to buy me a small student scope and a box of slides for Christmas that year. He even asked Mrs. Pernot for any of the leftover slides and supplies from class so I could study them more at home." She paused and sniffed, holding back the tears that often threatened to fall when she thought of her father.

"It wasn't just knowing what was inside a thing that called to me, not just the beauty of that microscopic world, but the knowledge that there was more than what was just on the surface, more than what the naked eye could see. Something that complex, that perfect, could not be happenstance. For me, it was proof that God existed, proof of a higher power in control of a world that often seems so daunting and chaotic. My dad understood that. And even later when life spun out of control and I lost him, I could look to science and my microscope for reassurance that all was still in order."

Beth sighed deeply and returned to her documentation. "Mr. Crisp, you are an excellent listener; you didn't interrupt my meandering stories even once. Thank you for being so patient."

Beth grinned and sat in the guestroom chair to record her findings in her laptop. While his nose was still not entirely covered by skin, the structure had returned with the soft tissues, providing a good idea of what it was to be. His lips had begun to heal in a few places, suggesting a pouting fullness. His ears, mostly lost in the fire, were also regenerating, the cartilage providing a more natural shape. Small ringlets of brown-black hair had appeared in a patch of new skin just above and behind his right ear. Where the skin was mature over his chest, she noticed a faint pink-red flush after the units of blood began to infuse. Despite the cool temperature of the refrigerated blood, Mr. Crisp's skin temperature increased with the transfusion, another interesting finding to add to a string of curiosities. At this rate of healing, remarkable for the few days Beth had cared for him, he would be fully recovered very soon.

"I certainly hope we have the chance to meet, Mr. Crisp. I've told you much about myself and would so like to hear about you. I suppose you won't remember any of it though, will you? That'll be odd, somehow, telling you about myself all over again when it feels... well, it feels like you're already listening."

CHAPTER 23

LUCIANO

LUCIANO HAD AWAKENED ONCE again as he felt the transfused blood coursing through his veins. Though still quite weak, he could feel his strength beginning to return. But the pain was intense, and he knew movement would be agony.

She was once again at his side. Her scent had become familiar and delicious. Her blood called to him, but she was obviously still caring for him.

Il Diavolo either believed him dead or did not know where to find him. Either way, it was not in his best interest to harm her or let her know he was awake. Feigning a coma would allow him to continue to heal and learn about her without requiring him to answer questions he wasn't prepared for. The less she knew, the easier his departure would be when he had healed enough to care for himself.

She changed the dressings over his wounds, and in the few areas where she cleaned away the damaged tissue, the pain was so intense he nearly cried out. But then came the soothing cool of the ointment she applied and more healing blood. All the while, she spoke to him, and in the midst of the pain, he focused on her voice. She spoke with a quiet confidence for the most part, telling him about how he was healing, speaking her thoughts about the regeneration and her theories about its origin.

She was intelligent, perhaps a doctor or researcher, and clearly sought to understand his condition. She had accepted that he was a vampire and seemed intent on understanding what that meant. But it was when she spoke of herself, her innermost thoughts, her past, her dreams for the future, that the vulnerability was apparent in her voice. In many ways, she reminded him of his bride of so long ago with her quiet strength and stubbornness acting as a shield for her tender heart. Her loneliness and hesitance to reach out resonated with him, the heaviness of his own loss centuries ago still a fresh wound on his heart. He did not dare risk opening his eyes to look at her, though he did wish to see her face. He imagined that she was beautiful, a soft face with gentle bright eyes.

But he knew well he could not hide for long. If il Diavolo had any idea that he lived, he was in danger, and so was she.

He had purchased the house that il Diavolo had burned about sixty years ago and, along with it, another in what was then a countryside on the south end of the metropolitan suburb called Olathe. But if il Diavolo knew of the house in Overland Park, he likely knew of the Olathe home as well. It wasn't safe.

He knew she was experimenting, her curiosity over what fueled his abilities growing. It was dangerous for her. There were two camps in the vampire world. The majority relished their existence and the perks that came with it. They kept their existence a secret and would happily kill anyone that threatened it. And scientists poking around to understand, harness and exploit their superior abilities were an obvious threat.

The second camp did not feel as threatened. They shared the curiosity of the scientists and would happily give up their thirst if not the other abilities. Most who felt the lingering guilt over the lives they took to feed didn't survive long. The blood banks had alleviated some of the reliance on live, face-to-face donors, but situations still arose where a life must be taken. If a vampire failed to feed regularly, they could lose control, like he had when waking from his death with so severe a thirst he had taken the life of his own new bride. The years had softened that wound, assuaging some of the guilt. Luciano knew that il Diavolo had been the cause for his actions, but the memories of her screams still occasionally haunted his dreams.

The woman sat next to him in the chair, and he heard her laptop chime as it began to load. He dared open his eyes just enough to watch her as she entered her password, *F-i-n-d-t-r-u-t-h-5-2-**. He committed it to memory, knowing that if he didn't take her life, he would need it to remove all the information she'd gathered about him.

When he was healed, he would also have to clear away her memories of him, but perhaps they could speak for a short while first. She deserved a few answers for her efforts and, to be honest, he just wanted to have a conversation with her, eyes open, so he could watch her as she spoke and have a look at her face.

CHAPTER 24

BETH

"ONE SUMMER WHEN I was young, my father saw me watching *National Geographic,* one of my favorite shows at the time. A whale had beached itself and died. Scientists were investigating its cause of death. After many examinations, they were still uncertain. I remember asking my father why the scientists couldn't figure out what killed the whale. And he said to me, 'I don't know Beth, but if they can't, I'm sure you will figure it out for them!'"

Luciano struggled to be still, stifling laughter, trying hard to think of something, anything else. He even conjured memories of the night he lost his wife to curtail the laughter. It was so difficult to lie still while Beth told him the stories of her life, but he couldn't let her know he was conscious, couldn't answer the questions she asked him or reassure her when she seemed uncertain of herself.

It was obvious to him she missed her father by the emotion in her voice when she spoke of him. Despite her pride in her independence, Luciano could also tell she longed for someone to see her for who she was at her heart. She would never call it loneliness, and in many ways, she was content in her solitary life. She didn't need another for happiness or approval, but she did want it. Although, from her stories, he could also tell she didn't trust easily. Losing her father so young, the one person in her life she loved and trusted, had left a mark.

While the blood she provided was slowly healing his wounds, he knew that the more blood he consumed, the sooner he would regain the strength he needed to defend himself. It would only be a matter of time before he was discovered.

With the bandages placed and the second bag of blood now coursing through his veins, the woman said, "Goodnight, Mr. Crisp," and left the room. He heard the light switch click off and could see the darkness through his lids. He listened as she brushed her teeth, then heard the lamp click off. It wasn't long before he heard her breathing become deep and regular and he knew she slept.

Luciano decided that it was time he rose and helped himself. He opened his eyes and began to rise from the bed. The pain was excruciating, and he winced, freezing the motion to regain his composure. Every tiny movement was like a burning, searing pain, nearly as bad as when the flames themselves had licked at his flesh. But he pushed on, knowing the danger he was in.

At the time of the fire, he was alone and had believed, even accepted, he'd reached the end. But fate had intervened. Now, with Beth, as she called herself, caring for him and his body regenerating, he felt obligated to continue. He had been given another chance to right some of his past wrongs and to honor the memory of his wife. Whatever happened, when he was adequately healed, he would return the kindness she had shown him and protect her as best he could before leaving to escape the Master.

He slowly made his way to Beth's bedroom. She slept curled on her side, her right arm bent beneath her head. Her curtains were drawn and only a small sliver of daylight made its way around their edges. But with his night vision, it was enough.

She *was* beautiful. Her hair was dark and hung loosely around her face and chin, spilling over her exposed shoulder. Even in the dim light, it shone. He knew it would be like silk to run through his fingers. Her skin was pale, perhaps even more than his, but perfectly smooth, almost porcelain in the pale light. Her lips pouted in her sleep, a soft petal pink. He found himself wishing she would open her eyes so he could see their color. Long but light brown lashes extended from her lids and lay on the skin beneath. He could see the curves of her body beneath the thin cover of the sheet, and could tell that she had a small but athletic frame. Her arm lay atop the sheet, fingers curled beneath her chin, but the outlines of the muscles of her upper arm were visible even as she slept.

He saw a wallet on the dresser in the corner of the room and slowly, silently made his way to it. Her license was inside and read, "Elizabeth Ramsey, 5 foot 5 inches, eyes blue, weight 130 pounds, address 1582 South 41st Street." Assuming the address was correct, he was in the north part of town, one of the bedroom communities just south of the river. So at least he knew where he was.

The bedside digital clock said 2 p.m. on April fourth. Now he was getting somewhere. He had been in and out for four days. He couldn't leave the house during daylight hours, so he would have to hope she decided to venture out.

He slowly and painfully made his way back to the second bedroom and was careful to return himself to the same position in which he started before allowing himself to give in once again to the sleepiness of the daytime hours.

CHAPTER 25

BETH

BETH AWAKENED, ROSE SLOWLY, and threw her legs over the side of the bed. She sat for a moment, running her hand down the curve of her jaw wistfully.

She stood, gathering her robe from the end of the bed and wrapping it around her, then strolled into the next room to check on Mr. Crisp. He lay in the bed exactly as she left him, sheet folded neatly across his waist. His healing in just a few short hours was amazing, with the majority of the flesh of his chest now covered in smooth new skin.

Beth walked to his side, admiring his exposed chest. She reached out her hand and gently placed the backs of her fingers on the skin of his neck. It was cool but slightly warmer than the day before. Memories of her dreams of the dark-haired man flushed her cheeks. Her hand glided slowly over his collar bone, down his chest to the nipple, taking care to only touch intact skin. Her hand continued to make its slow, languorous path to his abdomen, the taut muscles underneath the baby-soft skin such an enticing combination.

Beth's fingers continued their exploration, tracing the small curves of his abdominal muscles to the edge of the sheet and a small curl of brown hair that had found its way from underneath.

Beth felt the muscles tighten beneath her fingers and quickly pulled back, her cheeks hot and pink. She turned to Mr. Crisp's face to find it unmoving, eyes closed as always. Certainly she'd imagined it. He was clearly still unconscious, but she felt embarrassed nonetheless.

"I am certainly glad you weren't awake. I don't usually molest comatose men. I do apologize."

Beth took a deep, calming breath. "Time for a run and a shower before I head out for your breakfast."

As her feet fell in the familiar rhythm on the belt of the treadmill, her mind wandered. Her dreams were so vivid, kissing the dark-skinned, brown-eyed hunk, the sparks she felt as his lips touched hers. She wound her fingers in his shoulder-length, wavy mahogany-brown hair, her other hand tightly planted on his muscled chest. There had been no blood this time, the only red in her flushed cheeks.

Beth nearly tripped, having drifted to the edge of the treadmill belt and stepping on the side rail before stumbling back into her rhythm. It pulled her reluctantly from her thoughts.

All of this time caring for Mr. Crisp was getting to her. It wasn't as though she had never seen a man naked. Through her work and medical school, she had examined many men from top to bottom, just never intimately. Dating had always been difficult and uncomfortable. She had fumbled around the front seats of cars in college, but it just had never felt right to keep going. She hadn't planned to wait so long to have sex; the right person had just never found his way into her life.

So what? Now she was attracted to a burnt-up dead guy? A vampire was Mr. Right? And who was to say he was the man monopolizing her dreams? In all likelihood, if he ever awakened, he would try to drain her dry too, not ask her for a date. He was beginning to look a lot like the man in her dreams, though. Could vampires do that? Put visions in your head through dreams? Could they even have sex? In some novels vampires were impotent.

Novels, what reliable scientific literature she was referencing these days.

Beth forced the dreams and the sight of Mr. Crisp's bare chest from her thoughts.

As she reached the three-mile mark, Beth slowed the treadmill to a gentle walk to cool down. If Mr. Crisp was more friendly than bloodthirsty when he awoke, what would he do? Would he awaken startled, not knowing where he was, and bolt? Beth supposed he might, and then she would never have a chance to see what he was like or ask him questions about how he had become what he was. If he was friendly, how could she let him know that he was in no danger from her? She had nursed him back to health and kept him safe while he was unconscious, but that might not occur to him until much later. What could she do? What would he be looking for when he awakened?

Well, clothes, for starters.

She had brought him home in items from the morgue lost and found. The clothes didn't exactly fit him and certainly did not scream style. She didn't know if vampires even cared about such things, but surely having some decent clothes and shoes that fit him couldn't hurt. It was a good start, anyway. A shopping trip was in order, but first she would need measurements.

Thank goodness clothing sizes for men were far more standardized than those for women.

Beth had showered and dressed in khakis and a lilac soft cotton tee. She left her hair down since she was going out. In the shower it had occurred to her that she didn't own a tape measure other than the retractable one she kept in the drawer that she used for small projects around the house. It was metal and not exactly useful for taking body measurements, but she had a solution. She had a ball of string that she'd purchased a year ago for an experiment. She'd used it to tie cuts of meat together to approximate a mass of human muscle and soft tissue so that she could study the rate of decomposition in various waterways around the area. The experiment had gone very well, and she'd published her study last fall.

She unrolled about two arm's lengths of string and cut it off. Starting at one end of the string, she placed it from the center of Mr. Crisp's right armpit to the center of the left and then placed it along the metal tape measure.

Twenty inches, which would mean forty inches to go completely around.

Beth then placed the string edge at the right of his waist. As she carried the string across his waist, her hand grazed over his abdomen and she noticed the same tightening response she had noticed before, only this time it was accompanied by goosebumps.

She glanced quickly at his face, but his eyes remained closed. There was nothing else to suggest he was awake.

She completed the journey to the other side of his waist and measured fifteen inches even; a thirty-inch waist. Now she just needed the inseam.

Beth felt for Mr. Crisp's hip bone and moved down to the groin to place the tip of her string. She held her hand there and then stretched the string to his heel. She glanced back at her hand near his groin and noticed that the sheet near her hand looked fuller.

Clearly, Mr. Crisp had an erection.

Beth froze for a moment before quickly removing her hands from his body. "Well, that settles that," Beth said, thinking of the novels suggesting vampires were impotent. She couldn't help but notice that it was quite adequately settled too.

Mr. Crisp didn't stir otherwise, and Beth thanked her lucky stars that he was still unconscious. She guessed this could be chalked up to a wet dream. Apparently, vampires had them just like humans.

Thirty-four inches, the inseam, she thought. She couldn't help the smile that crossed her lips any more than she could help the one last glance below his waist as she measured his foot: size 11.

Beth went to the mall on 95th street. She had never shopped for men's clothing before, unless you counted the hideous tie she bought her dad for Christmas when she was twelve. Hoping to avoid a mistake like that again, she decided on the Gap.

She walked into the store and headed for the men's side. A mannequin was wearing a pair of khakis and a button-down shirt. She touched the button-down, but it felt a little rough in her hands. Mr. Crisp's skin might still be a little sensitive if he awakened soon, and something softer might be more practical. Beth decided on a cotton Henley in a turquoise blue. It would go well with his coloring. She picked up a large and headed to the rack of khakis for a 30/34.

As she approached the register with her selections, she passed a rack of men's briefs and paused. He would need underwear, but somehow standard briefs just didn't feel right. There was a pair of stretchy black boxer briefs with small foxes all over them. Why not? She also picked up a pair of size 10 to 13 white socks. She used her debit card to pay for the items and headed toward the closest Hibbett sports store.

Beth debated for a while on dress shoes versus tennis shoes but decided in the end that you could never go wrong with a pair of Chuck Taylor All-Stars and went with white in size 11.

She couldn't help thinking he would look really good in that blue Henley.

CHAPTER 26

BETH

BETH WAS ENCOURAGED BY her previous success with the sample she had collected and looked at under the scope. On her daily run for blood, she had stopped by the university pathology lab for a vial each of glutaraldehyde and RPMI. After a moment's consideration, she grabbed a second vial of each, just in case. The glutaraldehyde would hold a tissue sample for electron microscopy and the RPMI for chromosome analysis. Beth thought they might be a long shot, seeing how Mr. Crisp's tissue had reacted to other things, but it was worth a try.

Chromosome studies could give her an idea as to where the abnormalities that made him a vampire were located, which, down the road, might mean targets for gene therapy to remove the undesirable parts of his existence, like drinking blood. And with electron microscopy she could see inside his cells and perhaps identify the differences in his cells' machinery that made his remarkable regeneration possible.

After logging Mr. Crisp's progress for the day, she took a small bit of granulation tissue from his right arm and dropped it in the glutaraldehyde, holding the vial back from her face as far as possible. She once again waited, eyes closed, but after a minute the tissue was still intact in the vial with no visible reaction.

So formalin and glutaraldehyde, both fixatives, had worked just fine.

She took a second sample from Mr. Crisp's shoulder and plunked it into the RPMI, again keeping the vial at arm's length. The tissue seemed stable at first but then started to disintegrate with a faint popping noise.

Blood, she thought. It was clearly all about blood.

Using the second vial of RPMI, she added a couple of milliliters of blood from the most recent unit and then added the tissue.

This seemed to work beautifully. The tissue remained intact. She would have to mention this oddity to the techs in the cytogenetics lab somehow. Bathing a tissue in blood to get it to grow was not the usual practice. Assuming the regeneration with blood and the rapid degradation without blood meant rapid cell growth and turnover, then stimulating the cells and growing them should take very little time. And the less time hanging out in the lab with Mr. Crisp's secrets, the better.

CHAPTER 27

BETH

AND THERE IT WAS. *There... it... was.*

A virus fractured open before her eyes under the electron microscope. Externally it was round, with a roughly cone-shaped inner capsid—the heart of the virus which contained all the information to replicate itself.

And she found not only one but, as she scanned around, many, many more. So what did this mean? That Mr. Crisp was suffering from a cold? HIV? Or could this be the reason for the way he was? She was beside herself with excitement, her mind racing through the possibilities. It was one step closer to the answers she needed to come up with a cure or to harness the possible healing powers for humanity.

For lack of more reliable sources on the matter, she returned to Bram's account of the transformation of vampires. If that was accurate, repeated feeding and sharing of blood caused the host to transform while others were simply drained and died. The bloodletting would certainly weaken the host, making them more susceptible to a virus. Both the bite and feeding of the vampire's blood to the victim would aid in virus transmission. Although the ingested blood would be a far larger exposure, surely some viral particles would be destroyed by the body's defenses, especially stomach acid.

Blood itself didn't bother Beth, but destroyed virus or not, the thought of being force-fed vampire blood made her a bit queasy.

Now, the Jonathan Harker character was a bit of a conundrum because he had been fed on repeatedly by Dracula's "brides" but never turned. So perhaps it was the feeding of the blood after all. Perhaps the virus was not transmitted in the saliva. Or possibly Jonathan Harker was naturally immune? There were still unexplained gaps in her theory. And she still didn't know with certainty if this was the culprit or a passing infection she'd happened upon.

Perhaps vampires were actually born, not turned from human form, and all was myth. But somehow the virus theory felt right.

Now, how to prove it?

If she could show human DNA in Mr. Crisp, would that be enough? Would it mean they were transformed into vampires by the virus or that they were an offshoot of one or the other from some point in the human family tree? And if they were a separate species with genetic overlap, why were there so few of them? They were clearly more powerful, more resistant; they could easily overtake humans in significant numbers and use them like cattle. Were they just controlling their numbers to not outgrow their food supply? Or were there far more vampires than she imagined with a completely other blood source than victims off the street? That would be a shock, realizing that vampires were all around and humanity had never noticed.

Prisoners would certainly be ready victims, but if her virus theory was correct that would have inevitably created some rather nasty criminal vampires who would surely not all remain quiet and behind the scenes with their regenerative abilities. So maybe the blood supply was controlled like in some of the movies. Maybe vampires owned the research donation sites and used the collected blood for a ready, inconspicuous food source.

Mr. Crisp would know those answers and hopefully would be willing to share them if he ever awakened. Her curiosity knew no limits, and with a nearly endless list of questions, she very much hoped he did. For now, Beth would head home, continue to care for him and pray for the best.

CHAPTER 28

LUCIANO

ABOUT AN HOUR AFTER dusk, Luciano listened as Beth began the infusion of another unit of blood. Skin had begun to cover the muscle over his shoulders, chest and thighs. It at least partially extended over his scalp, and he could feel the growth of new hair. Beth hadn't changed his bandages yet today, but he could tell there was far less fluid on them than the day before. Although he was careful to stay perfectly still in her presence, he bent and straightened his hands and fingers, feet and toes when she stepped out of the room to discard another empty blood bag. Although still very painful, the movement was bearable.

"My cupboards are bare, Mr. Crisp. I'm going to have to make a run for human food," Beth shouted from the next room. Luc was pleased, thinking it would leave him a nice little window to explore his surroundings and perhaps feed, if he was lucky.

Luciano heard Beth shuffling her keys followed by the soft thuds of her tennis shoe-covered feet. She poked her head in the bedroom doorway and said, "Goodbye, Mr. Crisp, be back soon!"

He heard the click of the lock and the raising of the garage door followed by the sound of a vehicle engine starting, again the closing garage door, then silence.

Luciano had rarely been alone with his own thoughts since arriving under her care. Her banter while caring for him was endearing. Several times, he had wished he could respond to her and ask questions of his own. He had nearly given himself away when Beth had unexpectedly run her fingers along his body, clenching instinctively as she neared his pelvis. She had recoiled quickly and sounded embarrassed, startled. He wondered what it meant. Could she be attracted to him? It was more likely that she was just curious, especially given his current physical state.

He felt a bit of guilt deceiving her by pretending to be unconscious, hearing her stories but sharing nothing. And there had been several uncomfortable moments in which he thought he would give himself away. But it was for the best. The less she knew, the safer they would both be.

He rose and saw new clothes neatly folded at the foot of the bed with shoes on the floor nearby. He considered putting them on but feared his wounds or stains from the excursion he was about to undertake might ruin them.

He searched further and found a pair of scrubs nearly his size folded neatly in the top drawer of the dresser and shoes on the closet floor. They looked well-used, likely hand-me-downs or discards, but at this point he had little concern for appearances. He needed to feed. While the units of blood Elizabeth infused for him at night were allowing healing, the full volume of a human would heal his wounds so much more quickly.

Luciano struggled with the motion of dressing himself, pausing after bending to pull on the scrub bottoms to pant away the pain. Even with the scrubs finally on, his arms were uncovered. He grabbed a hoodie hanging in the closet and put it on. It was gray with what looked like old paint spots across one sleeve. The front said "BITE ME" in large black letters with a Joe's Crab Shack logo emblazoned across the back. Not exactly what he would have chosen but certainly ironic.

Exploring the house would have to wait, so he quickly found a door and slipped out the back.

The night air was cool but typical for a night in April, with enough humidity to be comfortable. He could smell rain, though, coming from the west. He certainly would not want to try and hide damp clothes and bandages, and until he had a good plan for shelter and had enough skin to cover the usually visible parts of his body, he needed to lie low. Even with skin, it would take blood to restore his strength and allow him to defend himself.

The glow of the downtown high-rises and the sounds of the cars passing on the interstate allowed him to orient himself. If he was where he thought he was, the KC Southern track bridge near 635 was just a short run away. There were always gatherings of homeless men there, drunk on five-dollar bottles of wine, cheap beer or whatever pure grain alcohol they could get their hands on. The blood was tainted by their high alcohol levels, but blood it was and would serve his needs as well as any. And, while he didn't enjoy taking a life, another missing homeless man wouldn't draw the attention he desperately needed to avoid.

He began a painful jog toward the bridge, slower than what he could normally muster, but still faster than any human could achieve.

A block from the bridge, he slowed to a walk. He could see figures of men moving in the remaining moonlight and smell the stench of cheap liquor and sweat.

Luciano had not been forced to feed on humans for many years. In the mid '90s, plasma donation and collection sites began to open in the US. Some also collected blood for research purposes. It was then that he started New Horizons Blood Research. It was modeled after the original plasma research sites, and after a few short months, the center was up and running. It was a legitimate research facility, using the vast majority of collected units for study. But there were always units that didn't make the cut. For whatever reason, the donated units were unsuitable for use and would be destroyed. It took just one man on the inside willing to make a few extra dollars to ensure an endless supply of rejected units.

As a vampire, he was immune to infection by any bloodborne pathogen or other human ailment. A few units a day kept him well-fed with no harm to the donating humans. The business investment had proved lucrative as well. Every fifty years or so, he had to create a new identity, which, for the right price, wasn't difficult. All monies were funneled into a trust which he passed from identity to identity as if from one generation to the next, creating the next before the "death" of the last. The last few years had been good ones indeed, with income to secure his future for at least a century and no human casualties.

He found himself angry and saddened by what he was now forced to do. But the Master could not yet know he lived, and if he knew of his home, he likely knew of the donation center as well.

Few of the men beneath the bridge spoke, most having settled into their customary places for the evening. There were two on the north end separated from the rest, loners, and for the hunter he was, easy prey.

He walked silently to the one furthest north. The man half sat, half lay on the uneven ground next to the steep fifteen- or twenty-foot slope leading up to the train rail. Bottle in hand, "Kentucky Deluxe" was partially visible between his filthy fingers. His face was smeared with dirt around the scraggly brown of his unkempt greasy hair and dark brown beard. His eyes were only partway open and glazed, the lids blinking sluggishly in his drunken state. He drank from the bottle, sloppily trickling the contents down his beard-covered chin. His clothes were disgusting, brown of course, but whether they were actually brown or brown from months of filth could not be told. All were ill-fitting, and the outer coat and pants, clearly too large, hung from his frame. Other than his protruding belly, his limbs seemed quite thin, likely the effects of liver disease and wasting from long-term alcohol abuse.

The things humans did to themselves, to their fragile bodies and short lives. To think this same fragility was once his destiny as well. But il Diavolo had changed that. It had been out of spite, not a gift, and in the death of his bride he had paid dearly for it. It had taken him years to see it as not a curse but an amazing opportunity to see things no other would. The coming and going of complete generations was his to watch, interacting with as he chose. He was no longer bound by the pressures of time, the cycle of growth, marriage, accumulation of wealth and children followed by the pains of aging and death. Time had little meaning, and he could enjoy it all without the sense of urgency felt by humans to leave their mark, a legacy, a fortune. It was quite simple to amass a fortune when you could wait centuries. This man's brief life would fuel his and he would know of him, remember him, long after his expected years had come and gone.

He had never enjoyed the killing and tended to take the lives of those dangerous to others, near death, or like this man, on a path that would soon result in his death. He was a hunter now, pure and simple, and like the animals in the wild, the old and weak were the readiest targets.

Standing mere feet away, the man still did not see or sense Luciano.

Luciano prepared to pounce, pulling the hood down to his eyes to be sure his face was shrouded for any possible onlookers, when he heard heavy footsteps and the scraping of gravel.

"Please let go of me! I promise I didn't take no money. I gave you everything I got. I been out for hours but I only got three parties. I swear!" It was a woman's voice, and she quickly came into view. She wore a skintight blue satiny dress. It was cut to her waist, showing a lacy hot-pink bra beneath. The dress would barely have covered her backside even if it hadn't ridden up as she struggled against the man dragging her toward the underpass. She teetered on what had to be six-inch clear stiletto heels as she tried to remain upright.

"Bitch, I know you made more than four hundred dollars," he said, dragging her the last few steps to the bridge support. He stopped, grabbing the lapels of his red leather jacket and tugging it straight. He leaned in nose-to-nose and raised a gold ring-covered hand to point in her face. "You lying to me just like the last time. This time, you ain't gonna forget the lesson."

He grabbed her arm with his left hand and drew the right back, fist balled. The woman raised her arms, eyes closed, bracing for the blow.

But as the man's arm came forward, it was stopped by Luciano's ironlike grip.

The man screamed in pain, releasing the woman, who saw her chance to escape and fled without so much as a backward glance.

"Who the fuck do you think—" the man began, but in a fraction of a second, Luciano had his neck to his mouth, one hand covering his screams so he couldn't alert the rest. The other hand was on the back of his head, tilting it away from him to reveal his carotid artery, bulging and now pulsing rapidly beneath the skin of his neck.

Luciano's extra set of canines were already down in anticipation, and he sunk them quickly into his flesh. The heat of the fresh blood was intense and spread like fire through his body. Luciano could feel the regeneration it allowed, the pain of movement subsiding, the strength returning to his limbs.

Feeding was always a pleasurable, exquisite sensation, nearly erotic.

Tonight was no different, even with the severity of his injuries. Luciano drained the man dry. The man struggled only briefly before he became sluggish, then limp in Luciano's arms.

Luciano heard the drunk behind him drop his bottle, shattering on the cement beside him. He discarded the pimp unceremoniously to the ground, turning to look at the man as he struggled to stand, feet scraping back and forth, unable to gain ground.

"No, please, don't kill me, please don't kill me," he said.

Luciano turned back to the pimp, bending to search his pockets and finding two large wads of cash. All told it had to be upwards of four thousand dollars. Cash in hand and hood pulled down to his eyes, he walked toward the man, who began to cry.

"Oh, God, no, please. I didn't see nothing..."

Making sure his face was in shadow, Luciano knelt in front of him to be at eye level. The man stopped struggling, sitting roughly and turning his head and pressing his back tightly to the cold cement behind him.

Luciano held the money out to the man, who flinched as Luciano's hand raised.

"Take it," Luciano said as he thrust the money toward the man a second time. "I will spare your life tonight only if you use it to get help and clean yourself up. I will be watching you. If you don't use the money for rehab, if you don't stay clean or if you say a single word about what you saw here tonight, I will make sure you are my next meal."

The man slowly reached for the cash, hand shaking so badly it took a couple of tries to grasp it. He was scared beyond speech, bulging wide eyes staring wildly up at Luciano, but he nodded profusely.

Luciano picked up the man's broken bottle, walked over to the dead body and dragged it several yards. Then he slashed the dead man's neck with the jagged bottle edge, almost completely obscuring the wound he'd created on the side from which he had drunk. He turned the man's pockets out and emptied them, throwing the remaining contents as far as he could into the distance. To the quick observer it would seem to have been a fight between rivals or perhaps a robbery gone wrong. These deaths were frequent, and little investigation would follow. No one would take the time to wonder why there was so little blood. Normally, he would spend more time concealing the body—decomposition was very helpful in obscuring injuries—but not knowing how quickly Beth would return, there was no time to be wasted.

He turned and began his return, movement much easier, much faster, and the pain less distracting. His body was warm from the feeding, a sensation he much enjoyed since he generated little body heat of his own.

He was surprised to realize how fond of Beth he had become. When he had first awakened, he had considered feeding on her and taking her life to preserve his own. Now, the thought of needing to kill her to preserve his safety was disturbing... More than disturbing, it was unacceptable. His unwillingness to kill her would place him in more danger. But she had shown him such kindness, he had to return it.

Since he had chosen to keep her alive, he would have to remove her memories of him. And if he was wiping her memory, where was the harm in talking with her first? The thought of actually having a conversation with her, looking into her eyes as she spoke, put a smile on his face. The happiness in the anticipation was something he hadn't felt in quite a long time. He would stay in town long enough to ensure her safety as best he could before once again fleeing to evade the Master.

He found his way again to Beth's back door and went inside.

CHAPTER 29

BETH

As BETH ENTERED THE guestroom, her body froze.

The bed was empty and stripped, the sheets in a pile on the floor.

Her heart pounded in her chest, blood pulsing in her ears. Mr. Crisp was awake.

Fear slowly gave way to disappointment and anguish as she realized she may never get a chance to see him awake, a chance to ask his real name, to know how long he'd lived and where, to know what had brought such an amazing creature to lie as a vulnerable corpse on her autopsy table.

Beth sighed as she began to accept that this was the end of the adventure. She had known it could end like this, with more questions than answers. The disappointment was bitter; even though they had never actually had a conversation, she had opened herself to him. She had told the sleeping Mr. Crisp things that she had never told anyone else. She would sorely miss the one-sided conversations.

Beth placed the infusion tubing on the end of the bed and turned to go back to the kitchen. She would have to dispose of this unit later.

As she passed through the door, again her heart leaped to her throat.

In the kitchen, looking directly at her, stood Mr. Crisp. He'd been beautiful as he slept, but it was nothing in comparison to seeing him now.

His brown eyes moved carefully over her. Despite his surveillance, his eyes were soft and full of light. His head was slightly lowered, and he looked at Beth in part through his heavy, brown, thick and full lashes, the kind that women always wanted and never seemed to get. His jaw was square and strong; cheekbones high on either side of his long but thin nose. His mouth was closed, hiding the intimidating canines; his full lips soft and deep red against his pale yet still olive-tinted skin. The color in his cheeks suggested he had recently fed. Considering that breakfast was still in her hand, she surmised he had ventured out before returning to meet her.

Beth found herself wondering who he had chosen and, for a moment, felt some responsibility for the life that may have been lost. She had nursed Mr. Crisp back to health and had known full well what he was. Any deaths that may occur at his hand now would be on her hands as well. As a physician, this was difficult to square. If there was ever a time when their conversation was familiar enough to allow for detailed questions of feeding, she would remember to ask how he chose his victims.

Though Beth had measured Mr. Crisp at the time of her attempted autopsy, the reality of his six-foot frame had not really set in until she saw him standing before her. He was impressive. Muscles rippled below the thin cotton of his shirt. Everything about him conferred an appearance of raw strength and power, a predator.

"I should introduce myself." She startled at his words, his voice a rich baritone. He spoke softly, but the strength of his voice easily carried to her across the room. "My given name is Luciano Verde. Do not be afraid. I wish to thank you for your kindness."

Chapter 30

Beth

Beth willed her muscles to close her mouth then swallowed hard. *You're a scientist for goodness' sake. Get a grip and seize the moment.*

After clearing her throat, she said, "I'm Elizabeth Ramsey; my friends call me Beth. Please forgive my surprise. I had no idea what you might be like or if I would ever have the chance to speak with you."

"I'm sure there's much you would like to know, and I am pleased that we have the opportunity to have this conversation. It's not safe for me to stay here any longer, but I wanted to meet you formally," he said.

With this he walked slowly toward the couch, and Beth followed. His movements were graceful, and she couldn't help notice how the khakis she'd bought him hugged his thighs and rear end as he walked.

They sat, facing one another. It seemed he never blinked and held her gaze, almost as though he was looking for something in her eyes.

"I have so many questions, I scarcely know where to begin," she said.

"So, let's begin at my beginning. It was in Venice, Italy in 1722."

Beth couldn't help a small gasp. While she had considered the longevity his regeneration might provide, three hundred years was a very long time.

The corners of his mouth rose in a small grin before he continued. While she had been startled by his voice when he first spoke, its rich tone was inviting, like that of an actor reading a very sultry scene in an audiobook or a late-night DJ playing the tracks to put young lovers "in the mood." It was a sound she could get used to.

"Venice was a city alive with arts and theater. Gondoliers could be heard singing in the canals as they carried the many tourists which came from all over the globe to see the unique architecture and to buy fine glass and lace. I was a nobleman, and at thirty, old to be unmarried." Beth could relate to that and found herself oddly pleased to hear he was unmarried.

"I had finally met and fallen in love with a beautiful woman. She was stunning, with long blond hair and such kind eyes. Much like yours," he said, then dropped his gaze to his hands. Beth knew she had no reason to feel jealously over his love for another woman, she had no claim on him, but she felt it nonetheless. She told herself it was ridiculous and tried to focus on the rest of his story.

"It was our wedding day. I still remember the lace pattern of her dress and the flowers in her hair." He seemed lost in the memory.

"We shared our vows, and after our wedding party, headed home for our wedding night. As we prepared for bed, the vampire that turned me barged through our bedroom door. He drained me and fed me his blood."

Beth raised her hand over her mouth, stifling another gasp.

"As the hours passed, I died and turned to become this." He gestured toward his chest with both hands. "He also caused the death of my wife." Luciano paused; his voice had wavered, and he closed his eyes. There seemed more to the story, but Beth didn't want to push after they had only just begun to talk. She felt so sorry for him and wasn't sure what to say. She very tentatively raised her hand to place it on his forearm. Through the sleeve of the blue Henley, she felt a small twitch in his muscles beneath, but he didn't look up.

She waited a few long seconds before speaking. "I am so sorry for your loss." It didn't seem like nearly enough, but they were the only words she could find.

"Does he still live, the one who turned you?"

"Yes. I believe he is almost certainly the one who tried to take my life." He raised his head to again meet her eyes but didn't move his arm from her hand.

Afraid continuing to touch him would be awkward, she slowly drew it back to her lap. "Are there many of you?" Beth said, trying to shift the subject away from this memory which was clearly upsetting to Luciano.

"No, not many. Most of our kind don't make it through the first year. Taking lives to continue their own is something that most just cannot get past. Rather than live like that, most decide to greet the morning sunrise one last time. But those of us who find a way to deal with our need for blood lead fairly solitary lives. It's difficult to hide what we are from human acquaintances for long, and with our longevity, we eventually watch all our friends die. Being alone is easier."

Beth could relate to that. The pain of losing her father was not something she wanted to experience again. Truly opening your heart to another meant leaving it completely unprotected from the hurt of losing them.

"How long have vampires existed and where did they come from?"

"The first vampires were created by the Vampyre, at least that's what our legends tell us. The story has been passed down among vampires for millennia and says the Vampyre were an advanced race that flourished, even before the time of the Egyptians. It is said their knowledge and capabilities would surpass even those of modern day.

They were a superior but peaceful group with physical strength and speed that far surpassed those of other men. They were almost never ill and lived far more years than surrounding villagers.

"As the legend goes, tribesmen from a local village sent their warriors to help fight with the Vampyre in battle when they were attacked but asked for nothing in return. The Vampyre felt they owed a debt to their brave friends and sought to find a way to thank them for their loyalty. They decided to offer them a gift, a process by which they could give the warriors their physical attributes. The grateful warriors accepted and went to the Vampyre city. Whatever the Vampyre tried to do to them, the warriors became very ill.

"When they finally felt well enough to venture outside, they found their pale skin immediately burned in the sunlight, even turning to flame and ash if they did not flee the sun's rays. They were also ravenous and the only thing they could eat was human blood. The warriors hated the Vampyre for what they had done. They killed every last one of them and swore that the new race of evil monsters they had become would forever be known as Vampyre to disparage their memory. While the pronunciation has changed over the millennia, the name has remained."

"Have they attempted to find a cure?" Beth asked.

"Until the last century, the technology to examine what happened to the warriors didn't exist. Even the Egyptians never had technology or knowledge to rival that of the Vampyre."

"It had to be a retrovirus." Now Beth was even more convinced the virus she had seen in Luciano's tissues was part of the process and not some passing infection. "That would explain much of it; the fevers and sickness. Bram Stoker's description of multiple bites causing the victim to turn might actually be accurate, with the draining and sharing of blood causing a faster change. The Vampyre must have tried to use a retrovirus to insert their genetic material into the warriors' DNA. Only something went wrong. Perhaps they weren't entirely genetically compatible or the wrong genetic fragments were chosen, or maybe the virus was unstable and mutated."

"Many have been killed trying to discover the truth. There are two sides, those that wish for a cure so they might once again see the sun and be free of the thirst. The second group, the one who turned me included, believes in the superiority of the Vampyre race. They seek out and kill all those who would attempt to find a cause or cure for their affliction. It's why your knowledge of me must be erased from your memory. It's too risky for you."

With this Beth leaned back from him, suddenly feeling defensive. To have all this taken from her after what she had learned would be a tragedy. And she had just found out he wasn't some mindless bloodsucking monster. How could she lose this chance to get to know him? "Erased from my memory? How do you intend to do that?"

"It is a skill all vampires possess to some degree. It is much like hypnosis. We can suggest to your subconscious that the events never happened and you simply forget them. It isn't perfect, but it works on most."

"But I don't want to forget. I've finally met you; I don't want to forget that. And I've learned so much. What if I could find the cause, a cure even? Then those of you who are turned and want to go back could. They wouldn't have to die."

"Beth, it isn't safe for you. I have put you in enough danger as it is. If il Diavolo, or the Master, as he calls himself, is behind this attempt on my life, as I believe he is, why would you think he would hesitate to kill you? I don't want to take away your memories of me, quite the opposite, but it is the only way for you to remain unharmed, and that's what matters most." He held her gaze, his eyes intense, as if trying to will her to believe him.

"Since when has knowledge and science been safe? How many people have been killed by the very diseases they investigated, or become ill at the very least, studying them and hoping for a cure to end the suffering? Shouldn't I get to choose which is more important?"

Shaking his head, he said, "Not this time, Beth. I can't. By allowing you to help me, I have put you in danger. I will not allow you to die for this. Please, let's enjoy what time we have left to talk and stop arguing."

Beth relented, not because she was resigned to his decision, but because she hoped to learn more. Perhaps he would tell her something that would bolster her argument and listening would also buy her time to think of a way past this.

Taking a deep breath and settling herself, she moved on. "So, are there limits to your regeneration? What other abilities do you have?"

"As long as my heart beats and my brain is intact, my body will regenerate with enough blood. The faster I get it, the quicker I heal. Compared to humans, I can move much faster, beyond the limits of your capability to see me in motion." With this he was suddenly gone from the couch and standing back in the kitchen where she first saw him. Then again, before she could blink, he was standing next to her.

So, running away from him was definitely out.

"I am also much stronger than when I was a human." With this he stood and lifted the couch, with Beth on it, about four feet off the floor, seemingly with no more effort than she would exert lifting a pencil. He gently returned the couch to its original position and once again settled onto it in front of her but closer, his lower thigh now touching hers. Beth tried to ignore it. He surely meant nothing by it, but the skin of her thigh warmed to his touch in response.

Pushing the thoughts aside, she asked, "Can you fly or shapeshift?"

"No," he said with a laugh. "That is just myth. But that would be fun. Vampires do have exceptional hearing, though. I can hear a human heartbeat from many yards away. And while I can't make out clear thoughts from humans, I often get a sense of emotion and an occasional word if the thoughts are emotionally charged. Some are easier to hear than others."

Beth's eyebrows rose. The thought of him being able to sense her feelings made her self-conscious to say the least. Had he read her thoughts when she admired his physique? Was he reading them now? She felt her cheeks color.

Luciano continued as though he'd heard nothing. "It becomes easier to sense the better I know a person and seems to work best from vampire to vampire, although not all of us have this gift."

Beth decided moving on to more details about vampirism would keep her mind off more sensitive thoughts she wanted to keep to herself.

"So can you eat regular food as well, or only blood?"

"Just blood, unfortunately. Everything else tastes like dust and my body will reject it."

"What about blood from animals? Would that work in place of human blood?"

"Only for a short while. It doesn't contain all the nutrients I need to live on long-term. Over time I would become weak and sick. In this age, however, we can obtain donated human blood from privately owned blood banks and research facilities. It's not often that we would need to take a life to feed."

"I believe the virus you carry can likely be passed on in your saliva.

So, if you feed on someone, will they turn if you don't kill them?"

"If I feed on a human but don't kill them, there is a good chance they will become a vampire. And the more times they're exposed, the more likely the change will happen. So, to preserve our secret and prevent another person from suffering from this affliction, it is best to kill."

Beth flinched despite her efforts to hide it. She had known what he was and what he likely did to sustain himself, but hearing it so harshly put rekindled the guilt and responsibility for his future kills that she already felt. And though he said he didn't wish her to die, would the day come when it was "best" to kill her?

"I know that sounds harsh, but it's only in the last seventy or so years that I have had other options. I used to choose the sick or criminals to feed on whenever I could. I don't like to kill, but it was the only way I could survive. When research centers started collecting blood from voluntary donors, it all changed. I saw an opportunity to get what I needed without harming anyone. Over time, I invested in some of these places and eventually started my own research centers. I keep the units that are undesirable to research that would otherwise be discarded until I need them. I have made similar arrangements for other vampires across the country to try to prevent human harm. I believe it's one of the reasons the Master may have tried to kill me. By supplying vampires with blood they don't have to kill for, I have gained the respect and loyalty of many. The Master is powerful, and if he's discovered my network, he certainly won't want it to continue."

"Why would the Master not just do the same? Wouldn't he prefer to feed without killing?"

"No, the Master is cruel and sadistic. He enjoys killing and believes it is his right. He believes he is a superior being and that humans are like cattle."

It was difficult for Beth to imagine someone taking a life out of anything but necessity, especially with better options. It was a level of cruelty she couldn't really wrap her head around. What could make a person, or a vampire, so full of hate that taking a human life would mean so little? There had to be more to the Master's story. Even knowing his reasons, Beth doubted she could ever accept his choices. The more Beth learned of the Master, the more she hoped they would never have cause to meet.

"Do you age or are you truly immortal?"

"I think we do age, just so very slowly we may as well be immortal. I cannot imagine living long enough to ever die from old age and cannot guess at how many millennia that might take."

Beth couldn't imagine a life spanning centuries, let alone millennia, and the experience and knowledge that would come with it. It made what she had learned in thirty-two years seem so miniscule in comparison.

"So, do you ever seek out other vampires? Surely there are others leading solitary lives that would welcome another's company." Beth had no reason to think there could be anything between them, especially with him planning to wipe her memories, but she couldn't help hoping the answer was no.

"Yes, I have spent time with several through the years, but just because we are all vampires doesn't make us any more compatible than those you have dated. Even though they are human, it doesn't mean they are someone you could spend a lifetime with. Or in my case, many lifetimes."

Beth nodded at this. She did understand all too well. As a vampire, she would still be thirty-two and single.

CHAPTER 31

LUCIANO

LUCIANO WAS SURPRISED THAT Beth had reached out to him. And the comfort in her touch was more soothing than he expected. He relished the warmth of it. It wasn't as though he hadn't touched a human recently, but this touch was offered in kindness. He knew he shouldn't, but he wanted to touch her again. When he moved closer, so their thighs met, he heard her heart speed. Was she scared of him? He tried to search her face, to read the emotion, but she seemed deep in thought. She sat quietly for a moment, seeming hesitant to ask her next question. He glanced at her wall clock, his heart heavier seeing that the precious hours they had to talk were quickly ticking away.

"So there are no humans who are allowed to know vampires exist?"

"There are a few," he admitted, "but they are servants, almost slaves, to a vampire; sworn to do his bidding or die. Some accept this role in exchange for the promise that the vampire will one day turn them, but that rarely happens." He could see the energy drain from Beth's face and feel a hint of revulsion.

"Have you ever used humans in that way, as slaves?"

He leaned closer and steadily held her gaze, wanting to be certain she knew there was no question about his answer. "No. I would never do that."

"And you have never broken the rules to have a..." Beth paused, seeming to search for the right word. "Friendship with a human?" Until meeting Beth, Luciano had never spent enough time with another human to want a relationship of any kind. Humans were fragile, and a vampire and human together would surely result in death, just like his wife.

"No," he said. "I would never wish to put someone I care about in harm's way."

"Have you ever considered creating another vampire?"

"No," he said shortly and then paused, gathering his thoughts. "I have considered it, yes. But to put another through the pain of death and condemning them to this life of night and blood seems... selfish."

As they spoke, Luciano could feel the dawn approaching, each passing moment gone even faster than the last, the inevitability of what must come a heavy weight on his heart.

"Dawn is coming, Beth, and as much as I would like to continue our conversation, our time together is almost up."

She frowned and lowered her head, seeming to consider her next words carefully. "Why have you decided not to eat me?"

Now it was Luciano who paused. Should he admit he'd considered it at first? It could reveal that he hadn't been in a coma but only pretending to sleep. He had felt it necessary to remain silent, but telling her now would seem like betrayal. There was so much vulnerability in her eyes as she waited for his answer. What was she hoping his response would be?

"You saved me from being discovered and nursed me back to health. I am grateful for that. I don't want to harm you." He wanted to say that he felt he had come to know her while listening to her talk about her life; that he was talking to her now because he felt closer to her than he had to anyone since his wife. But they were thoughts he was only just realizing himself. For Beth, this was their first meeting, a first meeting that would also be their last. It was too much to say.

"Why did you decide to help me?" he asked in return.

"I wasn't sure what to do at first. I knew that if anyone else in the medical field found out what you were, you would likely be treated as a lab rat and tested. Or they wouldn't believe you were a vampire and treat you like a human, which wasn't what you needed." She dropped her eyes briefly before returning to meet his gaze. "A part of me was also curious about what made you a vampire. I wanted to study you without any harm coming to you." She was being very honest, sharing even her not so altruistic motives, and he felt even more guilty about deceiving her with his "coma."

"But the more I've thought about it, I think a lot of it was that I believed I really did have a chance to save you. I lost my father to cancer when I was sixteen and I didn't have the knowledge or skills to do anything about it. I couldn't allow that to happen to you if there was any chance I could stop it." There it was again, her love for her father and regret that she didn't know enough to save him. It seemed to drive her forward, to learn all she could and to use it to help others.

"It's why I can't stop now. Think of all the people who could be saved if I understood how your regeneration works. Please, don't make me forget you... or my research." With her plea, she placed both of her hands on his. She seemed to add the last three words as an afterthought. Could she have feelings for him? How could she since until now they had never really met? He tried to push the thoughts from his mind. Her hands on his, her blue eyes pleading, he struggled to keep his resolve. But he couldn't allow her to keep her memories of him or her research. He had to stop indulging thoughts about what could not be.

Luciano took a deep breath. "It is time for us to say our goodbyes.

I wish very much it didn't have to be. You are someone I think... I know... I would like to know better."

"Then don't do this. I know the risks. It should be my choice. I want a chance to know you too."

To this he only sighed. He looked in her eyes and raised his hand to brush a few stray hairs from her cheek, the touch again precious and nourishing, like water in the desert. Lowering his voice while deepening the pitch, he said, "Beth, this is for the best." It was as much to convince her as it was to reassure himself. He felt a connection with her that he hadn't experienced in three hundred years. Of course, he would find it with a human, beautiful and fragile. *But humans and vampires cannot mix*, he reminded himself. *If you care for her, let her go.*

He let out another sigh in resignation.

"When I am gone, you will not remember me. You will not remember bringing me home or nursing me to health. You completed the autopsy on a burn victim and left on vacation. You have spent these last several days catching up on reading and even watching a few old movies. You have been running experiments on units of blood from the university blood bank, but unfortunately the experiments failed and you will have to begin again, if you wish. Vampires are only a myth."

He knew he would never have the opportunity to touch her again, so with those last words, he leaned slowly forward and placed a kiss on her forehead.

CHAPTER 32

LUCIANO

LUCIANO WATCHED THROUGH THE living room window as Beth looked to the kitchen and blinked. She stood and grabbed a scientific journal from the small coffee table in front of her, "New Insights into Drug Resistant Bacteria" in large letters across its cover. Placing it on the counter and opening the fridge door, she pulled out a bowl containing the leftovers of chicken fettuccine alfredo she'd made the previous night.

Luciano watched as she placed the bowl in the microwave and leafed through her journal while waiting for it to finish, then as she sat and picked at the leftovers while reading. He almost wished it hadn't worked, but Beth needed to move on. She needed to be safe, and there was no way that knowing vampires existed could be good for her.

Luciano slipped the flash drive from her drawer into his pocket. He had wiped all the research files from her computer before she'd arrived home. All the supplies she had purchased, including the daylight lamp, were safely discarded. And he had placed the units of blood she had retrieved from the blood bank in the refrigerator. She would be safe now and better off if he stayed away.

Pausing for one last look at her, he turned and left.

Beth sat at the kitchen table, eating leftovers and trying desperately to read the journal article in front of her. She had to look like nothing had happened, knowing he was likely watching her. Beth hoped he wouldn't notice how her heart pounded and the little smile she could hardly contain.

Luciano's hypnosis had failed. Beth remembered everything.

CHAPTER 33

BETH

HER DRIVE TO THE address provided by the first responders led her south of Kansas City and into the suburbs. Even with some answers, Beth's mind swirled with questions. Did Luciano live a normal life? Was he just a squatter in the house he was found next to? Had il Diavolo really set the fire as Luciano believed? Beth thought that perhaps going to the scene of the crime might help explain not only what had happened to Luciano, but also more about him and his life. With their time together cut short, Beth wished more than ever for more information about him, how he lived and perhaps even where he may have gone.

Luc, Beth thought, and smiled at the nickname. "Luc" seemed to fit him.

New neighborhoods were springing up, but she could tell the area where the remains of the house stood had not long ago been rural. The old farmhouse was two stories, a simple white and sat on about ten acres of relatively untouched farmland. It was blackened by the fire with tongues of gray soot extending from the basement and main level windows.

Beth parked her car near the end of the gravel drive and walked to the front of the house, camera hanging around her neck. The front door appeared to have been rammed open, likely by the firefighters.

Splinters of the doorjamb remained around the broken lock.

Walking to the side of the house, Beth peered in one of the basement windows. Inside, the area was littered with debris and was still damp with water from the fire hoses, but she could see what remained of a large wooden rectangle on the floor. It was charred, but the door was thrown open. It was nearly seven feet in length and roughly four feet wide, and with the lid maybe two- or two-and-a-half-feet tall, judging by what fragments remained. What looked like chain lay partially covered by rubble beside the large box. The walls of the basement were burned gray-black, and Beth couldn't make out any details of what had hung on them, if anything.

She continued her walk around the house, taking photographs as she went, and found an area in back where the ground was charred and the grass scorched or flattened as though something hot had been dragged across it. This pattern began at one of the narrow basement windows and continued for about thirty feet. The "path" ended in a blackened area, roughly the size of a man. She assumed this was where they had found Luc. It was impossible to tell if he had been dragged to this location or if he had managed to crawl this far by himself. For a normal man, she would have assumed he had been dragged. But Luc was clearly no ordinary fellow.

Beth knew the house was probably less than stable, but she wanted to see what remained of the upper levels. It appeared that the skilled response of the fire department had left at least the front of the upper levels largely intact. Since the majority of the damage was toward the back of the house, Beth entered through the front, ducking the yellow caution tape.

The entryway smelled strongly of burnt wood, and the walls were discolored by smoke. The heat from the fire below had bubbled the wood floors toward the back of the room, and Beth avoided that area for fear that the damaged wood wouldn't hold her weight.

The room was large, maybe fourteen by twenty feet, with a couch taking up the majority of its center. It appeared to have been covered by a floral pattern fabric, but the colors were muted by the smoke damage and soot. An overturned coffee table abutted the couch, which was framed on each end by small wooden end tables. One appeared to have held a glass lamp, now entirely shattered on the floor save for its gray-stained lampshade. In front of the couch, seemingly the focal point of the room, was a large brick fireplace with a thick wooden mantle. Several pictures lay fallen and scattered over its surface, and a large frame lay on the floor at the foot of the mantle.

Beth walked to it, glass crunching beneath her feet. She lifted the frame to find the glass cracked but largely intact.

It stopped Beth in her tracks.

The image was very old, a painting of a man and a woman in what must have been contemporary dress centuries before. The man was standing to the woman's right, left hand on the back of her chair. He wore what appeared to be a dark blue velvet jacket, belted at the waist, and close-fitting tights or trousers, largely hidden by the chair. His hair was shoulder-length, brown and wavy, and surrounded high cheekbones and dark eyes. The eyes were kind, soft and mesmerizing. Clearly the painter was drawn to them, painting them with such depth. He was handsome by any standard.

The man was Luc.

The woman was blond and very beautiful with long ringlet curls flowing over her shoulders. Her face was small and porcelain with pink doll-like lips. She was seated in the chair and wearing a ruby-colored gown, shining like satin. Her waist was tightly cinched with her

U-shaped bodice full but modestly covered by white lace. Her skirts were full and spilled over the sides of the small chair. Neither smiled, but their faces appeared warm and welcoming nonetheless. There was no inscription to provide a hint at the age of the painting, just the illegible squiggles of what was likely the artist's name at the bottom right of the image. But Beth didn't need an inscription to guess this must be Luc's wife.

Beth felt a strange pang of jealousy at this thought and immediately felt like an idiot. She didn't even know Luc well, let alone the woman in the picture. Beth had no right to be jealous.

It was likely one of the last portraits of him before he became a vampire, a happy moment before his life was so irrevocably changed. What had he been like then? And how was the Luc of today different than the one his wife had known?

Beth stood the painting up, gently leaning it against the fireplace. The remaining undamaged pictures on the mantle were more recent although still old, showing Luc in what appeared to be '50s and '60s dress with various others. The same striking dark eyes followed her from picture to picture. Beth looked at the images through her lens as she photographed the room. She longed to hear the stories of these photographs, to hear about the many decades he had experienced firsthand. What had he seen and lived through over three hundred years?

A staircase to her left held more promise than the open doorway to what was clearly a kitchen to her right. The stairs were not obviously damaged, and Beth decided to give them a try. They creaked under her weight but held as she climbed.

At the top of the stair was a small balcony with two closed doors. The first opened to what could have been a small bedroom, but it was empty of furniture with a single uncovered window. The walls were covered by faded and focally peeling floral wallpaper but otherwise bare.

The second doorway opened to a similarly papered room, but this one was furnished with a full-size metal-framed bed. The bedspread was ruffled at the bottom but faded to a dusty blue. A small dressing table with a mirror sat against one wall and a painted wardrobe against another, thinly carved vines adorning its front. The windows were curtained in the same fabric and ruffles as the bedspread. And next to the bed was a valet chair with a place to hang a man's jacket and a seat for putting on shoes. The last piece of furniture was a small wooden stand with a towel rack on its side, containing a single neatly folded hand towel. On the top of the stand was a wash basin and water pitcher for washing. The room, while furnished, had the feel of never having been used. A layer of dust covered every visible surface.

Beth opened the wardrobe, disturbing the dust of the handle and wiping it on her jeans. It was empty, further supporting her impression of never having been used. There were no decorations save for a vintage-looking hand mirror, brush and handkerchief with the initials "LV" on the surface of the dressing table. As far as Beth could tell, no one had even entered this room in quite a long while.

Whatever had happened in this house, it was all focused on the basement. She returned to the main level and entered the kitchen. There was a refrigerator but no hum of electricity. She supposed that it could have been turned off by the firefighters, but opened it up anyway.

The inside was pristine and smelled like musty plastic. The freezer also appeared to have never been opened, let alone used. Dishes filled many of the cabinets, but none contained food. A door to the left of the fridge stood ajar and was darkly charred, the remaining paint bubbled and peeling.

As she walked closer, the floorboards creaked loudly underneath her weight and a loud crack stopped her progress. The boards were bowed and warped, probably from the water used to squelch the fire. The few upper stairs she could see through the doorway gave way to an open space below where the rest of the staircase had fallen away. There was nothing more to see from this angle.

Beth tried again from the outside, returning to the window that Luc appeared to have used as an exit. The glass was gone, but the metal frame still looked menacing. Beth knew she shouldn't try it, but she had come here for answers and the only way she might find them was to take a closer look.

Beth wrapped the ends of her sleeves around her hands and pushed and wiggled her way through the broken window, feet-first. She dropped to her feet on the floor below, but lost her balance on the debris and ended up on her backside in it and the damp wood. Thankfully, her camera banged against her chest but nothing else during her fall.

With nothing injured but her pride, she stood and glanced around the room.

It was difficult to tell what the room had looked like or what had been where. What remained of a broken wooden chair was visible next to the large wooden box. She slowly made her way closer to it, being careful not to fall again over the litter on the floor. The walls of the basement appeared to be the original brick and cinder block with no other remaining covering. The ceiling was down to what remained of the wood floor in the kitchen above. It was deeply charred and appeared to have taken the brunt of the flames which, as far as Beth could tell, had been focused on the large wooden box. The walls of the box were mostly destroyed, but a portion of the base remained and consisted of wood at least an inch thick. Whatever this had been it had to have weighed a ton.

She got a closer look at the chains and small bits of singed rope around the box and realized that the chains continued beneath the box, which stood on chunky clawed feet. With the amount of chain lying on the sides of the box and one length lying across what remained of the base of the box, she had to conclude that it had been chained shut. So what had been chained inside? Luc? Was this where he was when the fire was started? It would explain the severity of his burns and why he hadn't escaped sooner. She could only imagine the fear he must have felt realizing he was trapped and burning.

She took photographs of the box and chains, proof of the agony he must have endured.

With the sun beginning to set and no other obvious clues, Beth decided to make her way back out of the basement. Piling what was left of wood debris and climbing on the precarious mound, she managed to pull herself back up and through the window in the rear of the house.

Returning to her car in the driveway, she watched a set of headlights go slowly past the end of the drive before speeding up to continue on down the road.

Beth felt her heart skip a beat. While she hoped it was neighbors wondering who could be visiting the burned-up farmhouse, she remembered Luc's warnings. Could it be il Diavolo's human slaves, watching to see what she knew?

She glanced in her rearview mirror at every turn on the way home to be sure she wasn't being followed. She had found the UV light Luc had tried to dispose of in her outdoor trash can at home. While it wouldn't help against humans, who knew if il Diavolo had other vampires under his thumb? She would keep her trusty aluminum softball bat and the UV light handy from here on out.

CHAPTER 34

LUCIANO

LUCIANO AWAKENED SLEEPILY JUST before dusk in the boxcar that had been his home since revealing himself to Beth. He stretched his sluggish limbs and could hear the grinding and clanking of the last few evening trains at the nearby rail yard.

Luciano had found this abandoned boxcar, off the tracks and surrounded by overgrown brush, several years before. He'd placed a mattress inside which allowed him to rest up off the floor. It was minimalist to the extreme, but it did keep out the rain and, more importantly, the sun, which now shone in a fading sliver of light from the closed edge of the door.

He should stay away and he knew it. But what if she was in trouble? What if the Master and his men had gone after her anyway? Surely when they realized she knew nothing they would stop. But Luciano was kidding himself. If they even suspected she might know something, Master would kill her on the spot.

He couldn't let that happen. He couldn't let another woman die because of him.

It would be taking a chance, going there. If they were looking for him, and had put it all together, they might be watching her, just waiting for him to show up. His efforts at hiding these last few days would be for nothing.

Luciano was healed but really didn't savor the idea of another injury. And who was he fooling? He wanted to see her again. He had held closely to his promise to himself not to get involved with another human since the death of his wife. But Beth was different. He knew he couldn't have her, but it didn't change the wanting.

Either way, Beth was in danger, and so was he.

Luciano didn't need to breathe but sighed deeply anyway. The sound was his white flag, a surrender that might go badly for both of them.

When night fell, he rose to leave his tiny boxcar apartment. The door still worked but required the strength of several men, or a vampire, to break the bonds of rust and heave it open. While most of the outside of the car was covered in rust, he could see small bits of red paint, curled at the edges, clinging like moss to a tree. He had hidden a metal box behind it where the brush was thickest. It was just as rusted and would draw no attention if spotted.

He opened the box and found the items he'd hidden in it in case of such an emergency untouched. A Missouri identification card with a social security card and passport to match, five thousand dollars and a change of clothes. He had several similar stashes in town and in neighboring states. Whenever he moved, it was the first order of business. And when he was convinced Beth was safe, he would gather the items from his various stashes and move on.

He secured the box and headed for the nearest bridge.

Luciano hated killing again, but until he had pieced together what had happened and what needed to be done, he couldn't chance being seen at any of the local blood and plasma centers. Not only would they likely be watched, endangering him, but it could also be dangerous for whatever humans might be working there when he arrived. Tonight, there would be more blood on his hands though, something he still regretted and avoided even if he did choose those already on their way to death.

Luciano found another drunken homeless man passed out beneath the tracks, and quickly drained him before heading towards Beth's. He never woke.

Beth was just finishing a shower when he arrived at her window. He knew her schedule well already and knew she had just completed her daily run. Her hair hung in damp brown-black clumps around her face and shoulders; a fluffy white towel was wrapped and secured just above her breasts. She walked toward her dresser and tossed the towel thoughtlessly on the bed.

Luciano dropped his eyes immediately, not wanting to invade her privacy any more than he already had, but the flash of her slender, leanly muscled body and perfectly smooth skin would not leave his mind as quickly.

After she'd dressed, he watched as she returned to the bathroom. He heard the hum of her hair dryer. When she returned to her bedroom, her hair was pulled neatly back into a ponytail, which seemed her default when there was work to be done. A pale blue cotton T-shirt hung loosely from her shoulders and draped over her breasts. It was tucked neatly into her faded Levi's. Despite being loose, they accented her waist and small hips. Luc tried not to notice the way the back pockets seemed to hold and curve over each side of her butt and instead followed them down to her thighs. He remembered her uncensored comment about the seams from when he was supposed to be unconscious and smiled to himself.

From here she walked to her desk, opened her laptop and waited for it to boot. After entering her password, she pulled a flash drive from her pocket and inserted it into the computer. It must be a new flash drive, as he had destroyed the one with her detailed files of him. He hadn't wanted to take her memories of him, of the science that was clearly so precious to her, but it was for the best.

As the drive opened, he saw her open a Word file and begin typing. Even with his vision, he couldn't read the page from the window and was curious to see what had her working so intently. But that was her, wasn't it? There was nothing she didn't do with that same intensity.

She opened a second file, this one with images all in shades of black and white. There were all kinds of structures, and one in particular that seemed to be in the center of all of them, a sphere with a cone inside. They were clear, but he had no idea what they were. Perhaps it was medical, related to something she was researching.

She pulled some of the images into the Word file. As he watched, she took a small digital camera out of her desk drawer and inserted its SD card into her computer. She opened a file and began viewing the images.

They were familiar in some way, pictures of a burned house. As he continued to watch, an image of a portrait popped onto the screen... his wedding photo.

My God, how does she have pictures from my home? It was badly burned, but the portrait of his beloved had been spared. And Beth had been there.

Luciano's mind returned to his wedding night. The familiar guilt returned, and he vowed that would not happen to Beth. Why would she have these? He had cleared her mind of him but not of the autopsy itself. Perhaps these were images she had from the scene investigator, but if so, how would they be on a card from her camera? Could she have gone there looking for more answers about the body? This had to be the case, didn't it? He had to know. As soon as he had a chance, he had to get a look at that file.

He had been fascinated with this era and the digital advances. He was certainly computer literate, but a computer hacker he was not. When she was caring for him, he had watched her enter her password more than once. Believing he was unconscious, she'd had no need to be careful and conceal it. He had used it the last time he was in her home to delete the files pertaining to him and her research on her hard drive. He would wait until she was gone and take a look at that new file.

CHAPTER 35

BETH

IT WAS HER FIRST night back on duty; a slow night and exactly the kind Beth hated. It left a lot of time for thinking, and as much as she tried, her mind kept wandering to Luc. Ever since hearing him say his name, *Luciano*, in that sexy voice, she couldn't stop thinking of him. She guessed she should be thankful that he hadn't eaten her, that she'd had a chance to talk to him and that the hypnosis had failed... and of course, again, that he hadn't eaten her.

But the truth was, she wanted to know more. She just hoped she had the chance to see him again.

Trying to stay on task, she decided to go over some dictation completed on cases she'd done before vacation. Beth had submitted several corrections and needed to sign off. The first case, though, was the transcription on Luc. Beth read over the case, and that first night replayed in her mind. She had broken how many rules and maybe a couple of laws to keep him alive? She couldn't count but knew every single one had been worth it.

She made minor corrections to the summary and then signed off. She wanted to put this case and its paperwork behind her as quickly as possible.

Rifling through the rest of her files, she noticed one of Peter's cases had been put in her queue by mistake. It had a case number but no name or other identifying information. *We must have a new transcriptionist*, she thought. It was tough to find good people. The pay wasn't a lot and many of the new hires just couldn't take reading about the gunshot wounds, stab wounds and missing body parts. This field clearly wasn't for those with weak stomachs.

Beth walked to the cooler and slid her finger down the list, finding the case number by drawer number seven. She slid it out and lifted the sheet to look for the toe tag, but the body had been put in feet-first. The corpse was a young blond female, maybe twenty-five. Beth's eyes were immediately drawn to two small punctures on the left side of her neck, each maybe five millimeters in diameter and three and a half or four centimeters apart right over her carotid artery.

That was odd. Could it be a vampire bite? Beth had never seen one before, but the spacing and size looked consistent. The dead flesh was slightly raised and pink around the punctures, but there was minimal bruising. She couldn't have lived long after they were inflicted; there would have been more bruising and tissue reaction.

Beth decided to take a look at the report to learn what had caused the wounds.

She flipped through Peter's autopsy report and found nothing. There was no mention of the wounds at all. He listed the cause of death as cardiomyopathy, an enlargement of the heart muscle that could be a cause of sudden death in young people. Beth saw no mention of it in the woman's included medical records, but sometimes people did make it to adulthood without it being discovered. Sometimes family history could give clues, but she couldn't find any evidence of that either.

Beth didn't really have a reason to second-guess Peter; perhaps it was just an omission. But what if it really was a bite? Could it have been

Luc? Could Peter know him and be covering for him? It was probably just her being paranoid. Beth was sure there were things she missed in dictation even though she worked hard to make sure they were few. Given their recent run-in, she wasn't on the best of terms to be calling him on the carpet for a simple omission. It could be an honest mistake. And drawing attention to this would make him wonder why she was looking at all.

"If he isn't working with Luc, or worse, il Diavolo, he'll think you are a total nut seeing vampire bites in two small neck wounds," she said aloud. And if he was working with il Diavolo, she certainly didn't want to raise more suspicion.

Her toe tag read: Neveah Summerland. Another victim of parents trying to be clever with "heaven" spelled backward. Beth jotted the information onto the report and took the file to Peter's desk.

His desk was stark and sterile. He had taken the space vacated by her previous coworker, Henry. He had no pictures of friends or family, just his diplomas from college, medical school and residency, along with his forensic pathology fellowship. His certificate for anatomic pathology boards hung next to them on the wall behind him. All were perfectly aligned, evenly spaced.

While Beth could relate to his organized space, much like hers, that was where their similarities stopped. He was intense and overbearing, sometimes downright rude. Compared to him, she was a social butterfly.

His laptop sat in the center of a large paper desktop calendar with nothing written on it. A stackable file tray, full of case files for autopsies he had performed in the last two weeks, occupied the upper left corner just to the side of his Olympus BX45 microscope.

Beth paused. She knew she shouldn't look through his files. It was thirty minutes before shift change. If her day shift partners arrived early, they would certainly be concerned about her snooping, not to mention Peter himself. But her curiosity had been piqued; she needed to know if he was up to something and who he might be helping.

She picked them up and started flipping through, being careful to maintain the order and direction. Seventy-four-year-old male, traffic accident with transected aorta; twenty-two-year-old male with multiple gunshot wounds (thanks to their local gangs); twenty-four-year-old traffic fatality, motorcycle versus 18-wheeler (never a fair fight); and then twenty-six-year-old Molly Vitelli, cardiomyopathy.

Beth had been practicing as a forensic pathologist for three years outside of residency. Through medical school, residency and fellowship, she had never had a case of sudden death from cardiomyopathy. The odds of Peter having two in two weeks were slim to none. So, either he was an idiot and missed something, despite his fancy credentials, or he was hiding something.

Molly Vitelli's available records showed no history, personal or family, of cardiac issues save for a heart attack in her grandfather. She had been found at Walmart in the driver's seat of her car by police. This file contained the initial police report. While the officer hadn't touched the body otherwise, he had felt for her pulse and noted she was extremely pale and had two small round wounds about an inch and a half apart on her left neck. Now what were the odds of that?

She heard the soft beep and click of the outside doors as someone scanned their ID card to enter. Beth hastily returned the files to Peter's desk and went to sit at her own as quick footsteps reached the office area.

It was Peter. She knew Peter was still investigating the disappearance of the body that he would never find, and while moments before she had hoped the day shift wouldn't arrive early and find her sifting through Peter's files, now she hoped they'd arrive quickly. Being alone with Peter was not something she was comfortable with right now.

"Good morning, Beth," Peter said as he passed in front of her desk.

"Good morning," Beth said, pretending to be engrossed in her open autopsy report.

"Any more revelations on our missing body or what might have gone awry?"

"It's always a series of errors when something goes wrong, Peter, never just one. I started it, signing for release by mistake, and it kept snowballing." It occurred to her that if he were working with Luc, why would he care? It would have been in Luc's best interest and therefore Peter's. For il Diavolo, however, the search for Luc would keep him hot on the trail.

Beth's skin blossomed with gooseflesh, but she tried to act unshaken.

"You're sure there was nothing odd about the case?"

"I'm not sure what you mean by 'odd.'"

"No unusual findings?"

"Other than his extensive burns, no. What are you implying?" Why would he otherwise be so curious about this particular case? Apart from a paperwork error, had he found something she had missed?

"Nothing, nothing." He seemed to backpedal, quickly dismissing her concerns. To Beth, it seemed strange. "Just trying to understand what could have gone wrong here."

"I made a mistake, Peter. I'm not sure what else you want me to say."

Another beep and click let them both know the next day shift pathologist had arrived. Beth dared to meet his gaze.

With a disgusted "Hmph," he turned and stomped away. Seriously, he stomped. He was like Hitler on his way to a staff meeting.

CHAPTER 36

BETH

"Hello, Amanda. It sounds like you are seeing a lot of abnormalities. Can I have a look?" Beth said, entering the cytogenetics bench area. It was a narrow room with multiple workstations where several techs sat, sorting out the images of chromosomes on their computer screens.

"Sure. I remember how you like to try to match them up, so I haven't sorted anything yet. But just from a quick glance, multiple chromosomes are involved. And it involves every cell I've photographed, so it is certainly clonal or congenital. You said this was from a fetus?"

"Yes, a stillborn with obvious malformations," Beth lied.

"Well, these parents have to have some serious issues. I haven't seen this many combined abnormalities even in offspring from siblings. And the cells matured much more quickly than usual. It only took a few hours to get them into metaphase."

"Sounds like this might take a while. Mind if I use that workstation?" Beth asked, pointing to the computer next to Amanda's. Given Luc's regenerative abilities, Beth wasn't surprised by the rapid growth but decided to let it go without commenting.

"Not at all. Let me know if you need help."

Beth thanked her and got to work.

Amanda wasn't kidding. Beth had paired the chromosomes decently but had a great deal of difficulty identifying which pair was which. At metaphase, Luc's chromosomes looked like X's, just as a normal human's chromosomes would, with two short arms on one side and two long arms on the other side of a central point that joined them, the centromere.

Beth had tried aligning chromosomes again from time to time since that original attempt, with the friendly techs encouraging her interest, but these were a complete mess. What she believed to be chromosomes 1 and 9 were especially a mess, but many of the chromosomes had additional material in one arm or the other. After lining them up as best she could, Beth enlisted Amanda's help to finish the job. The abnormalities were far more extensive than she had hoped. She would certainly need the cytogeneticist's help to decipher even a few of the abnormalities. Beth decided to ask the director of the lab, Dr. Thorben Fariha, to provide a little insight into Luc's complex mutations.

After thanking Amanda for her help, Beth headed to Dr. Fariha's office. He was seated at his desk, a patient folder open before him, deep in thought. He was a very conservative man in his mid-fifties, always impeccably groomed right down to the V-neck sweater-vest and bowtie. With his head bent, Beth could see his sandy-brown hair that laid flat against his head thinning, but not yet showing his scalp.

Beth knocked quietly. "Dr. Fariha? Do you have a moment?"

Dr. Fariha looked up from his paperwork, his face drawn, as usual, into an expression Beth could only describe as mildly stressed. "Beth, good to see you," he said and smiled as he rose.

His lips formed a nearly straight line beneath his cleanly shaven face. Although Beth had seen him smile on numerous occasions, it never really seemed to belong there. While not anyone's version of an extrovert, he was approachable and clearly motivated to teach any eager student.

Beth stepped forward, extending her hand, pleasantly surprised that he remembered her name. She'd found cytogenetics fascinating as a resident. It showed, and Beth's interest had won his in return.

"Dr. Fariha, it's wonderful to see you again as well."

"Please, have a seat," he said, motioning to the chair across from his desk. "What brings you our way? I am quite certain your chromosomes were normal in medical school. Are you here to check again?"

"No, thank you. I still have the printout of my karyotype in my files at home, as proof that, at least on a genetic level, I have no major defects." This drew another straight-lipped smiled from Dr. Fariha.

"I brought a sample to the lab from a very abnormal fetus I received for an autopsy." Yet another small lie to remember. For someone who valued truth, Beth was certainly getting better at bending it. This was uncomfortable ground, and Beth hoped the need for deception would soon be over.

"It's not for an official review, but merely to satisfy my curiosity," she added. "I've looked over the karyotype and attempted to pair up the chromosomes but couldn't manage it because of the extensive abnormalities. I left it with Amanda. I was hoping, if you had a few moments after they're grouped, that you wouldn't mind taking a look and giving me your thoughts on what the abnormalities might mean."

"That sounds intriguing. I would be happy to. It may take me a couple of days to get through the current pending cases. But when we have a lull, I'll take a look, jot down some notes for you and send them over."

Beth stood and again offered her hand. "Thank you so much. I look forward to it."

"You, and your curiosity, are always welcome here."

Beth hoped he would feel the same way after reviewing Luciano's karyotype and not see through her lies. He was a brilliant man, and she hoped he couldn't read more from the sample than she was willing to reveal.

CHAPTER 37

BETH

BETH SETTLED INTO HER desk, ready for her shift, and flipped through her file tray. It had been two days since her visit to the cytogenetics lab and, true to his word, a manilla envelope had arrived from Dr. Fariha. When Beth flipped the envelope over, the flap was creased and only loosely stuck down in multiple places, not unmarred as if it had never been sealed but rather like it had been opened and then it didn't reseal well. Someone had already read her mail.

No one knew that she had helped Luc or that the tissue she had submitted for study was from him. Who but Peter could have expected something and gone snooping? Could there be someone else she hadn't yet suspected? Beth looked around to see if anyone was watching and immediately felt silly. Both day and evening shift personnel should have been long gone by now, just her and whatever bodies had been brought in over the last forty-eight hours.

At least there was nothing in the information she had given the cytogenetics lab to link the cells to Luc, unless Peter knew of some of the vampire abnormalities. Given Luc's description of how harshly a good segment of the vampire community dealt with those who attempted to research them, she doubted he could.

If Peter worked for Luc, which seemed less and less likely, would this information be enough for Luc to realize she still had her memories of him? Would he try to wipe her memory again? Even though he seemed to want to protect her, would this be enough for even Luc to turn against her? And, if Peter was working for il Diavolo, would this be enough evidence for him to come after her?

If Peter believed her cover story of a malformed fetus and was just snooping, she would be in no more danger than she had been. If she confronted him, it would reveal how suspicious she was of him, and she just didn't have enough proof yet of what he might be up to. It felt like a chess match. She hoped she was the one two moves ahead, waiting for her opponent to make a wrong move.

Beth opened the envelope to see Dr. Fariha's notes on Luc. As Amanda and Beth had thought, there were numerous abnormalities, and extra material was present on many of the chromosomes in locations that didn't have specific diseases or abnormalities associated with them. There were changes on the short arms of chromosomes 1 and 13, though, in areas related to TP53, a gene relating to programmed cell death. And the one on chromosome 13 was commonly seen in familial porphyria cutanea tarda, a disease where unfortunate carriers had extreme sun sensitivity relating to the body's inappropriate utilization of the products for hemoglobin synthesis and buildup of its byproducts. Luc's sensitivity was beyond extreme, more like explosive, but perhaps this was the culprit.

There were also other abnormalities in areas sometimes involved with muscular dystrophy. But with so many of the abnormalities having no known significance, this was far too complex to sort out. The enormity of the changes would only be seen in a human who had had generations of compounded mutations or who had been purposefully genetically mutated. She was a pathologist and butting up against the limits of her training. But Peter was a pathologist too, and if she was struggling to understand this information and how it pertained to vampirism, he would be also. It was becoming very clear that if she wanted to sort out what the abnormalities meant in relation to Luc's abilities and morbidities, she was going to need help. And asking for help would mean more risk of exposure, not to mention endangering other humans.

Beth sat back roughly in her chair with a sigh. Luc had forty-six chromosomes, just like a human. They clearly shared a significant amount of genetic material, and she knew that Luc had been turned into a vampire, not born one. She also knew he was infected with a virus and that the circumstances around his being turned certainly sounded like infection.

The story of the Vampyre that Luc had shared again came to her mind. If the Vampyre's "gift" to the tribesmen had been an attempt at genetic modification, the easiest way to do that was by using a retrovirus as a kind of mailman, adding all the new genetic material to the virus and then letting it deliver it to the host's DNA after infection. Except those viruses were then programmed to die, not stay intact and continue to replicate for hundreds of years. Obviously, the Vampyre's attempt had gone horribly, horribly wrong.

This could take geneticists and virologists a very long while to sort out, assuming they ever discovered that vampires existed. And the only way that was likely to happen was if Beth decided to share.

CHAPTER 38

LUCIANO

LUCIANO WATCHED THROUGH BETH'S living room window as she headed out to the garage. A moment later he heard the engine start and the garage door open. A flash of headlights told him she was on her way to work. Now was his chance to see what she knew.

In less than thirty seconds, he had picked the lock on the back door and was inside. He could smell her scent lingering in the air and on everything she had touched. It was a warm inviting smell, like clean linen dried in the sun. Nothing was changed, apart from the made bed, done to military perfection, where he had spent his recovery.

Her desk was neatly arranged just as it had been when Luciano watched her from the window the night before. He sat at it and pressed the computer's power button. When the laptop had booted, he entered the password he had seen Beth type so many times before, *F-i-n-d-t-r-u-t-h-5-2-**.

"Incorrect Password," the screen spat back at him.

He entered it again, thinking he must have typed something wrong, but got the same response.

Beth had changed the password. Was this a part of her routine and the old password's time was up, or did she change it because she remembered and knew he could once again access her files?

He looked though the drawers of the desk but found no notes to suggest what it could be.

He found the small digital camera he'd seen Beth use and turned it on to view the images. There were almost forty in all. It looked like she had entered through the basement and had photographed what remained of his grandmother's wardrobe. A pang of sadness at its loss and anger at the insult washed over him. If the time came when returning home was safe, he would gather the remains along with the portrait of his wife. So little of his past remained, he didn't want to lose those too.

He returned everything to the way he had found it and walked to Beth's room. Her scent here was stronger, and it clung to her hairbrush in the bathroom along with a few long brown hairs. Luciano touched them, wishing he'd had a chance to touch her hair during their all-too-brief meeting.

Her nightstands and drawers contained nothing unusual, no duplicates anywhere of the research that he had deleted, just medical journals and a book on nutrition. He paused by a photograph on her bureau. It was of a man who looked to be in his thirties. He had a gentle smile and dark brown hair on either side of Beth's blue eyes. It must be a photo of her father. From her friendly ramblings as she cared for him, he knew her father had died when she was young, leaving her alone to spend two years in foster care.

It was one thing they had in common—neither of them had anyone else left.

Luciano returned the following night just after sundown, hoping he would arrive shortly after Beth awoke and before she had a chance to log on to her computer.

She was finishing her run and really moving tonight. She was clearly deep in thought about something and running nearly full-out. The screen said *5.8 miles*, a long one today. He wondered if she had ever considered a marathon. Her shorts and sports bra were soaked in sweat, and drops beaded on her forehead. Even with the effort, he could see her breathing was smooth and regular. She was in excellent shape, and the muscles of her calves and lower thighs rippled as she ran.

She slowed to a walk to cool down and blotted her face with a towel slung over the rail. Her customary ponytail was in disarray with little wisps having escaped to stick to her neck and forehead. Luciano could see small curls at the base of her neck and felt the urge to wind them around his fingers. He waited for her to shower and dress. Yes, he was watching her, but he would respect her modesty.

She approached the desk dressed for work, with loose-fitting black scrubs and purple Brooks running shoes. Her ponytail was back in place, the loose hairs neatly tucked away. She booted the computer and pulled a folder from her messenger bag. Finally, the computer screen asked for her password, and he watched her keystrokes closely as she typed.

L-u-c-i-a-n-o-3-0-0-!.

His heart was a roller coaster of emotion. It fell, knowing she remembered and the danger it meant she was in, then soared to think he may have a chance to talk with her again. Then it was another steep drop as he wondered if her interest in him was anything more than a researcher with a lab rat. The night they had spoken, Beth had asked about friendships with humans and she had asked about his relationships with other vampires. He knew then he would have to wipe her memory, but now that he saw that the attempt had failed, he hoped she had been fishing to see if there was anyone else in his life.

He watched as her fingers raced over the keys, adding information from papers in the envelope to her research file. He took a step, intending to leave, as a photograph of him opened on her screen—a head shot. It had been taken while he pretended to sleep.

He watched as she stretched out her hand to the screen, running her index finger from his ear to his jaw and then back up to his lips. She outlined them with her finger and sighed.

It was all he needed.

He was a boy again, giddy with the excitement a boy feels when he goes to see a girl, a girl he hopes will be just as excited to see him. It was 9:07 p.m. and Luciano was once again standing outside Beth's bedroom window. He made a quick run around the block, looking for any sign that he could have been followed. There were no vehicles parked along the street on Beth's block to suggest her house was being watched. He stopped back at her window and stood completely still, listening for anything out of the ordinary. Then he breathed deeply, searching for any scents that could suggest humans or vampires nearby.

Nothing. It was as safe as it could be.

CHAPTER 39

BETH

THERE WAS A LOUD knock. Beth jumped and turned quickly, trying to locate the sound. It came again, and she focused on a face in the window. Her heart beat rapidly in her chest, nearly as fast as when she was running. Fear and excitement overwhelmed her.

Oh my God, it's Luc. Her thoughts raced along with her heart. Was he here because he knew she remembered? He had to know. Otherwise why would he ever see her again? How could he know? Had he been the one to open her mail? Did Peter know and tell him she was still investigating? Did he have someone else watching her?

She paused and took a deep breath as she walked to the back door of the house. She had to let him in. Surely, he was being kind to knock. He could easily have knocked her door down and forced his way in. He had been in her house before, and if the legends were true, he clearly wouldn't need her permission. Kidnapping him and dragging him into her house would probably be considered an invitation.

She focused on steadying her breathing and shaking hands, then opened the door.

He smiled down at her. Surely this was a good sign, right? He didn't look angry.

"Hello, Beth. I hope you don't mind me dropping by."

Mind? Seriously? Beth felt her cheeks flush as her eyes fell to his full lips. Lips she had been mooning over just moments before. What do you say when a three-hundred-year-old vampire "drops by?"

"Not at all, Luc—I'm sorry, Luciano—"

"No, Luc is good," he interrupted. "I like it. No one has ever called me that before."

Beth blushed, the fact that she had a nickname for him surely revealing that she had thought about him more than she wanted to admit.

"Please, come in." Beth waved her hand to the left and stepped aside. "I'm surprised you're here," she blurted. "I didn't expect to see you again."

Luc chuckled. "I didn't expect to see you either. But I am glad I have."

Beth hoped the heat in her cheeks and her heart's skipped beat weren't enough to be noticeable.

"You're not disappointed the hypnosis didn't work? I thought you might be angry with me or..."

"I'm not angry. It would have been safer for you. But I'm not angry."

His eyes looked so soft, so gentle, and he held her gaze.

Afraid her eyes showed too much, she looked down and turned to walk toward the couch. Beth needed to keep her emotions in check. She was sure he was not there just to say hello.

Trying to act nonchalant, "So, what brings you back?" *And please don't say it's because you are going to try to wipe my memory again or because you've had Peter or someone else follow me and I have to stop studying you.*

"I'm concerned about your safety. I told you, there are others like me that would have you dead just for knowing we exist."

"What about you?"

"Me? You saved me. I owe you my life and will do whatever I can to be sure no harm comes to you."

And there it was. He didn't want her harmed because she had saved his life. He was here only to repay a debt.

She turned her back to him to be sure he couldn't read her disappointment and moved to the chair at one end of the couch. Sharing the couch with him might be a bit too unsettling.

Beth tried to focus and center herself. "So where do we go from here?"

"Well, I am aware that you are continuing your research and—"

"Why do you think that?"

He was seated but shifted and dropped his eyes before regaining her gaze. "I've come by before to be certain you were safe and I saw you working on it through your window." With this he pursed his lips and smiled sheepishly. Had he seen her looking at his photo? Oh, please, no. Anything but that.

"I saw you viewing pictures of my home after the fire."

Oh, thank God! Beth struggled to hide her relief. "Yes, I was trying to understand what happened to you and how you survived."

"I was chained into... a large wooden box while I slept. The men who did this could be the same men that come after you if your research is discovered. The one who I believe is behind all of this is very powerful and older than any other vampire I have ever encountered. He could have men watching you from almost anywhere."

Beth's mind went to the lights she had seen at the end of the drive at Luc's burned home and then to her opened mail and Peter. "What about you? Do you have people helping you and watching me?"

"Of course not, why would you think that?"

He looked genuinely surprised, and she decided to just be blunt.

"I found a couple of autopsy cases, young women, with puncture wounds on their necks, but my new partner didn't mention the wounds in his report."

"What did the wounds look like?"

Beth was relieved; if he didn't already know what the wounds looked like, surely he couldn't have inflicted them.

"Two small circular wounds, maybe five millimeters each and about thirty-five millimeters apart. They were over the carotid artery."

At this, Luc's forehead creased and he looked away.

"And I think... actually, I'm fairly certain that someone went through my mail at work." She may as well come clean at this point. "It was a report on your karyotype."

Beth closed her eyes and waited for the tongue-lashing that would likely follow, but Luc was silent. He almost looked pale. He sat completely still for about thirty seconds before speaking.

"What's a karyotype and did the results contain any links to my autopsy results? And you said this partner was new?"

Beth was relieved; clearly Luc didn't know Peter. But the thought was quickly followed by the knowledge that her concerns about Peter covering for someone else, and very likely the Master, were confirmed. She felt a little knot in the pit of her stomach.

"A karyotype is an analysis of your chromosomes and any abnormalities they might contain. I labeled them as if they came from an autopsy on an abnormal fetus. And yes, Peter James is new. He seemed to drop out of thin air. He submitted an application just before another of my partners, Henry Adams, died in a car accident. We hired him a couple of weeks later and he started just before you were injured."

"Have you said anything to him about the suspicious autopsy cases?

Or the mail?" Worry lines were etched across Luc's forehead, and he leaned forward, waiting for her answer.

"No, I wasn't certain on either and I just found the second suspicious case last night." She dropped her eyes, avoiding eye contact, and admitted, "I actually thought he might be working for you." She peeked up at him through her lashes, wanting to gauge his reaction, but his expression hadn't changed.

"So, for now, he probably doesn't know you suspect him of anything, right?"

"No."

Luc's shoulders were rigid, muscles occasionally twitching beneath his shirt, and the intensity of his gaze was making her anxious. "Beth, you need to stay away from him, avoid him at all costs. If he is working for the Master and they are watching you, you have to be certain they don't find anything that could tie you to me and cause them to come after you. The Master's resources are extensive and he buys or takes whatever he needs. Is there anything else you can think of out there that could link you to me?"

"I don't think so."

"What were the black-and-white photos I saw you looking at?" So he had seen those too, had he? How many times had he watched her since he left?

"Electron microscope photos. I processed the tissue and took the photographs myself. No one else knows about them. Did you know your blood contains a virus? I think it may have been how you were turned."

"Beth, no, I don't know about any virus, and you shouldn't either." His voice was impatient, flat. She knew it was because he was focused on their safety and not interested in the details of her research right now, but it still felt dismissive. "Is there anything else that's happened that you haven't told me?"

"No," Beth said coldly. "There is not a single other thing you need to know."

"I'm sorry," Luc said with a long exhale. "I don't mean to sound cold; I'm just trying to understand where things stand, what the risks are and what I need to do next. I've been trying to figure out why the Master would come after me now and if he's still looking for me. If he believes I am still alive then he would suspect that I had help. If he discovers you're searching for information about me or investigating vampires, he will come after you. He will kill you, Beth, and without a second thought. He made me..." His voice wavered, and he paused to gather himself. "He killed my wife. I don't want him to take your life as well." With this he paused again, seeming to need to say more, but holding back. After a moment, he continued, "You will be late for work. And I'm putting you at risk being here. I should go."

Whatever reason brought him here, Beth didn't want him to leave. Though she was certain it was one-sided, she felt a connection to Luc and didn't want to give that up.

He stood and looked toward the door, shifting his weight on his feet, seeming to hesitate. Could he feel her reluctance? Why would he want to see her again? What could she say that would make him come back? She had so many questions, but mostly she just wanted more time with him.

"So, where could we meet that would be safer? I would like to share what I've found with you."

Considering this, he said, "Yes, I would like to understand what you've found and why you find it so fascinating."

Good, it was a start. "How about the medical library or a casino?

Maybe a coffee shop several miles away?"

"The library, tomorrow, perfect. What time?"

"Fifteen minutes after sunset?"

"It's a date," he said with a grin.

Beth smiled back, thankful to know he was looking out for her and truly happy she would see him again. But she couldn't help thinking that there were a lot of daylight hours where he couldn't watch over her between now and then.

CHAPTER 40

BETH

BETH ARRIVED HOME AT 6:25 a.m. after her shift at the morgue. She changed into jeans and a simple blue polo shirt and tugged on her gray-and-white Brooks running shoes. She released her hair from its ponytail and smoothed it. She glanced at her appearance in the mirror and decided the outfit would work; nothing flashy, nothing memorable. Then she grabbed a small duffle bag from the closet and placed all of the hardcopy files from her investigation of Luc inside along with a new flash drive containing all the digital files she had collected.

She had a shoebox-sized fire safe on the shelf of her closet. She worked the combination lock and pulled out all the cash—five hundred dollars in twenties—her passport, social security card and birth certificate. They would be safe at the bank, and if things really got ugly, she would need them to start over somewhere else. She also added her emergency credit card to the stack. She mostly used her debit card for day-to-day but had a card with a fifteen-thousand-dollar credit limit for emergencies. Though it could be tracked, it may become necessary in a pinch. She also tossed in her battery-powered UV light, the only weapon she knew would work against a vampire if she had to face one. She could pick up another for home on her way.

She zipped the bag and began to walk from the room.

Beth paused at the edge of her dresser, looking at a picture of her father and her taken on a sixteenth-birthday trip to SeaWorld just a few short months before he died from metastatic colon cancer. His arm was draped over her shoulders and they were both smiling broadly.

Beth grabbed the photo with a gentle touch, smiling sadly back at her father, and added it to her duffle. If something happened and she couldn't return home, she wanted a picture of her father to remember him and the good times they had shared. He had been the only person in her life she had truly trusted; the only person who had ever really understood what made her tick. And she only had him for such a short time. The pain of losing him was still fresh after all these years. Loving someone meant opening up to the possibility of that hurt again.

She blinked slowly, clearing the thoughts so she could focus.

She had chosen a Central National Bank location in Lawrence, about a thirty-five-minute drive from her home. It was on South Iowa Street where the majority of the chain stores were, which seemed like a good idea if she truly was in a lurch and couldn't return home. She hoped it would be far enough away that she would be able to get to it unnoticed if needed. She would rent a safety deposit box, paying with cash, and know that all the information she had gathered was held in safekeeping should she need it.

While she had suspected Peter could be involved with the Master before, the discussion with Luc the previous night had confirmed it. She had come up with a plan to give herself an option to run as well as to protect her research if the Master did decide to come after her. The fact of the matter was that she had gone about as far as she could go on her own, at least for now. She would continue to study whatever could be behind Luc's odd genetics as well as the virus that infected him. But ultimately, she would need the help of a virologist or a geneticist at the very least to begin to decipher the meaning of the changes in Luc's DNA as well as to examine the structure and RNA or DNA of the virus itself. But until everything quieted down, she didn't dare reach out to other scientists.

Instead, Beth came up with a sort of insurance plan. As she had driven home from work, she had left a message with a local law firm. She would meet with one of the lawyers tomorrow and put together a plan by which, if she notified them or she didn't contact them weekly, a set of letters would be sent to scientists of her choosing with access to both the research she'd accumulated and a sample of Luc's blood or tissue stored at various tissue banks near the scientists she had chosen. If and when the letters were sent, all records of her interactions with them would be destroyed so the Master would have nothing to track should he discover her plan. It at least could give her a bargaining chip. If the Master harmed her or Luc, his secret would be released to multiple others with no way for him to track down and retrieve the information.

CHAPTER 41

BETH

BETH WAS READING THROUGH the primer on retroviruses, refreshing her memory from her last studies in virology from medical school and waiting for Luc to arrive. She had forgotten a little, but there was new material as well. So much was discovered in medicine from year to year. Being in the medical field was a commitment to lifelong learning. Most states required at least fifty hours a year for continuing medical education to maintain a license, but it barely scratched the surface of all the new research that became available. Retrovirus treatments had become far more specific and now targeted specific markers. Those markers that were only on cancer cells meant that a patient could receive therapy with far fewer side effects since the drugs targeted only the cancer cells and not all of the patient's cells as earlier chemotherapy agents had.

As Beth turned the next page in the summary, she noticed Luc had arrived. He had seated himself silently across from her and was gazing intently at her jeans. She glanced down to see if something was amiss but found nothing.

"Is everything ok?" she asked.

Luc, caught staring, quickly averted his eyes. Beth thought she saw a faint change in his coloring. Did vampires blush?

"Yes, everything is fine."

"Is something wrong with my clothing? Do you not like blue jeans?" she said as she closed the text. This particular pair were Beth's favorites, fitting well in all the right places. But surely Luc wouldn't know about that. He had been unconscious when Beth had talked about them. Maybe he didn't like the way they looked on her.

"I have never worn them," Luc said, still not meeting her eyes. "They weren't available before I was changed. When they did become more commonplace, they were typically for construction workers or worn by rebellious teenagers in the '50s. It seems they are a wardrobe staple these days."

So that was it; Beth felt the self-consciousness fade. She decided to buy Luc some jeans as a gift for their next meeting.

Still looking a bit uncomfortable, Luc asked, "Anymore questions from Peter today? More opened mail or other strange things?"

"No, thankfully. My shift was uneventful."

"Good. Then explain to me what you have discovered so far."

Beth moved to the seat next to him and leaned in close, her shoulder brushing his, so she could whisper and be certain they were not overheard. She knew with Luc's hearing he could easily hear her whisper from across the room, but it was a good excuse to get close to him.

If he minded, it didn't show. He leaned his head closer until they were nearly nose-to-nose. His eyes were even more beautiful up close, the deep brown also containing flecks of yellow and green that seemed to flicker as he listened.

She explained what she had found so far and what it told her about vampire physiology. It took a while, answering his questions about the science as they went along. When she was finished, Luc asked, "Do you have any other studies waiting? Anything else that Peter could find?"

"No, that's it."

"Okay, so no more suspicious fieldtrips. Peter must not have put enough together to firmly tie you to me. If you can lie low and not arouse any more suspicion, perhaps he will move on."

"So, if experiments are on hold, can I at least ask you a few more questions?" Beth still had much she wanted to know about Luc, but it also gave her another excuse to continue to meet with him.

An indulgent grin formed on Luc's face, and Beth's eyes lingered on his full lips for just a moment. "Ask away."

"I have wanted to ask you about when you... well, eat. Is that ok?"

Luc nodded.

"I know you can't eat regular food, but when you... eat... your stomach digests the blood..."

"Well, when I drink blood, most of it goes through my fangs. Some does go into whatever is left of my stomach, which digests it."

"Through your fangs?"

"Yes, how can I describe it?" Luc paused to think. "My fangs are like sharp straws. When I feed, there is this warming sensation that travels quickly from the initial explosion of warmth in my mouth to the rest of my body. It is a very pleasant sensation..." Luc dropped his gaze again. "Almost... erotic."

Erotic. And he seemed shy about it. Their close proximity was suddenly more noticeable, but if it made Luc uncomfortable, he didn't move away. Was sex and drinking blood intertwined with vampires? And what about the donor? Did the bite have any effect on them? Other than the sheer terror they must feel? Did vampires even have sex? That was definitely a conversation she wasn't ready to have... well, yet anyway.

"So, when you are finished... drinking, do you feel full like you've had a big meal?"

"No, I feel satiated... satisfied... but not full like I did before I was turned."

Beth wanted to know about other bodily functions too, but thought maybe something a little easier would be good to break up the difficult and more embarrassing questions. "You said you were in a wooden box sleeping when the Master's men chained you into it. You didn't have an enclosure while you were recovering at my house, though. Do you usually sleep in a box, and with your house gone, do you have a place to stay?" Beth knew her place wasn't safe for him but wondered if he would have considered it otherwise.

"No, I don't need to sleep in a box, but I liked that one because it had sentimental value and completely kept out the light. Right now, I am sleeping in a boxcar down by the rail yard. It is certainly not fancy, but as long as wherever I sleep keeps me out of the sunlight, I can make it through the daylight hours."

Her curiosity getting the best of her, Beth asked, "Have you ever slept in a coffin?"

"No," Luc chuckled, "although I did spend a few nights in a tomb once while traveling."

"I'm around death all the time but for some reason that sounds a little creepy."

"Actually, it was very quiet," he said and shot her a playful grin.

"So, forgive me for being direct, but while you were in a coma, you never passed urine or feces. Is that normal for vampires?" Beth hoped she wouldn't embarrass him, but the question had nagged at her.

"Yes, it is. I haven't had those bodily functions since I was turned."

"So your body must use the blood very efficiently; there is no waste. Perhaps your fangs drain directly into your circulatory system or maybe you have another digestive organ all together." Beth wondered to herself how she could test for this. In CT scans, radioactive iodine was used as contrast material to highlight the circulation or they had patients drink barium to highlight the digestive tract. In nuclear medicine there were PET scans that used radiolabeled glucose to see areas of increased metabolism like in tumors. Beth didn't know how iodine might work in Luc's system, but the radiolabeled glucose certainly wouldn't harm him. Glucose was just a sugar that all human bodies used for energy. It would already be in the blood of the humans he was feeding on, but by adding the radioactively labeled form, she might be able to see how it traveled through his body as he drank. Figuring out a way to get him into the PET scanner without raising eyebrows wouldn't be easy, though. A test for another day, she supposed.

"So what about other body fluids. Do you have saliva?"

"Yes, I do. My mouth is not dry."

"And your nasal passages, are they moist too?"

"Yes."

That left only one. Beth paused for a moment, trying to think of a matter-of-fact way to ask the question without embarrassing herself...

"The answer is yes. I do make semen too."

Did he get there by process of elimination or had he read her thoughts?

Beth nodded her head, and they both shifted a bit in their seats. Flashbacks of uncomfortable physical exams with male patients when she was a young medical student passed through her mind. But they had broached the subject, and he seemed open to questions, so...

"Can vampires have children? I mean, other than by infecting humans with the virus?"

"No, I don't think so. I've never heard of two vampires producing offspring in the usual way. I've never heard of one having a child with a human either. And turning children is not tolerated. It would be cruel. Their minds would age and grow, so they would at least mature intellectually, but their bodies would always remain weaker and child-like." His voice lowered as he spoke of children, and his shoulders slumped ever so slightly.

"Luc, if you had a chance to be human again, to get to be in the sun, to be free of the thirst but give up your near-immortality, strength and regeneration, would you choose—"

"In a heartbeat. There have been times through the years when I have thought about dying. Three hundred years is a very long time." Beth couldn't really imagine three hundred years of loneliness. And hearing Luc so certain of wanting to be human again, she was even more determined to continue her research as soon as possible.

"Seeing the new inventions and exploring the world is exciting at times, but watching everyone you once knew die is difficult. Forming relationships with humans is painful because I know in the end I will watch them die too."

Was Luc referring to a relationship with her or was he bringing it up to warn her away? She didn't know how to ask without revealing her feelings.

"What about other vampires? Those relationships would last."

"It is true, they would. When you consider that it could go on for many centuries, it makes 'till death do us part' sound even more serious."

At that Beth had to smile. "I'm guessing there aren't a lot of vampire divorce lawyers out there either."

Luc returned her smile. Beth loved how the corners of his eyes turned up when he grinned. It occurred to her that she had never heard him laugh. "So, what do three-hundred-year-old vampires do for fun?"

CHAPTER 42

BETH

"HERE, I GOT YOU a present," Beth said, holding out the Gap bag.

Opening the bag and removing the stone-washed, button-fly jeans and orange rugby Beth had bought him, Luc grinned. "Thank you! I'm curious to see how they feel. I'll wear them the next time we meet."

Beth hadn't bought him more boxer briefs. It felt too intimate now that he was awake, but she couldn't help wondering how he looked in them.

"And speaking of meeting, I was thinking that perhaps we should arrange to meet at a different location. We've been fortunate to not be discovered here but I am concerned about being so close to the university, especially with Doctor James already keeping you under watch. There is a park on Sixty-third Street east of Mission Road. Do you know it? We could meet there after sunset."

"Yes, I know it. I've gone there to run from time to time. I can meet you at the benches near the front entrance. It'll give us a couple of hours to talk before I have to leave for work." Beth didn't know what Luc's goals were, but she hoped it wasn't just to check up on the Master's progress in tracking him through her. She knew keeping them off her trail was paramount but wanted more time with Luc just getting to know him. She hoped it would be more of a date than a meeting.

"Perfect! I've been thinking about your work as you have taught me about what you are discovering with your research. I can tell you love your work, but doing autopsies seems like a strange career choice. You haven't mentioned how you ended up becoming a forensic pathologist." Luc, who was sitting on a bench seat, scooted over and patted the seat beside him.

Her heart sped. Did he want to be close to her too? She sat down as close as she could without being obvious and turned to meet his eyes. He shifted to face her more directly, his knee now touching hers, and she wondered again if he could read her emotions. He didn't seem the type to toy with her, so if he could, he must feel the same. Or maybe he couldn't and she was reading too much into it.

"I guess I was just born for it. I was always curious about how things worked. I wanted to understand what made all living things tick and have always been curious about what caused their deaths. Learning about it all, finding the answers to all my questions, became a bit of an obsession. I would dissect things that I found—worms, frogs, birds, anything that I found already dead. As I grew, I would study anatomy from library books. My father understood my curiosity and encouraged me." Beth remembered a story she had spoken aloud while Luc had been unconscious, but knowing he wouldn't remember, she decided to share the story with him again.

"One summer when I was young my father saw me watching *National Geographic*, one of my favorite shows at the time. A whale had beached itself and died. Scientists were investigating its cause of death. After many examinations they were still uncertain. I remember asking my father why the scientists couldn't figure out what killed the whale. And he said to me—"

Luc chimed in, "'I don't know Beth, but if they can't, I'm sure you will figure it out for them!' I loved that!"

Beth paused, looking directly at Luc with her forehead creased. The smile faded from Luc's eyes. The realization of what it meant made her head swim.

"I told you that story while you were unconscious. How can you know that unless you weren't really unconscious? Luc, how long were you awake? How much did you hear?" She had to know. Was it moments, a day, the whole time? *Oh, God, please not the whole time.*

"I was in and out, so I did hear a few things."

"Luc, *how long*?"

"On and off the first day or so..."

"The first *day* or so? So you were awake and pretending for all the rest? For everything I said?" Beth paled and sucked in a deep breath. Suddenly she felt very foolish, then angry, and then just plain mortified.

She stood and backed away a couple of steps, needing space to breathe.

As she retreated, Luc stood, reaching out both hands to gently grasp her shoulders, but she dropped her head and wouldn't meet his eyes.

"I'm sorry, Beth. I didn't know who you were or what you wanted from me. It seemed that I was safe. I needed a place to stay that was under the Master's radar while I healed, so I pretended to be unconscious. As I heard you talk, things changed. I learned about what kind of person you are and I started to... I began to—"

"I need some time to think." Her cheeks flared red as she thought of all the things she had told him. All the things he knew about her. She had let herself talk about things she would never have said otherwise. Her blue jeans, which was of course why he'd stared at them; the day she had run her hand down his chest...

The color left her face and she thought she might be sick. She was beyond embarrassed. She quickly gathered her things and hurried toward the door. This was her own fault and she knew it, but she didn't feel any less humiliated.

CHAPTER 43

LUCIANO

Il Diavolo was laughing... laughing beyond his bedroom door. Luciano burst through it, the door exploding into small fragments of wood, and faced him. In his anger Luciano attacked, screaming incoherently, guttural noises forced from his mouth as he ran and leaped at him.

Il Diavolo sidestepped his lunge, and Luciano plunged into the nearby wall. It crumbled beneath him as though it was made of paper and sticks. Every time Luciano came at him, he deflected his blows. He was much faster than Luciano, and Luciano only succeeded in moving il Diavolo about the house, knocking down walls as he missed him over and over again.

Il Diavolo began to chuckle once again, fueling Luciano's anger, and this time he caught him full in the middle, catapulting them both into the wall dividing the kitchen and living room.

Il Diavolo laughed aloud. As they both rose to their feet, Luciano realized that even this direct hit had done no damage. Luciano couldn't hurt him by hitting and tackling. Luciano grabbed the leg of a broken kitchen chair and flung it at il Diavolo's chest with all his strength, only to watch him move from its path with amazing speed to leer at him, completely unharmed.

It was no use, and the battle was only making Luciano feel more furious and pathetic. Luciano was no more able to harm il Diavolo than he was able to protect his wife.

In desperation Luciano turned and ran from the house, hearing il Diavolo's mocking laughter as he fled. Luciano wanted to run until the exhaustion freed him from his fury, until the pain of his body overcame the pain in his heart.

But the physical pain did not come.

He realized he had reached the next town, some three days' ride by carriage, and felt no more strain on his body than when he had begun. He turned back the way he came, stopping at a grove of cypress trees just outside of the village. In anger, Luciano swung at the closest tree and was taken aback to see the top of the tree fly off, broken clean from the trunk in the direction he had swung. Luciano grabbed the trunk, wrapping his arm around its full base and, with little effort, ripped it from the earth and heaved it to the side. He approached the next tree and did the same, finding that its destruction gave him some bit of relief. He tore tree after tree from the ground, ripping away the large branches as he went.

After a small forest of trees, the anger was gone and he half fell, half sat on a large tree trunk in the center of the mess he had made. Luciano let his face fall into his hands and wept in loud anguished sobs. He had saved his wife from il Diavolo only to take her life with his own hands. The life they had planned together was gone, his dreams with her never to be. He cried from a pain within him that he could have never imagined.

After several hours, the tears stopped and he began to realize what he had done there. Ripping tree trunks easily from the earth with nothing but his hands. He was strong. He was a monster but very, very strong. Luciano remembered the way il Diavolo had easily dodged his advances, how he had so effortlessly flipped him about the rooms of his house. How strong he must be in comparison was daunting.

And Luciano had covered the ground from his house to the edge of the village in such a short time. So not only was he strong but also quite fast.

Luciano realized that his vision was perfect; nothing was dim. The light of the waning crescent moon was more than enough for him. He could see with as much detail as he could in daylight, more even.

He looked to the trunk he sat on. Every ridge of the bark was so clear, so intricate, subtly colored by the growing moss. There were shades of green and brown he was certain he had never seen before. Luciano looked out across the field and could see the same level of detail on the trees of the next grove, even from a great distance away.

And hear! He could hear everything. Luciano had been so absorbed in his sorrow before he hadn't heard the sounds of the night over his sobs. The crickets and locusts sang their songs that rose and fell in unison like a choir. An owl called, and he turned to find him. The bird sat, preening in the tall branches. He could hear the near-silent rubbing of his feathers together as he moved. To Luciano's left he could hear an opossum moving through the underbrush, searching for his next meal. The night was alive with sound and smells of the warm grass, decaying leaves and the sweetness of the few blossoms that remained on the trees. He could tell there was water nearby. The peeper frogs called softly, and he could faintly smell the damp moss. Luciano had been damned, that was certain, cursed to live with the memory of his wife's death. He had become a night creature, a monster from the terrifying stories he believed myth, that drank blood and was condemned to a life in the shadows.

Luciano awakened slowly from the nightmare as the sun dipped beneath the horizon, the sorrow slowly dissipating as his thoughts turned to Beth. Luciano knew he could tolerate what remained of the light, so he rose and ran toward the park. At his top speed, evening in the waning light, human eyes would never see him. They would assume it was a breeze in the trees or an imagined motion caught in the corner of their eyes.

As he ran, he reflected on the dream. Much had been taken from him with his wife's death. And he had vowed to understand his abilities and their limits to be sure il Diavolo would never harm another soul. And right now, that soul was Beth's.

In a few short minutes, he had reached the entrance to the park. One last walker was unlocking her car to leave. Hers was the last car in the lot, and he felt the disappointment of Beth's avoidance once again. He had waited last night for several hours before leaving to feed. He wanted to respect her privacy and knew this was his fault. He should have just come clean from the beginning, but he never intended for her to even remember him. The hypnosis had failed. He wasn't certain why. Perhaps it was his hesitance to do it at all, or perhaps Beth knowing it was coming had helped her resist. Whatever the reason, he was selfishly thankful she remembered him and prayed now that she would forgive his deception.

He waited in the dark, watching as two young lovers hurried giggling into the park and down one of the trails, cell phone flashlights and a blanket in hand. Luciano knew even thinking about such things with Beth was dangerous, but he wished for it just the same.

She wasn't coming, that was clear. But he would not give up. He would come to the park each night at dark for as long as it took. But if she didn't come tomorrow night, he would go by her home. It would be as much to check for her safety as it would be to see her face again, but he would not disturb her. She clearly wanted space and time and deserved both. It was possible she may never forgive him or wish to see him again. As much as he hoped that would not be the case, he also knew that it would be best for her.

But for tonight, he couldn't bear to dwell on that.

CHAPTER 44

BETH

LUC WAS WAITING FOR her by the train station. When she approached, he reached out his hand, and she took it. His hand was cool in hers, but she didn't mind.

He pulled her up and on board the train, and they walked to their own cabin. When he closed the door behind him, he pulled her into his arms and kissed her. She could feel her fingers curled in his hair and his tongue against hers. She felt his lips against her neck as he moved from her chin to her collarbone. His hands were on her back, one low and the other between her shoulder blades and pulling her closer...

And her alarm sounded.

She didn't want to leave and fought to stay in the dream until she could no longer pretend her alarm was just part of the background.

She raised her hand to her mouth. His lips had been so full and soft. She imagined they would feel just like her dream. She hoped one day she would get to find out.

It was 6 p.m. Beth crawled from her bed and pulled on her running clothes. It seemed she dreamed about Luc most every time she slept now. It had been two days since Luc had told her he'd been awake for most of her time caring for him.

She hadn't been able to bring herself to meet him at the park.

She tried to distract herself with her run, but her mind just kept going back to their last meeting. She wasn't mad at him, even though he had pretended to be comatose. He hadn't tried to hurt her. It was true that he hadn't known her or where he was. He had been in very bad shape and needed a safe place to hide out until he figured out what had happened and was well enough to deal with it. Given the circumstances, she probably would have made a similar choice.

The truth was she was only mad at herself and embarrassed beyond belief. She had shared many things that she had never told another soul and never would have entrusted to another, let alone a stranger, had she known he was listening. It left her open and vulnerable. Someone knowing enough about her to be aware of her weaknesses and use them to hurt her if they chose to was new for her and frightening. But it was done. And even though he knew those things, he had still come to see her. Either that meant he cared and was interested in the stories of her life, her thoughts and feelings or... more likely, if she was being honest with herself... he felt like he had gotten her into this in the first place and that he was responsible for keeping her safe. How to sort out the two, she wasn't sure. And she wasn't sure she wanted to if it was the latter.

He had said that human relationships were difficult since human lives were so short. Perhaps he had meant that as a way to tell her that was all she would be to him, a brief distraction in this century before he moved on to the next. Beth understood life was short—the loss of her father had taught her that. But thinking of Luc living for centuries on end, she truly felt how brief human existence was. She knew the pain of losing her father and thought how selfish it was that she would want Luc to love her knowing he would lose her in the blink of an eye.

But still, she missed him.

Time with him was precious and she was wasting it. She needed to know if there could be a future for the two of them, no matter how short. Tonight, as soon as the sun set, she would meet him at the park. Assuming of course that he hadn't given up on her already.

CHAPTER 45

BETH

THEY HAD ARRANGED TO meet at the park on 63rd Street just after sunset. Luc had said that the light after sunset felt prickly on his skin but that he could tolerate it and enjoyed the fading colors the sunset left on the horizon.

Beth didn't know if he would be there or not. She had avoided the meetup for two days, so perhaps he had given up.

She parked in the large lot outside the gates to the park, took a deep breath and turned off the ignition. She made one final glance around the parking lot entrance to check for headlights, making sure she hadn't been followed. However this went, she needed to know where they stood. She had never been one to hide from a problem; it only made things worse.

As she emerged from the car and headed down the path to the park and walking trail entrance, she kept her eyes down, hoping he would be there but not ready to look. She knew it was silly. "Just pull off the Band-Aid, Beth."

She looked up to see Luc about thirty yards in front of her. He was dressed in the jeans and rugby shirt she had given him at their last meeting. And even though he said he'd never worn jeans, she hoped it would become a habit. His brown curls touched the shoulders of his shirt, and the rusty orange of the rugby brought out the olive in his skin. She could see the fabric hugging the lines of the muscles in his chest. The jeans hung low on his hips and gently hugged his thighs.

He was, for lack of a better word, beautiful.

As she met his eyes, she saw him release a deep breath. Relief? Resignation? He dropped his chin slightly and looked at her through his upper lashes, and a tentative smile formed on his full lips. Beth returned the shy smile, and then there he was in front of her. He had crossed the distance between them before she could see that he'd moved.

"Beth, I'm so sorry. I should have told you right away."

"It's okay. I wasn't angry with you. I was embarrassed. It's my own fault for telling you all those things."

"I'm glad you did," he interrupted, and took her hand in his. His grip was firm but gentle and his skin cool, as she remembered it from when she had cared for him, but hers burned like fire.

He leaned in close. A few more inches and she could easily kiss him. Her heart hammered in her chest. She knew he could likely hear it and would know the effect of his touch. She could feel pink rising in her cheeks.

If he noticed, he didn't let on. He continued to speak with a little crease on his forehead just between his brows. Whatever he had to tell her was important to him.

"It helped me in ways you don't understand." Another deep sigh as the crease deepened. "I told you that the Master killed my wife. But I never told you the whole story." Luc told Beth about the night his wife died, leaving nothing out.

Beth held his gaze while he spoke. Tears for the cruelty of the Master and what he had made Luc do welled in Beth's eyes. All of the embarrassment and self-consciousness left her. She intertwined her fingers in his, and the little crease between his brows softened and disappeared.

"When you spoke to me and began telling me stories about your life, it touched my heart. You sharing a part of yourself with me showed me that I was still capable of caring for another. When I did speak to you the first time, I couldn't tell you that. You didn't even know my name, and as far as you knew, I didn't know yours. I knew it was safer for you if you could forget me even though it was the last thing I wanted. When I discovered that you remembered me... I couldn't stay away."

Beth was speechless for a moment. While she had been embarrassed before, pushing him away to preserve her wounded ego, she now wanted nothing more than to share her world with him. His words and his hand in hers gave her hope that he did too.

"Thank you for telling me. And I'm glad you came back," she said.

They turned toward the path and began to walk, hand in hand, headed toward the bench in the trees to sit.

"What the Master did to you and your wife, none of that was your fault. I cannot imagine what could make someone so unbelievably cruel."

"I don't know what happened to him, but there were times when my hatred for him nearly took me over. I spent the first many years of this new life chasing him and trying to kill him until I realized that it wouldn't change anything. It could never change what I had done. And it would never bring her back. I moved on, but I still can't forgive myself for what I did."

As they sat on the bench, Luc kept her hand, sitting close enough that their thighs and shoulders touched. Beth had never wanted to hold someone so much in her life. She longed to wrap her arms around his broad shoulders and reassure him, but it would be too much too fast.

"What if it had been me, Luc? What would you say to me?"

Luc sat silently, looking down at the ground but not pulling away.

"There is no way you could have known he would come after you, no way you could have imagined what he was let alone that he might turn you into a vampire. He knew you would have no control over your thirst when you awakened and left you there with her on purpose. The blame for her death rests solely with him."

CHAPTER 46

PETER

PETER HAD SEEN THE voicemail light flashing on Beth's desk phone shortly after lunch. But he didn't dare go snooping with the other pathologists around. He waited until 4 p.m. when the evening crew had come on and were busy with a case, pretending he stayed over to finish up on some paperwork. Hearing the two men talking about the case in the next room, he walked quietly to Beth's desk. He raised the handset to his ear and pressed the voicemail button. Passwords on the phone system had been set to their 5-digit badge number, and because he had copies of Beth's employee files and had spent time studying them, he had the number committed to memory.

He entered 85343 followed by the pound sign, 2 for messages and 0 to listen.

"Hello, Beth. This is Sherman in the blood bank. I was curious how your experiment was going. I hope the expired red cell units we were able to get you were enough for your study. Anyway, give me a call and let me know if you want us to save more for you. Goodbye!"

Beth had been getting expired units of blood from the university blood bank for an "experiment?" That was just a little too much of a coincidence. However she managed it, he knew she had helped Luciano. He was certain of it.

He hung up the phone and gathered his keys.

Peter sat down on his couch, the burn victim file spread over his coffee table. There was a television mounted on the opposite wall that he never used, apart from the occasional porno. It stood out in stark contrast to the pale gray walls and dark wood flooring. The only other piece of furniture was an upright black leather chair, sleek, simple, rigid and wholly uncomfortable. The couch was no better, but the overall effect was modern and industrial. A single row of track lights hung overhead and reflected off of the surface of the glossy prints of the scene and body. He'd poured over them a hundred times and could see nothing more of use.

Toxicology was negative, but the blood sample had been severely hemolyzed, making all other blood work appear skewed. The description of the body was accurate according to the report from the scene and available pictures. No prints were available, as the flesh had been burned from the fingertips. DNA was submitted, but there was no match as yet. He had reviewed all the available slides and the appearance of each sampled organ was consistent with Beth's report. There was nothing definitive there.

The odd cytogenetics report, the early release of the body and the units from the blood bank were very suspicious, but they weren't hard proof. Even so, if Peter shared these findings with the Master, he wouldn't hesitate to have Dr. Ramsey killed.

But if he killed her, Peter couldn't use her to lead him to Luciano.

Luciano had evaded the Master for years, and Peter feared he may not find another link. But the Master would expect results regardless. He had failed the Master in not being certain Luciano was killed in the fire, and he was not about to fail him twice. He needed something definitive, something he could confront Beth with and then, in her fear, she would lead him right to Luciano.

And, he had to admit, he didn't want Dr. Ramsey dead. He would much rather have her at his side, or rather, at his feet. If he had irrefutable evidence and she faced death because of it, perhaps he could convince her that joining him in working for the Master was a better option.

The only other item in the file was a sheet of dental films. Since there was nothing to compare them with, who they belonged to was anyone's guess. Perhaps Beth had taken a set of films from another of her cases or pulled some from an old file. But if it was another of her cases from the previous few days, how could she know there would be no previous records to raise suspicion?

Unless... Beth was smart. She would have confabulated the entire internal exam, gathered tissue from past cases with matching injuries where it counted, like the burned skin and smoke-filled lung tissue. She would have known she needed dental films that she could be sure would not match any prior cases or John Does. What if, to be certain, Beth had submitted her own? If the dental films were hers, it would put an end to all questions. He would have firm evidence for the Master and could confront Beth to set her on the run to Luciano.

Peter picked up the phone and called Alex Freeman, one of the Master's most loyal, who helped him with many marginal computer access issues.

"Alex, Peter. I need you to look into something for me."

CHAPTER 47

PETER

ALEX HAD COME THROUGH swimmingly. He had hacked the Blue Cross of Kansas mainframe and pulled down claims for Beth for the last five years, including bills for routine dental exams and X-rays. These showed the provider to be a dentist by the name of Henry McGown, DDS. Google gave his address and phone number as well as a photograph of the good dentist and his smiling office staff. "Making every smile your best" was beneath the practice logo.

While the other evidence Peter had gathered so far was suspicious, finding Beth's dental records in Luc's file would prove her involvement. Alex said the office computer system was antiquated and backed up on-site only, so he couldn't hack in from outside. He had done good work before, but Peter was certain Alex would be more motivated to get the job done if Peter himself were at his side. He had been absent for Luciano's burning and it had not gone well. He would take this opportunity to prove his worthiness for the Master and get the job done.

The same logo was printed on the front door of the office building. It was in an old strip mall, no cameras, minimal lighting, but Peter and Alex parked around back. Alex was tall and gangly, dressed in all black, which matched his hair and scruffy beard. Looking through his half-inch-thick glasses, it took Alex all of thirty seconds to navigate the door lock, and they were inside. He pulled out a handheld device, popped the cover off the alarm touchpad, plugged it in and cut power to the system. Peter held up his watch and started his timer.

"With this old model, that should give us twelve minutes for the system to fully reboot. We're on the clock," Alex said.

Apart from the hallway light, the office was dark, and thanks to an access door that blocked the lobby from the exam rooms, even that wouldn't be visible from the front of the building.

Dr. McGown's office was the closest to the back door. There was a simple oak desk facing a wall of shelving filled with books and a few scattered knickknacks. A computer monitor occupied the right half of the desk, CPU on the floor.

Alex immediately sat down in the black leather desk chair. He extended a small pullout shelf from beneath the surface of the desk and pushed the keyboard space bar. The monitor began to glow, showing a photo of the middle-aged dentist and his family all smiling at the camera with perfect teeth.

Peter glanced at his watch; twenty seconds had passed. While computer literate, Peter was no hacker. Alex was the best there was and perfect for a job like this. Peter expected Alex to pull out his fancy equipment and held up his wrist to monitor the time for him.

But, before bothering with attempting to hack in, Alex lifted the keyboard and flipped it over. Stuck to the back was a yellow sticky note with the letters "HENRY41556."

"The older they are, the easier they make it," Alex said. He typed in the password under the already-populated username field, and he was in. The same username and password opened the office's Cerner program where he searched for and easily found Beth's office record. Saved in the images file was her most recent set of dental X-rays.

"Three minutes."

"How would you like 'em?" Alex said. "Email?"

"No, flash drive," Peter said, holding out a 64GB flash drive still in the plastic. "I don't want to take a chance of leaving a trail if they discover the records have been accessed."

Peter watched the clock as the computer saved to the drive and Alex shut down the system. They left, flash drive with images in hand, and were finished with the entire operation in eight minutes.

Not waiting to return home, Peter pulled out his laptop and opened the file. He studied the screen, comparing it with the glossy photo in his hand.

"Game, set, match."

CHAPTER 48

PETER

PETER ARRIVED AT THE Master's current "home," a three-story, ten-thousand-square-foot mansion in Wyandotte County. It stood in the center of at least three hundred acres, fenced, gated and guarded.

He strode to the door with long, confident strides. He had Beth. He was certain she had helped Luciano, certain the Master would be pleased with his efforts, and hopeful that this would be the last piece he needed, his last proving ground, before the Master turned him. He also hoped that the Master would allow him to keep Beth for his own pleasure afterward. He would certainly have to keep her "contained" for a time, but he thought he could eventually persuade her that a life with him was far better than human death. But even if she didn't come around, he thought he would enjoy her resistance.

Peter rapped the heavy brass-handled knocker, gaudy with the oversized lion's head in its center, and waited.

Edmond, the Master's long-term human house servant, older than dirt but still far younger than the Master, finally opened the door. "Come in, Doctor James. He is waiting."

The Master sat in his study, walls lined with books, most shelved neatly in rows but some placed horizontally atop in the gaps where the shelves were already full. He sat behind a large rectangular walnut desk. The wood grain shone even in the dim desk lamp light. His white linen shirt was spotless and perfectly pressed. The Master's hands were tented in front of his chest, and he looked at Peter over the edges of his small wire-rimmed glasses. He didn't need them; his vision was perfect. But he seemed to like the effect.

"Well, what information do you have to share?" the Master asked.

Peter paused for a moment, collecting his thoughts. "I am certain Doctor Ramsey helped Luciano recover. I intercepted a call from the KU blood bank. One of the techs there was calling to see if Beth, er, Doctor Ramsey would like them to continue saving expired units for her ongoing experiment. I also found a very abnormal karyotype—"

"Karyotype? Speak English, Peter. I am not a physician. It is why I have you."

"A test that looks at a person's chromosomes, their DNA, to see what abnormalities exist. It was markedly abnormal. She submitted it as an abnormal fetus, but I found no records of recent fetal demise cases. I believe she was investigating Luciano, trying to see what might explain his condition."

With this the Master tensed noticeably, although he didn't budge from his seat. He folded his hands on the desk and met Peter's gaze, making Peter shift from one foot to the other, grasping his hands in front of him.

"Doctor Ramsey also submitted her own dental X-rays as those of Luciano to avoid identification. I believe if we confront her with the evidence, she will lead us to him."

The Master shifted, picking up a pen from the desk and lowering his gaze. He dismissed Peter with, "Take as many of my men as you need to gather her and bring her to me. It's time I met Doctor Ramsey."

"Yes, Master," Peter said as he turned on his heel and headed for the door. Though the Master had raised him and put him through school, the unease he felt in his presence after so many years was still fresh. He would see to his wishes adding his own orders that Beth was to be unharmed. The Master could be very... persuasive... and if he could make Beth see the benefits of assisting him, Peter may also be able to make her see the advantages of catering to his second-in-command.

CHAPTER 49

BETH

IT WAS NEARLY 10:30 p.m. and Beth was right in the middle of a case, this one a sixty-two-year-old woman found alone at home on her bathroom floor. She was naked with a large red, blood-filled knot, called a hematoma, over her right temple. From what Beth could gather, the woman had no significant history of illness, and her death was unexpected. She had been found by family who went looking for her when she wouldn't answer her phone. It appeared she had been dead at least two days. Her rigor had dissipated and livor mortis, the blood pooling in the most dependent parts of the body, was prominent on her left side.

Beth had made note of these findings, but there were no other visible injuries. She had even checked the neck for puncture wounds, just in case. She began by making the usual Roux-en-Y incision on the chest and abdomen to begin the internal exam. The woman was overweight but not obese. The odor of the fat was still strong, though. Fat had its own distinctive smell; greasy, mousy, not terribly pleasant but certainly nothing near decomposition.

Beth began by releasing the fat from the sternum and breast plate toward the neck and then outward to uncover the ribs. Using the Stryker saw, she made a vertical cut through each row of ribs from top to bottom, raised the sternum along with the attached pieces of ribs, then cleared away the fat and adherent tissue to reveal the lungs and heart beneath.

The woman's heart appeared large; a weight when it was dissected free would tell the tale. The lungs were a bit firm to the touch, perhaps a bit heavy with fluid. This, combined with the enlarged heart, could suggest congestive heart failure, a chronic illness where the heart muscle weakened and didn't adequately pump blood to the rest of the body. The blood would back up into the lungs and make them heavy with fluid. All that fluid would make it difficult to breathe. The continued stress on the heart could lead to all sorts of issues, one being a heart attack.

Beth cut across the aorta, the largest artery in the body, and began to dissect the heart free when she heard footsteps. She had said goodbye to Dr. Fluck on the evening shift at 10 p.m. and knew she was alone in the morgue.

"Lawrence, did you forget something?"

Peter strolled into the autopsy suite, his hands stuffed deeply into his pockets. He had a half-grin on his face that raised goosebumps on Beth's arms and reminded her they were very much alone.

She tried to sound nonchalant. "This is some serious overtime for you, isn't it?"

"Oh, this isn't on the books. I just thought you and I could have a little chat."

"What about?" Beth said, trying to sound unconcerned and returning her hands to the body as though she planned to continue the case while she talked. She watched him closely out of the corner of her eye all the while, her heart racing. She could hear each beat in her ears and her face felt flushed. She hoped if she kept her head down he wouldn't notice, but gripped the scalpel a bit more tightly.

"Just some inconsistencies, I suppose," he said.

"Oh? What inconsistencies?"

"Well, first there's the matter of the still missing burn victim..."

"I told you that was just an error. I never intended to release the body early and have no idea what the funeral home may have done with it following its release."

"... and then there are the unusual cytogenetics results you obtained on a 'fetus?' Beth, you haven't had a case on a fetus in over six months." He continued his slow pace, back and forth, inching closer with each pass.

"What are you doing going through my mail?"

"It wasn't sealed—"

"The hell it wasn't! I could see the marks on the envelope from when you opened it. What are you looking for? What are you trying to insinuate?"

"Oh, I think you know."

Beth did know, but she wasn't about to admit it and make it easy for him. In her anger and fear she'd stopped pretending to work on the cadaver and met his eyes, cold and dark, accusatory and completely infuriating despite her fear.

"You're quite beautiful when you're angry, you know," he said with a slight tilt at the corner of his mouth.

The goosebumps returned along with a wave of nausea. She still held the scalpel and prayed if he tried to grab her she could inflict enough damage to get around him and make it to the door.

"And then there was a very interesting call from your friend, Sherman, at the blood bank. He left a very pleasant voicemail to tell you that he had more expired red cell units for you if you needed them for your *experiment*. Just what experiment might that be, Beth?"

Beth hoped the expression on her face didn't give too much away. She felt like a rabbit in a corner with a predator pacing back and forth in front of the only escape route, salivating and waiting to pounce.

"Hey, Doc! I've got a fresh one for you!" Aaron the EMT shouted as he opened the double doors to the suite and began to push in a gurney with a covered body. Beth had never been so pleased to see him. "Sorry, Doc, didn't know you had comp'ny," Aaron said and walked to her side. "There aren't many visitors down here at night."

"Not a problem at all, Aaron. Doctor James was just leaving so I could get back to work." Beth could tell Peter was anything but pleased by this interruption.

"Aaron, was it?"

"Yes, Doctor James," sticking out his hand, "pleased to meet 'cha."

"The pleasure is all mine," Peter said as he briefly shook Aaron's hand. "I hope to see you around again soon." And with a far-too-toothy grin, he turned and placed his hands back in his pockets, whistling on his way out.

"You okay, Doc? That guy gives me the willies. And what is he doing here so late? He's day shift, isn't he?"

Beth moved her shaking hands below the edge of the table so Aaron wouldn't notice. The last thing she wanted was for Peter to decide Aaron knew something and come after him. Assuming he could be listening, Beth would be sure to keep her comments neutral.

"He is very... intense. And yes, he is day shift. He realized he forgot to sign a release that they would need for one of the mortuaries tomorrow. He was in the area and thought he would stop by to sign it and say... hello." Beth attempted a smile but doubted it looked more believable to Aaron than it felt on her lips.

"I'm not feeling very well. I thought it would pass, and I hate to leave a case unfinished, but I'm afraid I may have to go home sick. You might keep your distance in case it's catching." She turned her back to him for a moment to close her eyes and breathe, then placed the scalpel back on the mayo stand.

She wanted nothing more than to tell Aaron everything and to ask him to stay with her until dawn. At least then only humans could come after her, and the thought of that was bad enough. But Aaron needed to leave before he got entangled in this mess. Tonight, Peter had removed all doubt that he knew she had helped Luc and that she was investigating vampire physiology. He would use her to get to Luc. And because of her research, the Master would almost certainly kill her once they had him.

"Sorry, Doc. I wish you felt better. You do look a little pale. Anything I can help you with before I head out?"

"No, I can manage. I don't think you'll catch my bug, but you might. I hope to see you again soon, Aaron." And more than ever before, she meant it.

CHAPTER 50

PETER

PETER GLANCED AT HIS watch; 11:15 p.m. He had arranged for the Master's henchmen to pick Beth up as soon as she left the hospital. He knew he'd rattled her by confronting her, and while he was prepared to wait until the end of her shift, he didn't think it would take that long. He thought she might contact Luciano in her fear and ask him to come protect her, though it was more likely she would try to escape on her own to protect him. But from the stories of Luciano the Master had told him, he would surely come to intervene if they captured Beth.

Two bleeding hearts, ready to place themselves in harm's way for the other.

He couldn't risk being identified in the kidnapping and jeopardizing his job, so he stayed far enough back to be out of sight of cameras and watched as the Master's men within his view monitored the exits and Beth's Pathfinder. He fiddled with his cell phone, jostling it in his pocket as he waited for the call that Beth was in hand.

CHAPTER 51

BETH

NOT WANTING TO WAKE anyone so early, Beth left a message for her partner about her "illness" and unfinished case. She changed out of her scrubs and into her street clothes and tennis shoes. She found a KC Royals hat in the locker room and shoved all her hair into it, pulling it down over her eyes. It wasn't much of a disguise. She had no way of contacting Luc, but she wouldn't have called him anyway. It would draw him right into the Master's hands and she couldn't live with that. If they took her, she was fairly certain he would try to come for her, but at least it would allow him time to plan.

If she could somehow get free of them and make her way toward the train yard, perhaps she could fine Luc before sunrise. Otherwise, she would have to find somewhere to spend the daylight hours hiding. What were her options?

She could attempt to make it to her Pathfinder unseen, leave on foot or perhaps call a taxi or Uber. That could work. Peter or anyone with him wouldn't think a hired vehicle suspicious.

The closest exit to her car was at the front of the hospital. Surely Peter would be watching that one. Where would they least expect her? She thought they would likely anticipate her exiting through one of the unmonitored side entrances, but what about the emergency room? At this hour there was a fairly consistent flow of patients in and out, mostly drunk with lacerations from fighting or falling. In her street clothes, she might blend in.

She opened the Uber app and requested a ride.

The ten-minute wait felt like hours, but it was finally time; her ride was approaching. Beth left her backpack under her desk, placing only the essentials in her pockets. She always brought it with her to and from work, and they might be looking for it.

She walked to the outer locked door and paused. What if they were waiting for her in the hallway? There were no cameras just outside the morgue, but the exits were monitored. Surely they wouldn't want to be seen kidnapping her from the building.

She pushed open the doors, ready to run, and found the hallway empty. After her years at the university, she knew the winding corridors of the basement level well and covered them in record time as she headed to the emergency room underground. Constantly glancing around corners and over her shoulder as she went, she finally came to the stairwell nearest the emergency room entrance and opened the door. She stood still in the doorway and then, hearing nothing, covered the two flights of stairs, taking two at a time.

She paused at the door, peering through the narrow rectangle of glass in it, and could see the entrance. No one looked suspicious to her, but then again, she wasn't sure what she should be looking for.

Her phone beeped. Her ride had arrived.

Taking a deep breath, she pushed through the first door and walked quickly toward the motion-activated doors. As they opened, she could see the white Toyota Camry that was her Uber just beyond the circle drive that accessed the ambulance bay.

Head down, she started straight for it. Only a few steps forward, two men that looked like professional football linemen blocked her path.

"Doctor Ramsey?" one said.

"No, you must have mistaken me for someone else," Beth said, pulling her cap further down over her eyes as she tried to make a wide circle around them.

Undeterred, the man said, "We have orders to take you to meet with our employer. He would very much like to speak with you."

"I'm sorry, I already have plans for the day. Please tell your boss to call me and we can arrange a meeting at a more convenient time."

As the men stepped forward, trying to get her between them, Beth slowly retreated backward, matching them step for step.

"Our employer is a very busy man. He insists on meeting with you right away," Henchman Number Two said with an unnerving smile. He approached more quickly, extending an arm toward her.

Beth considered screaming for help, but if these men and their "Master" were as dangerous as Luc said they were, it would only mean placing others in harm's way.

They continued to close the gap, and she could tell there was no way she would make it around them to the Uber. As soon as they reached for her, she turned and ran. A hand grabbed at her arm, snagged on her sleeve and fell away.

It took only a few steps to be at top speed. Beth ran faster than she had ever run before. With each step she pushed with the balls of her feet, willing them to propel her forward even faster. Her arms pistoned, pulling her body forward. Her strides were long and smooth, and she could hear the men quickly falling away. Beth thanked God for her tennis shoes, she thanked God for her treadmill, she thanked God for every breath of air that filled her lungs and the steady beating of her heart. She thanked Him for every mile, every race, every step as they carried her away.

She didn't dare look back. She turned at every street corner, hoping it would make her more difficult to follow, winding her way north and west. If there was an alley, she took it, and when she could she ran across yards to cross a block more quickly. She avoided the street lights wherever possible and headed for the train yard. It would be a long run, some six miles or so, but with the fear and adrenaline coursing through her body, she knew she would make it in record time.

She turned her focus to Luc. Would he hear her if she called out to him? Would he pick up on her thoughts if she cried out with her mind? It was worth a try. Inside her head she screamed, *Luc, I'm in trouble, please hear me, help me!* It became her chant as she ran. She went for what seemed like an hour, every moment listening, turning away from any headlights or voices, fearful that they were waiting around the next corner to grab her.

As she cut through a back alley, she saw a dim pool of light shining down from a small porch, giving a faint glow to the tiny patio below. She heard a bottle fall to the ground and stumbled and nearly fell. She was moving so fast there was no time to change course before she passed the patio, adrenaline speeding her forward. Her heart hammered in her chest, thinking it must be the Master's men catching up to her.

Just as she was sure she would be caught, her energy nearly spent from the long run, a large black cat sprang from the alley trash can across from the patio, shaking loose another bottle that clanked to the ground below.

Tears of relief and fear stung her eyes as she pushed on.

She could hear the clicking of metal train wheels somewhere ahead and knew she had to be getting close to the yard. She turned the next corner, one side of the road lined with heavy trees, and ran close to them, hiding in their large shadows cast from the moonlight overhead.

Mid-step, arms encircled her, jerking her off her feet. A hand covered her mouth, forcing her to swallow her scream. She kicked and flailed but the arms held her like a vice, strong and unyielding.

Hope drained from her as the light faded and her captor dragged her back into the trees.

CHAPTER 52

BETH

BETH HEARD SOFTLY IN her ear, "Beth, it's me, Luc. I've got you. You're okay."

Beth's limbs went numb and she collapsed into his arms, stifling sobs. He quickly pulled her close, holding her up as her legs failed. She buried her face in his shirt and felt the hard muscles of his chest beneath her cheek.

"I could hear someone running and then I thought I heard you call my name. What happened?" he asked.

"Peter cornered me at the morgue and told me he knew I helped you. One of the EMTs came in and Peter left. But when I left the hospital, there were men there waiting to try and kidnap me. I outran them and headed for you," she said, breath coming in irregular bursts as she pushed back the sobs and tried to recover from the run.

"Did you know them?"

"No, but they said their employer wanted a word with me. They clearly were not taking no for an answer."

"Thank God you were able to get away! They had to be the Master's men. He must know that you're in contact with me, that you have helped me. You can't go back home, Beth. It's not safe."

"I'll have to get a hotel, but I have nothing with me. I have my ID and credit card but no cash, and I'm guessing using my card would be a bad idea. Same with my phone. With resources like the Master's, wouldn't those be easy to track?" With this she pulled the phone from her pocket and powered it down, taking no chances.

"Don't worry about that now. The important thing is you're safe."

"Safe? Safe! How can you even say that?"

"Come. Follow me," he said and took her hand.

Luc led Beth through the trees to the train yard and walked toward a single car at the edge of the yard. It had been removed from the tracks and sat by itself, tall grass growing up around its base. It had clearly been there a long while. There was an old gang tag on the outside that looked like a balloon art dog.

Luc slid the long door open just enough for them to enter. Night had fallen and the inside was pitch black, but Luc moved easily in the darkness, closing the door and switching on a dim battery-powered light. It was scarcely enough for Beth to see the ends of the boxcar inside, but it likely wouldn't show through any cracks to the outside. Luc had simple folding chairs and a low wooden table. A mattress in the corner with a single blanket was the only other furniture. The space was warm and smelled musty and damp.

Sweat continued to trail down her spine in small rivulets, causing her to shiver.

"It's not much, but it is safe. There's an RV park about three miles west where I've been going to clean up in the evening. This time of year, with the kids back in school, it's quiet. It won't work long-term but it will for tonight," Luc said. "Beth, you must come away with me. It's the only way I can possibly keep you safe. If the Master can't use you to get to me, he will kill you for helping me. The research you have done is just one more reason, as if he needed one."

"But my job, my work, this is all I have. Luc, the virus I found in your blood, that must induce this change in humans. I am sure the Vampyre were using it for gene therapy all those years ago. They must have thought they could change human DNA to include their own advances, their unique abilities. But the virus they used as a vector went horribly wrong. With enough research, I may eventually be able to fix this and actually use it to help vampires and humans. Or maybe it will give us something that we can use against the Master."

"If we leave, if we are careful and leave no trail for them to find us, you can start over somewhere else."

"Start over? Do you have any idea what you're asking? My research on this virus aside, I have worked for so many years to reach this point in my field. It's not so easy to just 'start over.' Unlike you, I don't have lifetimes to rebuild. I have local connections that could be useful in figuring this all out. I am so close to a discovery that could change lives. Science could take a huge leap forward. How can you possibly ask me to leave it all behind now? I just need to study the virus and then share my findings. If I share this with the medical community, the Master would have to back off, wouldn't he? It would be too dangerous for him to be identified. There has to be something we can do to hold him off."

Luc shook his head. "Beth, that's never going to happen. There is absolutely no way the Master will allow you to live long enough to complete your work, let alone share your findings. He already tried to kidnap you. When he realizes his men have failed, he will order your death with as much remorse as ordering fries at McDonald's. You must hide, leave, start a new life away from here and the Master."

"What life do I have away from here? How can you expect me to turn my back? What could be more important? This is bigger than me, bigger than my life. I am so close—"

"Close to dying. I don't care about the science, Beth. I only care about you," Luc shouted.

That stopped Beth cold. She could only look at him with wide eyes.

His gaze softened, moving from her lips and back to her eyes.

"I can live with being what I am and with never knowing why. But the world would be a much darker place without you in it."

Exhaustion from the stress of the chase and the physical exertion itself were taking their toll on her. She didn't have the will to argue and certainly didn't have more strength. She must look a wreck.

Luc moved to her and placed his hands on her shoulders. "Why don't you rest a bit? I'm sure you set a new speed record evading the Master's men. Take a nap. We'll talk more and come up with a plan when you wake." He led her to the mattress, fluffed the pillow and patted. "I'll be a perfect gentleman, I promise."

Beth knew Luc was right. She stretched out on the mattress and almost immediately felt the heaviness creeping over her limbs and eyelids. She was also certain he would be a gentleman, but not nearly so certain that she wanted him to be.

Chapter 53

Beth

Beth awakened disconcerted. Her sleep-hazy brain slowly began to clear and she remembered where she was.

"Good nap?" Luciano asked.

"Yes, thank you. I needed it. How long was I out?"

"Only about an hour. It's close to three a.m."

"Still plenty of time to come up with a plan before dawn, then."

"Yes, but first things first. You need food and water."

"I can wait. I'm not going to die from starvation or dehydration in just one night."

"You had quite a scare and you have to be dry after that run... and I need a bit of time myself," Luc said, dropping his eyes.

Beth understood immediately. He needed to feed. She wondered if it was difficult for him to be near her when he was hungry.

"You're safe here and I will be back in an hour or so. I didn't want you to wake up and find me missing." He rose and walked toward her with his hand out. "Here. It's my prepaid cell phone. I have the number. If anything changes, if I get suspicious that we may have been found, I will find a phone and call you on it. Keep it with you until I get back."

Beth held the phone in both hands, like a child clutching a favorite stuffed animal for comfort.

"What if you don't come back?" Beth said the words softly, not wanting to think about it happening but knowing she was in over her head with nowhere to go.

Luc knelt in front of her. He placed his hands on her shoulders and slowly ran them down her arms to cover her hands with his, bringing color to Beth's cheeks.

"We'll figure this out. But for right now you need to trust me and stay here." With that he leaned forward, kissed her forehead and stood up. He was outside and looking at her through the open door too fast for her to register the movement. "One hour," he said.

"One hour," she replied. And he was gone.

Beth touched her fingertips to her forehead where his lips had been. She remembered his words. *I only care about you.* It was all so confusing. He said human relationships with vampires didn't work, yet his behavior suggested he was thinking about just that. He had asked her to run away with him. Could it be for more than just keeping her safe? Would he really keep her with him just to protect her if he had no feelings for her?

Maybe she was just seeing what she wanted to see.

She stood, needing to move, even if it was just to pace back and forth in the boxcar. Her legs felt a bit wobbly from her long run, and she bent to stretch them. With all that had happened in the last few hours, Beth wasn't sure about much of anything other than the Master wanted both of them dead. What leverage could they gather against him? If she could cure the vampires that wished to be cured of their bloodthirst and sun sensitivity, would they join with them against the Master? If she could remove only the undesirable traits and leave the rest—strength, agility, regeneration and heightened senses—wouldn't that make the untreated vampires fearful of the treated vampires, knowing the treated could hunt them during daylight hours when they were weakened and confined from the sun's rays? And if there was a cure, the world could know vampires existed. Surely humans would band together with the vampires that no longer depended on human blood against those that did. But did she really want to put herself in the middle of a vampire war?

Who was she kidding, she was already in the middle of it.

Beth heard a rustling at the back of the train car and froze, heart racing, eyes wide. Had the Master tracked her here? Without Luc she didn't stand a chance. Another escape by running was out of the question until she had had more time to rest. And she had Luc's phone, so there was no way to contact him.

As she stood silent, waiting, the sound came again in the same place. And this time she also heard the wind whistling. The car was nestled against the tree line and the rustling must be a branch rubbing against it as the wind blew.

Beth wondered how much fright it would take to deplete her adrenaline stores entirely and smoothed her hair with shaky hands.

CHAPTER 54

BETH

IT HAD BEEN FIFTY-SEVEN minutes since Luc left and two minutes since she'd last checked the time when she heard the boxcar door slide open. Relief washed over her when Luc stepped in. He held a six pack of water bottles, a sandwich and a package of plain M&M's.

Beth couldn't help but smile. "You remembered."

A broad smile lit his face as he handed her the food and water, his hand brushing hers and lingering for a moment. It was warm, and combined with the color in his cheeks, she knew he had fed. She wanted to ask him about it, to understand what it was like for him, to know how he had chosen his "meal" for the evening. How was that something he'd become used to, especially when he clearly still valued human life? She decided, though, that these were deeply personal questions and there was limited time. It was probably best to focus on the now and plan for what came next.

She opened the water and downed nearly half a bottle. The cool liquid felt heavenly on her dry throat. Then she sat on the bed as she began eating her sandwich.

Luc asked, "Do you have anywhere you can go, Beth? Somewhere you haven't been for a long while that others wouldn't think of? Friends out of state, maybe? Someone with an apartment or house that they aren't using right now where you could stay temporarily without anyone knowing? The Master found my house and I'm afraid he may have discovered my other properties as well. We can't risk them."

Beth considered this for a moment. "My colleague that died, Henry Adams, had a cabin on Truman Lake. He took several of us up there for a weekend a couple of years ago. I don't remember the address, but I drove my vehicle there so I know where it is. I can't imagine his family would have sold it since they spent nearly every weekend there in the summer. And the weather is still a little cool this time of year so there shouldn't be many people around."

"That could work. Are you okay with breaking and entering?"

"I learned how to use a credit card to jimmy a lock in college since I had a classmate who kept locking her keys in her apartment. As long as there's no deadbolt, I can do it. If there is, then I'll have to break a window, but I'll manage."

"Okay, a cabin at the lake it is then. I have some cash. Just before sunrise I will call an Uber or taxi for you. Once you're out of the city, make a single stop at the nearest convenience store and buy a prepaid cell phone. I'll give you my number so you can text your new number to me."

"Wait, you're not coming with me?" Beth asked, confused.

"It's nearly dawn. You can leave but I can't. And I want you away from here as quickly as possible on the off chance the Master's men can track you, not to mention we will draw less attention if we travel separately. After I finish tying up a few loose ends here, I'll join you at the lake early Sunday morning. I'll call you for the address when I reach town. When I get there, we can talk about the different properties I have in other states and decide which direction we head next."

"Okay, but we need a backup plan in case something goes wrong." Beth thought for a moment and then nodded. "There's a little mom-and-pop hotel there called the Clinton Motorlodge. Some of Henry's relatives own it. If either of us is unable to call or contact the other, we should go there and rent a room. You register under the name Brian Hoffman and I'll register under Janice Hoffman. That way we'll each know who to ask for to meet back up."

Luc nodded his agreement.

"I need to make a stop as well," Beth said, avoiding his gaze. "I left cash, an extra credit card and other valuables in a bank in Lawrence just in case something like this happened. I need to go there and gather it all before I can make the trip to the cabin. Assuming the Master will be tracking me, I'll take out whatever cash I can get with my credit card and go. Maybe the charges coming from Lawrence will slow his search. And I'll take an Uber from there. It has to be harder to trace than a taxi."

Luc closed his eyes and exhaled loudly as he walked to the edge of the mattress. "Please just go to the cabin, Beth. I have what we need."

She rose to her feet in front of him. "It's more than that, Luc. My research is there, and I can't leave it behind not knowing if I will be able to return for it one day." Beth lowered her chin and looked at her feet, feeling vulnerable but needing Luc to understand. "And I put a picture of my dad there. If I can never go back home, it will be all I have of him."

CHAPTER 55

BETH

BETH KNEW HER VOICE was heavy with emotion but couldn't help it. The emotional toll of all that had happened had lowered her defenses. Tears threatened to fall, and she fought to hold them back. She didn't want to give in to her feelings now; she needed to hold it together to get through the mess ahead of her. She battled silently to keep her mind focused on what had to be done.

But Luc was quickly at her side and gathered her to him gently. Beth smelled his now-familiar scent. For the moment, thoughts of all else faded away. It was just Luc and the comfort of his arms around her. Perhaps he didn't mean it in the way she wanted him to, but for this moment, it didn't matter.

She nestled her forehead into his neck and felt his chest beneath her cheek. Her left hand melded against his chest. She imagined what it would be like to run her fingers along the lines of muscle that stood out so clearly beneath his shirt, but kept still, not wanting to give him a reason to pull away.

Moments passed and she waited for him to break the embrace, knowing it would become awkward if she stayed too long. Unwillingly, she lifted her head to meet his eyes to thank him for comforting her. When she did, she could see the flush of red in his cheeks from his recent feeding. The fleeting thoughts of what that meant, the price paid for her to enjoy such comfort with his touch, lasted only until his lips met hers.

The surprise of his kiss left along with any remnants of the sadness she had felt only a moment ago. His arms wrapped around her, gently but relentlessly pulling her closer, the muscles beneath his now-warm skin rock hard. A shudder tore through her as her breasts met the steel that was his chest. If it weren't for his arms, she would fall. Her limbs felt weak, unable to support her weight. Was this just her response to him, to something she had imagined a thousand times since she first saw him, standing in her kitchen weeks ago? Was it hypnosis? Did he have more control over her mind and emotions than he had let on?

Did she really care right now?

No. All that mattered in this moment was the fire she felt in her lips and the ripples of heat that spread through every inch of her body with each caress of his tongue against her own. It would be up to him to stop this now. She would give him whatever he wanted... her heart, her body... even her blood.

CHAPTER 56

BETH

BETH DIDN'T KNOW HOW long they stood there, locked together. It could have been an eternity; it could have been only seconds. Her mind slowly began to become aware again of the space around her. His arms loosened, and her head fell to his chest. Eyes closed, Beth leaned against him, trying to find the strength in her legs to stand on her own. The sweetness and warmth of his breath on her cheek was so alluring, tempting her back. It was almost painful to think of separating from him. His hands gently stroked her back and shoulders. His cheek and nose brushed her neck, sending another wave of heat through her. He lingered there, still for only a moment, his breath on her skin an arousing caress all its own.

The fingers of Beth's hand twirled in the wisps of his hair that she had, without a doubt, pulled over his shoulders in an attempt to draw him even closer. Her other hand explored the contours of his chest. She felt as much as heard him when he spoke.

"Beth, we should take this slowly. I don't want to hurt you."

Beth felt immediately angry and snapped her head up to look him in the eye and deliver her rebuttal. He'd started this. Was she so fragile, like some toothpick of a branch that would snap between his fingers?

The words froze on her lips when her eyes met his. The soft brown had changed to black. She could see the fangs pressing into his lower lip as he held his mouth shut tight over them. Only now did she hear the raggedness of his breathing. Was this what she aroused in him? Did she only stir his lust for her blood? Could he ever need her, as a woman, as she needed him?

"I'm sorry, I guess I... I misunderstood," Beth stammered as she slipped from his arms. Wasn't he the one that had reached out for her? Had it not been to kiss her but because he had wanted to feed on her? How could she have been so stupid, letting her emotions and active imagination get the best of her? It was the flush of embarrassment rather than passion that colored her cheeks now. What an idiot, imagining that he could want her.

Anger returned, realizing he could have fed on her. She would have let him! Beth became angrier still knowing that he had the will to stop. He was strong enough even to resist her blood. How pitiful that he controlled her so completely and she could scarcely tempt him as food! Beth was somehow offended. Ridiculous! A vampire doesn't want to eat her and instead of being thankful she was feeling what? Rejected? What a head case.

"No. No, Beth, it's not like that. You didn't misunderstand. Just give me a minute, okay?" He turned his head away from her and slowly stepped back.

Her knees threatened to betray her again, so she dropped back onto the mattress to avoid falling. She wanted to stand, to show she was unaffected, strong, but she couldn't. Sitting, even if it seemed to put her in less of a position of strength, would be a whole lot better than falling and allowing him to see the full effect he'd had on her. He was right; she didn't misunderstand... now, anyway. He had wanted to feed on her.

He seemed to regain his composure, and when he turned to face her, his eyes were softer, fangs now hidden. He seemed in control. Beth was sure her eyes and face burned with emotion which switched quickly between seething rage and shame for his rejection, her stupidity and the deep pain of aching, to accepting that there would be nothing more. He was a vampire, she wasn't. There would be nothing more than a tenuous friendship between them. Beth needed him to escape the Master, and he felt he owed her for helping him and placing herself at risk. *Deal with it.*

He settled next to her on the mattress, scooting closer to her. She stared forward, wanting to stand and leave, to not hear the lame excuses and apology that would make her feel even more insignificant. But her body, the traitor it was, responded to his closeness with another round of paralysis, trapping her next to him. Averting her eyes was her only means of defiance.

"Beth, you didn't misunderstand. I wanted to kiss you."

"To get me closer. To make it easier to feed on me," Beth quickly fired back.

"No. I didn't want to feed on you. You just don't get it!"

"Oh, I get it. I'm part of the food chain."

"Beth, that's just it. With vampires, everything is about the blood. As much as I care about you, when I'm close to you, it's still dangerous. I don't want to hurt you while I'm trying to..."

He paused, and she felt her heart skip. *As much as he cares about me?* Beth repeated the words in her mind, not making sense of them. "While you're trying to what?"

His face wrenched. "While I'm trying to... to love you."

Beth sat, dumfounded, trying to process those last words.

"I love you, Beth. But being a vampire makes it difficult. I want to be close to you, but feeling aroused for a vampire is complicated. I want you with every part of me. I want you physically, but I also crave your blood. Forgive me, Beth, but I feel like I have to explain. There is nothing in a vampire's existence that isn't in some way tied to blood. When vampires... are physically intimate, they also drink each other's blood. It's a nearly irresistible urge. That combined with my strength makes it very dangerous for me to be close to you. If I lose control for even a moment, I could hurt you. I could *kill* you. And I won't risk killing you just to indulge my longing for you."

Beth didn't know what to say. She had long forgotten about looking away from him and stared directly into his eyes. She could see he meant it all. He loved her. He had ended the kiss to protect her. He didn't want to eat her. Well, he did, but it wasn't his intention.

With that thought, and all of the stress she was under, she began to giggle. The ridiculousness of the situation sank in.

Luc looked at her, horrified.

Laughing so hard tears began to fall, she choked out, "I'm sorry, it just all seems so unbelievably ridiculous. I finally fall in love and it's with a vampire. And you love me back, but the kicker is we can't have an intimate relationship because you're afraid... you'll eat me!" With this last sentence she snorted, which caused another round of inappropriate but completely uncontrollable laughter.

Slowly the pained look left his face, and he began to laugh too. He shook his head at the impossibility of the situation, and Beth started to slowly regain her composure. After a few deep breaths, she settled. At least he wasn't just saving her for breakfast. A half-grin came to her lips with the thought, but the serious expression on his face stopped its progression.

"I never imagined I could fall in love. I thought that part of my humanity died when I was changed. Falling in love with a *human* was never even a consideration." He paused, thinking. "You said you loved me."

"I do love you," Beth said quietly, holding his gaze. "I have for a while now, but I didn't think a human, especially one like me, could even get your attention."

With this, he took her face in his hands and fixed his eyes on hers. "I never dreamed someone so beautiful could see me as anything more than a monster. I had stopped trying to be anything more. I don't want to put you in danger, and I know loving you *will* put you in danger. Forgive my selfishness, but since I've fallen in love with you, I know immortality would not be tolerable without you."

Beth leaned forward, pulling him to her again, pressing her lips to his. She knew she was tempting fate, but to kiss him again, maybe getting eaten was worth it.

CHAPTER 57

BETH

BETH SAT IN THE back of the Uber driver's Jeep Renegade. It was a few minutes before dawn and the driver, Mack, was far too cheerful for the time.

"So, what has you up and on the road at such an early hour?" Mack said.

"It's been an exhausting twenty-four hours. I've barely slept, and if you don't mind, I might nod off for a bit."

Mack looked a little disappointed, seeming perpetually cheerful and talkative by nature but also, thankfully, polite. "Not a problem. I hope today is much better for you. Rest up."

Beth wouldn't sleep, she couldn't with all the chatter in her head right now, but she pretended to rest anyway. Small talk was just a little more than she could muster right now. She hadn't wanted to leave Luc, but she knew it would be less noticeable for them to travel separately. Plus she didn't know the address of the lake property to give to him anyway, and it was nearly daylight so he couldn't have survived the cab ride.

They had both agreed that getting out of town before there was time for anyone to notice her missing and begin searching for her was best. If the Master's men returned, her being out of town would make the trail more difficult to follow. And if Luc had to suddenly run, he could do it more quickly without her. He, too, had business to take care of before leaving.

Now that she knew his feelings for her, her perspective had shifted. The feelings of loving and being loved in returned were new and overwhelming. While she wanted very much to continue studying Luc's condition, she also wanted to survive with him, to enjoy what they had together and see where it led. If she could figure out the science behind what had happened to him, perhaps she could fix it and allow him to be human again. As a human, nothing would stand between them and their relationship. They would figure out how to evade the Master together.

Her thoughts turned to their first kiss, and her cheeks flushed. Yes, a lifetime of those would be worth a life of running.

By the time Beth and Mack reached Lawrence, Beth felt more at ease. While the thought had occurred to her that Mack could be one of the Master's henchmen, he never veered from his course and attempted to wake her with a friendly, "We're here, sleepyhead!" upon their arrival in Lawrence. It was just before 7:30 a.m. by the dashboard clock, and Beth asked if Mack would drop her at the twenty-four-hour Walmart, which he happily agreed to do. Beth thanked him, paid him with a generous tip, and wished him well.

The sunrise had been clear and cloudless. The yellow light poked over the horizon, and Beth could feel the early warmth of it against her skin. She walked to the back of the store and looked over the prepaid cell phones. She found an LG for just less than seventy-five dollars and decided it would do.

She began to walk around the store looking for an employee and found one stocking shelves in the hardware aisle. He didn't look much over eighteen, thin and gangly with a few days' scruff on his chin that wouldn't make a beard for several years to come. He pulled his headphones from his ears when he saw her approaching.

"How can I help you?"

"I would like to purchase one of the prepaid cell phones," Beth said. The lanyard hanging from his neck said his name was Matt.

"Okay, I think I can help with that."

She followed Matt back to electronics and pointed to the LG she wanted.

"Okay, looks like that's on sale for forty-nine dollars if you buy a fifty-dollar prepaid plan. That work?"

"Perfect." Beth waited as Matt took her information and activated the phone while ringing up the purchase.

"That will be one hundred eight dollars and twenty-four cents." Beth handed him one hundred twenty dollars in cash from the money Luc had given her. She took the cell phone and paperwork and headed out of the store, texting her new number to Luc along the way. One task accomplished, she checked the phone for the time: 7:45 a.m. The bank wouldn't open until 9 a.m., so she needed to kill a little time before heading there. After the long ride, she wanted to stretch her legs.

The light was still dim as Beth left Walmart, and a cool breeze prickled the hairs at the base of her neck. Beth thought it was unlikely she was followed after her Uber ride—surely they would have tried to grab her by now. But she kept her cap pulled down, shielding her face. As she walked, her eyes scanned the streets for anyone that looked out of place. Only a few cars traveled the road beside her so early on a Saturday morning, but she watched each one closely, ready to run if they slowed or stopped near her.

She had eaten several hours before and was a little hungry. The temperature had dropped overnight and she was beginning to shiver. She was going to need to find a place inside to wait. There was a McDonald's not more than a block ahead of her. A hot chocolate and hashbrowns sounded good.

She sat in a corner table in McDonald's back near the restrooms where she could see both entrances. By 8:40 a.m. Beth had finished her food and was sitting alone. A staff member had already asked her if she would like anything else. The bank was a short walk, but the staff behind the counter had started to notice her, and, fearing they might remember her should anyone come looking, Beth decided it was time to leave.

She walked north on Iowa. It was still a little chilly without a jacket, but the heat from the movement kept her comfortable enough. At a slow pace, she still reached the bank a little before nine.

The Central National Bank of Lawrence was a small branch bank with the typical low-maintenance brick facade and oversized glass doors. Even though it was a few minutes before nine, one of the employees saw her waiting in the cool morning air and came to unlock the door.

Beth pulled her cap down a little lower over her brows and stepped into the bank as she thanked the woman, not raising her face to make eye contact. She pulled her driver's license and keys from her pocket and headed toward a desk in the center of the common area. She walked past the four teller counters to the left of the door, two of them occupied by bank clerks who smiled at her as she passed.

"I would like to access a safety deposit box, please," Beth told the somber woman behind the desk.

She rose slowly and said, "This way, please."

Beth followed her to the locked and barred door along the back wall. She asked for Beth's key and ID and entered the information in the log. She then unlocked the entry door and closed it, locking it behind her. Beth knew the lock was for security, but it didn't make her feel safe. Instead she felt trapped, and pangs of anxiety threatened her composure.

She followed the woman to the wall of metal drawers and watched as she placed the bank's key in the appropriate slot and turned it. She instructed Beth to do the same with hers to remove the box when she was ready. Beth nodded, trying to keep her face hidden as best she could. With this, the woman exited the room and left Beth alone.

Beth turned her key in the lock then took the oversized metal box to a single small bar-height table in the center of the room. Lifting the lid, she unzipped the duffle inside and could see that all of her items were just as she had left them.

She replaced the box and removed both keys. A knock on the door brought back the attendant, who unlocked it, allowing Beth to breathe a little easier. Beth handed both keys over, telling the woman she would no longer be in need of the box.

With this she walked to the ATM in the lobby and withdrew one thousand dollars in cash, keeping her gaze down at the keypad so as to avoid the camera at the top of the screen. She had to do it in two increments of five hundred, but the machine dispensed all she needed. Beth stashed the money in the inside zipper pocket of the duffle and headed out.

A few minutes later and her second Uber driver of the day arrived. Beth would be making this leg of her trip with Angela, a polite but quiet late-twenties woman with a compulsively clean late model Ford Escape. When Beth didn't start up a conversation, Angela asked if she minded the radio. Beth didn't, hoping once again to be left to her own thoughts, and settled in to FM 106.4 classic rock.

CHAPTER 58

DRUDGE TO THE MASTER

ONE OF THE MASTER's human servants, dressed in jogging pants and a white T-shirt, moved silently. Duke, the bloodhound he was walking, wagged his tail happily and dragged him along behind.

They had begun their long "walk" near the hospital campus, not far from the emergency room entrance where Dr. Ramsey had made her escape. After Duke had a few good sniffs of a jacket Beth had left in her SUV, he had her scent and tracked it with purpose, nose to the ground. He dragged the man along the edge of the road, winding in and out of neighborhoods but overall northwest. To anyone watching them, they were just a man and his dog out for a morning walk, Duke yanking on the leash whenever the man paused at corners or lights.

As they approached the train yard, Duke veered off the road and into a thick row of trees. The man ducked and dodged branches as the dog pulled him onward. When they broke free of the trees, Duke headed for an old derailed boxcar, rust-red with the painted "KC Southern" logo scarcely visible on its side.

Duke stopped at the boxcar and whined before turning toward a small gravel road and tugging the man along again. Reaching the road, he began to pace back and forth, trying to regain the scent but with no luck. The trail had ended.

Duke paced back the way he had come and began circling the boxcar, whining. Her scent here was strong. He jumped up with his paws on the base of the boxcar door and whined some more.

The man dug his cell phone from the pocket of his joggers, looking around and then taking Duke back the several yards to the road.

"Yes, did you find her?" the voice on the phone said.

"No, but Duke is keying in on a boxcar down here. Should I check it out?" the man asked.

"Send me your location and wait for the rest of the team. If the woman or Luciano are in there, you'll need backup. He'll be weak with the daylight but still stronger than most men. Stay put; they're on their way." The call ended abruptly.

The man texted his location and headed back through the trees to wait.

The team consisted of six men. They were all tall, thick through the shoulders and wearing polo shirts, jeans and dark glasses, which they pushed onto the tops of their heads as they lined up on either side of the boxcar door. One held a thick, ivory-colored canvas tarp and a chain heavy enough to serve as a leash for an elephant.

The man with the tarp gave a nod and they all tugged on the door, feet digging into the ground below, to heave it open before they rushed in.

CHAPTER 59

LUCIANO

LUCIANO LAY ON A mattress in the near corner of the car, still and flat on his back. He stirred at the sound of the door. Disoriented from waking and weak from the daytime hours, he attempted to rise, only to be tackled back to the mattress. Using his legs that had gotten curled up against the man's midsection, he flung him across the car and into the wall, still not certain what was happening in his grogginess.

The man hit with a loud thud that echoed in the small space and crumpled heavily to the ground, shaken.

The second one to reach Luc met Luc's fist with his jaw. Luc watched as his head snapped to the left, a molar and droplets of blood flying in the air.

The remaining four were not so bold as to rush him alone and came forward as a group. Luciano tore free from the grasp of a few, punching and kicking sluggishly, but still hard enough that he heard the crack of breaking bone.

But there was nowhere to go. He wouldn't last more than a few seconds in the midday sun if he tried to run, and the fight was quickly sapping his already diminished strength.

He deflected an attack from the rear only to be hit again from the side and knocked to the floor as the injured men rejoined the battle.

His head fell inches from the daylight streaming through the open boxcar. He saw his cell phone on the floor next to him, kicked to the center of the room in the struggle. Knowing it held a link to Beth, he pulled one arm free and flung out his fist to smash it but missed. In that moment, just before the tarp came down and he felt the weight of the men on his limbs, he saw one of his attackers pick it up and put it in his pocket.

He felt the chain encircle his feet and tighten. In seconds he was wrapped from toe to neck in tarp and chain. One of the men approached him with a smug smile on his lips and said, "The Master says hello." Then the tarp covered his head.

Luciano felt himself lifted and then dropped roughly into the back of a vehicle. He could feel the heat from the sun through the tarp, draining him. As much as he fought it, trying to stay awake to know where they were taking him, the daylight took its toll and he gave in to sleep.

This time he awoke in motion. He was on some kind of a cart with wheels, and after bumping over a door frame, he could feel he was inside. He pushed briefly against the chains, but they held firm, so he lay still, trying to gather what information he could.

After a short journey straight forward, they made a turn to the left. He heard a *ding* followed by the sound of elevator doors opening and closing. He felt the elevator shudder and then lower. He couldn't tell how far it went since he struggled to stay awake, but the trip lasted perhaps two minutes before the elevator *dinged* again and the doors opened.

They got off and took a right, bumped over another doorframe and stopped. Luciano felt himself lifted from the cart and placed on what felt like the floor, then heard the cart being wheeled back out. There was a tinkling of metal and then four quick footsteps before there was the sound of a heavy door closing with a rotating lock and a *click*, then silence.

Thinking for a moment he may be alone and able to free himself, Luciano bucked and twisted against the heavy chains and felt them fall loose from his neck and shoulders. He worked his arms free, though much more slowly than he could have mustered at night, and uncovered his head and upper body. Then he began to work on removing the binding from his lower body. As soon as his legs were free, he rose and surveyed the room.

It was small, maybe eight by ten feet at most. The walls were gray metal and smooth, without doors or windows. The doorway he had come through was approximately his height, narrow, also metal and fit smoothly into the wall. There was no doorframe or handle on this side. To the left of the door was another metal-covered opening, maybe a foot across and half a foot high; again, no handle on this side. He had freed himself from his bindings but clearly was still captive.

There was a narrow cot against one wall with a thin mattress and no bed linens. A single rectangle of sunlight lit the floor about three feet in from the opposite wall. This came from what appeared to be a skylight cut in the ceiling of the room that was otherwise the same sleek metal of the walls.

Luciano walked to the door and pounded twice.

"Who's out there?" No answer.

"Where am I?" Still nothing.

He pushed against the door and smaller opening beside it in turn. It was a useless effort, especially in his weakened daylight state. Neither gave in the slightest to his efforts.

The Master had him where he wanted him. This was his game, and Luciano would have to wait to hear the rules. Beth had made it away cleanly, but they had his cell phone. The same cell to which Beth may already have texted her new number. He only hoped that with not hearing from him, she wouldn't text the address and lead the Master right to her.

He dropped roughly onto the cot, hands over his face. All he could do was wait for sunset to try the door again with renewed strength, wait for when the Master chose to reveal his plans...

Wait.

CHAPTER 60

BETH

BETH MADE IT TO the lake cabin a little before noon. She told Angela it was her uncle's cabin and while she had been there many times as a kid, she couldn't remember the address. Angela was patient and followed Beth's directions to the beginning of the lane leading up to the cabin. Beth tipped her well and thanked her for the ride.

Beth slung her duffle over her shoulder and walked down the gravel lane. There were only four other cabins along the way, and all looked deserted with not a single car in sight. She walked around to the back of the little cabin anyway, wanting to hide herself from view as much as possible, then tried the back door. While it was locked, she was pleased to see there was no dead bolt. There wasn't much to worry about around here, particularly since the cabins were very simple and sparsely furnished. Not much to be had for anyone breaking and entering.

Using a grocery store membership card, Beth worked on the lock and after about thirty seconds had it open.

"Hello? Anyone home?" Beth called.

No answer.

She entered and found the place empty. Sheets covered the couch and chair in the living room. It looked like it had been closed up for the winter.

Beth relocked the door and propped a chair beneath the handle.

She had slept little the night before and knew Luc would be sleeping through the daylight hours. He'd promised he would call when he made it to town tonight so she could give him the address.

Feeling a little safer inside the cabin, the excitement and adrenaline of the journey began to wear off, and Beth was exhausted. Their plan was so far coming together, and she needed rest.

She found sheets and a blanket in the hall closet and spread them on the sofa. Taking time only to kick off her shoes before stretching out, she then pulled the new cell out of her pocket and curled it in her hand next to her head on the pillow. That way she'd be sure she heard the ring when Luc called that evening.

Beth was running but found each step barely moving her forward. Her legs churned and yet it felt as though she moved in slow motion. She could hear the Master's men closing in behind her. There were cold fingers grabbing at the back of her neck when she jerked awake, swinging her legs over the side of the couch and sitting upright in one motion. Her breath was ragged and drops of perspiration dotted her forehead and cheeks. For a moment she couldn't remember where she was. She was half-sitting on a couch in a dark room, the only light coming through a window from the single yard light outside.

Gradually her breathing slowed, and she began to remember the trip to Lawrence and the lake. She realized she was safe and alone, and her heart fell into its normal rhythm. It was dark, but Luc hadn't yet called. She felt on her pillow, but the phone wasn't there, so she looked to the floor beside the couch. Finding it and picking it up, she saw its screen was blank except for the time, 7:13 p.m. She checked that her initial text with her new cell number had gone through, and it showed that it had. To be sure, Beth texted the number again and waited.

Was he on his way? Would he have sent her away to the lake to keep her safe and then left without her? Perhaps trusting him was a mistake and he had decided in the end that running without her would be easier.

No, she thought, shaking her head. She pushed the thoughts from her mind. She trusted him. He would want to be sure she was safe, and as long as the Master was after them both, he would stay close. He said he had other things to take care of before heading this way, and she didn't know how long it would take him to make the trip here. She knew he was fast, but would he run or take a car? She hadn't thought to ask.

She picked up her duffle and headed for the bathroom to shower.

She hadn't packed extra clothes, never imagining she would have to run with only the clothes on her back. She would need something to wear after her shower. She had run at least five miles and spent more than twenty-four hours in the ones she was wearing already. In the master closet she found women's clothing near her size. Most were summer weight, but there were also two pairs of jeans, just one size larger than her own, and a black North Face jacket with a fleece lining. The jacket was loose but comfortable. They weren't perfect, but at least she could be clean and presentable when Luc did make it.

CHAPTER 61

LUCIANO

LUCIANO COULD FEEL THE sun setting even without watching the small patch of daylight fading on the floor of his cell. He could feel the strength returning to his body.

As soon as it had set, he rose from the cot and walked to what was really just an outline of the door. He laid both hands on it once again and pushed with everything he had in the chance that his strength, renewed by the setting of the sun, would make a difference.

It didn't budge. It didn't even shake or dent. He had expected as much. The Master would know his strength and wouldn't have wasted time with a prison that couldn't hold him.

He feared for Beth, and for himself, but he would not give in to it. There were likely cameras on him now. He would maintain his composure and not give the Master the satisfaction of seeing him fearful and lashing out. Luciano returned to the cot and sat with his hands resting calmly on his thighs. He set his face into what he believed was a dead calm and retreated into his thoughts.

He remembered holding Beth last night, the softness of her lips as she had kissed him. The faint sweet smell of her hair. The blue of her eyes as they met his and her breasts as they pushed against his chest. He would focus on these memories until he held her again. Whatever the Master's plan, he would find his way through it and go to her. Their relationship had not and would not be an easy one, but he had found love once again and he was not about to let it go.

***

After long hours waiting, he heard metal against metal and saw the small window slide open. He rose and walked slowly to it, peering through.

The Master's face looked back at him, smug, the corners of his mouth upturned ever so slightly.

"Luciano, I did not think I would see you again after your... accident. You are like a cockroach that refuses to die; a mistake I cannot erase."

Luciano wanted him to speak, to gloat, to tell his plan, so he held his tongue.

"I was surprised we found you again so easily. I thought you would be smarter after these many years. Women, it seems, are your Achilles' heel. We tracked her right to you. I was hoping to meet her, your lady friend, but I will in time."

Clearly the Master knew of Beth's involvement, but he didn't have her. Luciano felt a small bit of relief. He couldn't deny he knew her, but he could make her seem irrelevant. "I am nothing but a scientific curiosity to her. She knows after her encounter with your men that studying me is dangerous. Her only interest in me was is in how I could help her be free of this whole mess. She left town as soon as she escaped and has no interest in digging further."

With this the Master chuckled. "Three hundred years and you are still a terrible liar." He pulled Luciano's phone from his pocket and Luc's heart fell. What had Beth texted?

"It seems she is already trying to reach you." He held the phone close enough for Luciano to see the number of her new prepaid cell on the screen. At least she hadn't sent the address, and he prayed silently that she would wait for a response before she did.

"I'll tell you what I think. I think you risked coming out of hiding to help her run. I think you have feelings for this woman. She put herself at risk to save you once already, and I believe she will again. I have all the time in the world to wait. But how long can you wait? With each passing day you will grow hungrier until you are mad with thirst. We will find her, Luciano, and when we do, we will hold her until you can wait no longer and then offer her to you. It will be just like old times. You will either both die of starvation, saving me the trouble of killing you, or you will feed and live knowing you took her life to save your own. I will have to kill you then, but watching your torment will be worth the trouble."

Luciano's hands were clenched into fists at his sides, his jaw just as tight, but he fought to remain still, not wanting the Master to have the pleasure of seeing the rage his words were evoking within him.

Luc's phone rang.

"Well, perfect timing. That's Doctor Ramsey calling now."

Luciano's rage melted into anguish and fear, praying she would know something was wrong and run. He would never see her again if she did, but at least he would have the comfort of knowing she might survive.

The Master let the phone ring over to voicemail.

"Now she will begin to worry. She will begin to wonder why you aren't sticking to the plan, whatever it was. As I let her wait, she will become panicked, wondering what has become of you. And when people are stressed, they make bad decisions."

The phone rang again, emphasizing his words. The smug smile once again spread across his lips.

"I certainly have the means to track her down, but if I let her worry fester a bit longer before we speak, I won't need to. She will come to me believing she may be able to save you. But of course, that will never happen."

"What in your long life happened to make you so willfully cruel?" Luc spat through clenched teeth.

"The Vampyre made us what we are; no more, no less. We kill and we live on. Humans do the same to their prey. We are perfect predators, as I am sure the Vampyre intended. I will allow no one to change that. I will never eat from a bag of blood. I will hunt and take what I wish. And I will not allow anyone, human or vampire, to discover what makes us what we are and use it against us." He turned on his heel to leave and, with a flick of his fingers, the window slammed shut.

CHAPTER 62

BETH

BETH CHECKED HER NEW phone again. 8:05 p.m.; no calls, no messages.

She rummaged through her duffle and found the flash drive with a backup of all her research. It would be missing the most recent entries, but the majority of what she had discovered so far was there.

She put the drive in her pocket and headed for the kitchen. It was a tiny little galley kitchen with a stove/oven combo and refrigerator on one side and a sink on the other. A microwave was mounted under the upper cabinetry. There was very little counter space, but Beth supposed gourmet meals weren't really a focus at the lake. There was also a washer/dryer stackable unit at the end of the kitchen, so she went back for her discarded clothes and towel and started a load. Her own clothes would likely be finished before she left, and leaving as little behind as possible for others to find when she did depart seemed like a good idea.

Her stomach growled rather loudly, so she began to look in the pantry cupboards for something to eat. There was a box of macaroni and cheese, but of course no milk in the refrigerator to make it with. There was a bit of butter but most all of the other perishable items had been discarded. But she did find a can of tomato sauce, some dry pasta and a can of green beans and removed the ingredients from the shelves.

She opened the drawers and cabinets and managed to find pots and pans and utensils that would work. She also ran across a junk drawer with spare batteries, a flashlight and a roll of duct tape. These she sat on the counter for later.

She began cooking, relieved to have something to do besides check her phone and worry about Luc. The cabin was supplied with a good assortment of spices, and in just a few minutes Beth had the sauce seasoned to her liking, then returned to the couch with her plate and ate in silence. It wasn't Olive Garden, but it was warm and filling. She fished out what remained of the M&M's Luc had brought her the night before and ate a few for dessert. The fact that he had remembered her fondness for them made her heart ache for him to join her quickly.

The extra pasta and green beans she placed in the fridge for later, hoping Luc would arrive long before she was hungry again. She washed the dirty dishes, dried them and put them back where she had found them. Then she grabbed the roll of duct tape and headed for the bathroom. She made a little pouch out of the tape, placed her flash drive inside it and then taped the whole thing to the bottom of the trash can where it could wait safe and sound.

9:14 p.m. and still no call from Luc. It had been dark for a while now. What if he didn't arrive until closer to dawn? She should make sure as much of the house was shielded from daylight as possible in case they would need to wait out the day here before moving on. She walked from room to room, closing curtains as she went. The guest bedroom would be by far the safest, having only a single window with heavy curtains.

Beth wasn't much of a TV watcher and decided to look around for something to read. In the larger of the two bedrooms was a narrow bookcase with twenty or thirty paperbacks and a few medical journals.

A closer look showed the journals were from last year and that she had already read them. The paperbacks were mostly westerns, which she wasn't really into. She did, however, find a copy of Stephen King's *The Stand*. It was one of her favorites, and even though she had read it through at least five times, it never got old.

She took it down to bring with her, then checked a small wooden desk in the corner. The top drawer contained a deck of cards. She had never been much of a card player either, but she did know solitaire, and it might keep her occupied for at least a little while. The second drawer of the desk contained a legal pad and pens which also might be useful if she were here for long.

Back in the living room Beth sat on the sofa and curled her legs beneath her. 10:10 p.m. Beth opened the paperback and tried to focus on the Super Flu.

11:00 p.m.... and no word from Luc. She had checked her phone every five minutes for the last hour and now had reread the same paragraph at least five times but still couldn't remember what it said. She gave up and closed the book. Beth knew Luc said it may be early Sunday morning before he would arrive, but she at least expected him to call or text her before now. She had waited long enough.

She scooped up her new phone and dialed Luc's cell. It rang five times and went to voicemail, which consisted only of the computerized voice reciting the number and asking her to leave a message after the tone. She hung up and tried again only to go to voicemail for a second time.

Something was wrong. Luc wouldn't leave her alone in this. Had he been forced to run and either left or lost his cell? Perhaps he was already at the lodge like they had planned and waiting for her to call.

She looked up the number and pressed "call."

A sleepy-sounding gentleman picked up on the other end. "Clinton Motorlodge, how may I help you?" he said.

"Hello, a friend of mine, Brian Hoffman, was supposed to have arrived last night and I haven't heard from him yet. Can you tell me if he's checked in?"

"Let me check," he said. Beth could hear typing in the background as he entered something into the computer. "No, no Brian Hoffman here."

"Thank you for looking," she said. "Is there any way I could leave a message for him for when he does make it in?" Beth asked.

"Sure. Give me a sec to find a pen... Okay, go ahead."

"Please ask him to call Janice at 918-678-0121."

"Got it."

"Thank you again."

"Have a nice day!" he said before hanging up. Beth thought at this point that was pretty doubtful.

She attempted to call Luc's cell again with no answer. Had he been captured or hurt and his cell taken? If so, they would have her number. Could they track her location with it? She should turn it off just in case, but if she did there would be no chance for Luc to contact her...

She decided to play it safe and powered the phone off. She would turn it on once an hour, check for calls and messages and, if there weren't any, make one call to Luc's phone.

As much as she tried to push the thought away, it kept sneaking back in: what if Luc was dead? Beth allowed herself to consider this for a moment and just couldn't accept it. Until she knew for sure, she would assume he was alive and still trying to get to her. In the meantime, she needed to come up with a plan.

If the Master had Luc, he still might not know where she was. Luc would never share that information. But if the Master had Luc's phone, he also had her number. She just didn't know if he could track her new number or not. She could leave her phone off and move to the hotel, but that cost money that she would eventually run out of, placing her out in the open again. No, she would stay put and give Luc until morning to contact her. If he didn't, she would leave him a note saying, "Plan B." Luc would know that meant she was at the hotel. She would use cash to check in and stay one night. If Luc still didn't show, she would buy a new phone and leave the number in a note for him under "Brian Hoffman" at the hotel desk.

Considering what she needed to do, she had very little money. She figured if she had to run without Luc, her best bet was to take another Uber a few towns over and get as much cash from an ATM as possible. From there she would take another Uber to the closest city with a national bus service and buy a ticket to the farthest city on its route.

Beth prayed she wouldn't need to follow any of that plan. The thought of leaving without Luc and trying to make her way alone wasn't just terrifying, it also felt... empty. She realized that since meeting Luc and growing to care for him, her life had taken on a whole new meaning. The thought of living out her life now without him seemed like spending it in black and white instead of color.

Beth really wanted to go for a run—it was always the best thing for blowing off tension and clearing her head. She hadn't seen any cars or heard any voices outside so far. She looked out the windows from several rooms and saw no movement. The moon wasn't full, but there was enough moonlight for her to see where she was going while still being dark enough to hide her. She would rather not run in jeans again, but there just wasn't anything else.

She almost stepped through the back door and into the darkness, but then thought about Luc. What if he had just lost his phone and arrived while she was out? He would surely assume something had happened to her with her things left behind, and he would have no way to contact her. And, worst-case scenario, what if some of the Master's men arrived and she had to make a run for it? What few resources she had would be here inside the house out of reach.

No, as good as it would feel to run, it would have to wait.

CHAPTER 63

BETH

THE WAITING WAS HORRIBLE. Beth busied herself going through the kitchen pantry again to take stock of everything in it. Then she carefully went through every door and closet in the place to see if there was anything that might come in useful along the way. She desperately wished she'd had time to pack a few things before leaving or that she had planned ahead and been able to shop for more items at Walmart before leaving town, but she had believed she'd be meeting Luc quickly and this would be only a brief stop on their way. Now she was stuck with whatever she could get her hands on. Luc would certainly have access to more resources, so it was temporary, but she needed to gather what she could just in case she had to make another leg of the journey alone.

There weren't any weapons in the cabin, but she did find a hammer in a small toolbox in the bedroom closet. Only the UV light would work against a vampire, but the hammer would give her at least something against humans.

She found the right batteries for the flashlight in the kitchen junk drawer and put that next to the duffle as well. The Pop-Tarts and chocolate chips along with a small bag of peanuts she found in the back of the pantry went into the duffle too. It wouldn't hold her long but could serve for quick energy in a pinch. She found two water bottles in the kitchen cabinets, filled them and added them to her stash. She hadn't thought to include toiletries in her bag when she stashed it at the bank but found travel sizes of various kinds and an extra toothbrush in a small bin under the bathroom sink. It was probably a stash for guests or the owners themselves in case they'd forgotten something at home but would serve her well if she had to run.

Her little treasure hunt had taken only an hour. It was 1:13 a.m. And when she powered up her phone for her hourly check, she still had no texts or messages and her call once again went straight to voicemail. She looked out the windows of the cabin, being careful not to make herself visible from the outside. Still no movement from the surrounding cabins.

She decided to turn on the TV after all but to leave the sound low so as not to mask any sounds of approaching cars. She needed the distraction. An old *I Love Lucy* episode played across the screen.

If the Master's crew knew where she was, they could have easily reached her hours ago. She had to assume they didn't know how to find her or didn't care enough to chase her without Luc by her side. The area was quiet so far, and it appeared all the surrounding cabins were empty and likely would be until the fishing picked up or the weather warmed. So staying here, at least for now, seemed a decent option. Apart from food, she had what she needed.

She had easily broken into this cabin, and it occurred to her that perhaps she could also get into others in the area and find more to eat. She turned off the TV and peered out the front and side windows of the cabin. There were still no lights on. The closest cabin was to her north, and she could see its back porch door from the kitchen window. She put on the jacket from the closet and went out the back door, leaving it unlocked for her return. She walked nearly silently across the sparse grass and large rocks between the two cabins, stepped onto the porch and looked through the window on the back door.

No lights and no movement.

She opened the screen and jumped at the loud squeak from the hinges. She stood completely still, catching her breath and listening but heard nothing except her own breathing. True to the area, this door had only a simple doorknob lock as well, no deadbolt. She was able to jimmy it with little difficulty and let herself in.

This cabin looked more modern than the one she was currently borrowing. The door from the porch opened into an open main floor. A living room with chairs facing the lake was to her right. The chairs were covered by sheets, keeping out the dust until the owners returned. The floors were dark wood, but it was difficult to tell the color in the dim light. To her left was a door that opened into a bedroom with a dark, probably black, wood frame bed. The living room was open to a dining room table and chairs, also covered with a sheet. To the left of this was a modern kitchen with all the appliances, including a dishwasher and trash compactor, in shiny stainless steel.

Beth found a pantry next to the oversized refrigerator and looked through it. This one was fully stocked including, to her delight, powdered milk. She had brought several plastic bags from under the sink of her cabin and began filling them with anything that she thought useful. Checking the freezer, she also found frozen meats and hashbrowns. There was a package of Eggo waffles as well. It wasn't exactly bread but could work in a pinch. The fridge was largely empty but did contain some condiments, pickles, chocolate syrup and a box with sticks of butter. There was a wine rack on the countertop beneath the microwave, and Beth grabbed a bottle of Duckhorn Napa Valley Merlot.

Roughing it wasn't going to be half bad.

She turned toward the back of the house to return and paused a moment, feeling a little guilty for breaking and entering even though she was taking only a few food items. She thought for a moment, then took forty dollars from her wallet and left it on the counter. Treasures in hand, Beth headed back the way she had come, closing and locking the back door.

Back in her cabin, Beth put away the things she had "borrowed," placing anything that could help her on the run into or near her duffle.

It was nearly 3 a.m. Beth settled on the couch with a glass of the merlot. She turned on the cell phone, knowing it would be blank but needing to check anyway. It fired up with a chime and a green glow followed by a quick chirp and vibration.

And there it was. After many painful hours of waiting for a response from Luc were the words "Call me."

At first her heart pounded and she felt relief, thinking that Luc was alright and finally contacting her after working his way out of some tight spot. But another thought slowly took over: what if it wasn't Luc? Her breath caught and she felt her heart skip. If it wasn't Luc but the Master instead, it would mean they had him and his cell. But even if they did, she would have to call. She had to know. If he did have Luc, she had little to bargain with except to make the Master know that, unless they were safe, his secrets would no longer be his own.

Beth took a deep breath and dialed.

The person on the other end picked up after the third ring. "Elizabeth, how nice of you to call."

Her throat caught and the color drained from her face. It wasn't Luc's voice. Her worst-case scenario had just become reality.

She thought she might be sick.

"Where's Luc?" she croaked, voice little more than a whisper.

"Luc, a pet name, how sweet. Luciano is here with me. He is safe for now, but I can't say for how long. That depends on you."

The reality of losing Luc hit her with the force of a physical blow and took her breath. Her head spun, fear making it nearly impossible for her to process the Master's words.

After a long moment, she managed a shallow breath and, voice shaking, replied, "What do you want?"

"It's quite simple, Elizabeth. You have information you should not. I want it."

"Let Luc go and I'll give you everything I have."

"Well, I think we both know that's not going to happen."

"If something happens to Luc or to me, everything I know will be out worldwide in a matter of days." She had little to bargain with but hoped the threat would be enough to buy Luc time.

"Maybe, maybe not, but I can tell you that if you don't come to me, Luciano will die. You can run, but I will use my not insignificant resources to track you down. I think we both know you can't stay hidden on your own for long. I will find you, kill you and clean up whatever mess you might leave behind. Bring all you have to me and we can discuss... an arrangement."

Beth did not like the tone of his voice when he said "arrangement." It made her feel like she needed a shower. And the nonchalance with which he said "kill you," like reading from a grocery list, made her shiver.

But he was right. She had no experience running and hiding and no real resources without Luc. She was outmatched. The blood drained from her face; her mouth suddenly felt dry.

"You have one hour. Return home and I will send a man to gather you."

"That's not possible. I'm too far away. I would need at least six hours to travel." She wanted to buy as much time as possible.

"Very well, I can be reasonable; you have three." Smug, followed by a click. He knew he had the upper hand and he knew that, with Luc under his thumb, she would come.

CHAPTER 64

BETH

ON THE OFF CHANCE that she survived, to cover her tracks, Beth decided to jog the two miles to the marina and then find a ride or Uber in to town. She would borrow a phone there so as not to leave a number recorded on her own, then make one call, leaving a message for the law firm she had hired telling them that if they didn't hear back from her by the end of the week, her plan to distribute the research she had accumulated should be carried out. She would get another ride from there into Overland Park and then a final one from there to home. She hoped that would make the path back to where she had begun hard to follow should she ever need to return to the cabin again. The timing would be tight, so she didn't waste time cleaning up or even to change into her own clothes. She downed the last few remaining sips of wine in her glass to settle her nerves.

Her duffle was light as she slung it over her arm. There wasn't much use for most of what she had in it initially, so she had left much of it haphazardly discarded on the couch. She did take the duffle, though, in case she had been spotted leaving Lawrence with it. Beth didn't want them believing she had left anything behind. She was going into the lion's den and it would require an act of God to keep her life. The hammer and knife she had set aside to defend herself would be of little use against the Master and his group of thugs.

This was it. Either she would free them both with the threat of exposure and save Luc's life, or she wouldn't, but at least she would know she had done all she could.

The early morning air was chilly as she headed out the back door of the cabin, and she was thankful for the borrowed jacket on her shoulders. This was going to be a very long day.

CHAPTER 65

BETH

A TRIP HOME WAS something Beth usually looked forward to, but today, as the driver dropped her off in her driveway, she could only muster sadness, knowing this was likely the last time she would see it.

Mrs. Raintree, surely having been watching from her living room window, was out the door the moment Beth stepped from the taxi. Not wanting her to be involved in any of the mess, Beth called to her as she walked toward the front door of her home, "I'm sorry, Mrs. Raintree, some colleagues are picking me up for breakfast soon and I really have to run but I'll catch up with you later. Take care!" Beth thought of all the times she had been irritated by Mrs. Raintree's rambling but at this moment, she would happily have let her talk for hours to avoid what was to come. But she didn't want any watching eyes thinking that she had shared any information with her that would make her of interest to the Master's group of thugs.

Beth didn't look back, knowing she would see Mrs. Raintree's face and shoulders droop in disappointment, but it was for the best.

The door to the house had barely closed behind her when Beth heard the sound of an engine as it pulled into her driveway. They had been watching the house as she suspected. The color drained from her face, and she reached out to steady herself against the entryway wall.

Everything in her told her to run, but Beth fought the urge. She had to face the Master. There was no way around it.

Her laptop was missing from her desk—no real surprise there—and the paper files were missing from her file drawer. But the flash drive she had hidden with a backup of all her research was still tucked away under the master bathroom trash can. She knew they wouldn't allow her long and hurried to her closet and quickly slipped from her borrowed clothes into her favorite jeans and best pair of running shoes. It wouldn't hurt to be prepared if it did happen that she and Luc could somehow get free of the Master.

As she tied her second shoe string, taking far longer than usual because of the shaking of her hands, she heard a knock on the front door. She slipped on her own jacket and put the flash drive in her duffle. "Time's up," she said to her empty house.

CHAPTER 66

BETH

A BLOCK AWAY FROM her front door, the two men who had climbed into the black SUV on either side of her covered her head with a black cloth bag. She supposed, all things considered, this was a good sign. Why would they bother with covering her eyes if the Master had already decided to kill her? She wasn't any more comfortable thinking about the deal he might set forward for her, but at this moment, she would find hope where she could. Beth wasn't sure what the Master would want from her besides her research. Would he offer Luc's life in exchange for her help with the bodies that he dropped around town? He already had Peter covering up his murders, but would he want another doctor on the payroll?

The ride lasted for what seemed like forever but was in all likelihood about forty-five minutes. It began on I-635 and she was fairly certain continued west on I-70, but from there it became less clear. They turned off the interstate, but then the roads became gravel and seemed to meander right and left until she was no longer certain what direction they were going. The smells of diesel and exhaust fumes gave way to hay and occasionally manure, but there were no particular smells or sounds to provide a landmark. If they could escape on foot, she hoped Luc could navigate with the stars because there was no way she could provide direction. If there were enough trees, it was likely they would block the glow of the city lights. If all else failed, they would run until they found a road or something else to orient themselves.

The SUV slowed and she heard the driver's window roll down and a beeping noise. Beth assumed that was for access to a gate, because shortly after she heard a motor start up, the squeak of wheels and the popping of gravel beneath them as they rolled. The SUV moved forward slowly, and after about a minute she could feel the front of the vehicle dropping as though they were driving downhill.

Sound became louder here and the engine noise seemed to bounce back at them as they drove. Beth figured this must be some kind of enclosed or underground structure. After a few more seconds, the SUV stopped and she heard the driver shift it into park. She could feel the moisture forming on her tightly clenched hands. They hadn't bothered to tie them when she got in the vehicle. She guessed she didn't look like much of a threat.

One of the muscle-bound henchmen said, "Out of the car."

Beth slid to the edge of the seat and swung her legs out until her feet were firmly on the ground. The henchman grabbed her arm and led her forward.

She heard the sliding doors of an elevator and then stood inside it. The elevator took them down, although Beth couldn't say how far since it moved smoothly and quietly as they traveled. They had to be underground. She hadn't considered this possibility but supposed it might be a safe haven for a vampire to escape daylight hours.

To Beth it felt like a grave, and she hoped it would not be hers. Panic threatened, but she reminded herself why she was here and steadied her breathing. Luc was in trouble, and she was determined to do whatever she could to save him from the Master.

At the level of their choosing, they led her along again by the arm.

This level smelled sterile, like alcohol and bleach. The floor was smooth and hard like cement or tile, and Beth could hear classical music playing softly at a distance. It grew louder as they walked. At the end of a long corridor, they turned left and stopped. Then the man holding her arm knocked on the door in front of them.

CHAPTER 67

BETH

"Yes, yes, enter," said the Master's now-familiar voice.

Beth's muscles tensed. She heard the door creak softly as it swung open, and she was led forward.

"That will be all. Remove her hood."

The room before her was dimly lit by two floor lamps. The ceiling was remarkably high, which made the notes of the cello now taking center stage in the music echo eerily. The walls were a deep forest green and the ceiling a coffered dark wood that matched the floors. Despite the size, the dark colors made it feel as if the room was closing in around her.

Matching bookcases lined the walls from floor to ceiling, filled with books and what appeared to be old relics of stone and pottery, but there were no other routes of escape apart from the door from which they had entered. In the center was a large but simple desk in a similar dark wood. Beth could occasionally hear the crackling of burning logs over the music and smell the burning wood, earthy and smoky, but couldn't actually see the fire. The Master had attempted to burn Luc with fire, so the flames could certainly work on him as well, but Beth knew she could never reach it in time. Despite the heat she was sure it gave off, she was shivering.

Beth could see the Master's legs beneath the desk, dressed in brown pants, right leg crossed comfortably over the left. She could feel her hands trembling and clasped them together to keep them still, then raised her eyes to meet his.

He wasn't what she expected; a small man with dark skin and round metal-rimmed spectacles. Her fear of him had made him large and menacing in her mind, but he looked nothing of the sort. He sat with his elbows on the desktop, fingers touching, and appeared to be studying her as she studied him.

"So, finally we meet," the Master said. "I have been looking forward to it."

"I can't say the same."

"Well, now, we have business to discuss, but there is no reason to be impolite."

"I've brought all of my research to you. Let us go."

"Before we discuss terms, I need to see what it is you actually have." With this he pushed something across the desk toward her, and Beth realized it was her laptop from home. "Password, please."

Beth stepped toward the desk and reached for the laptop, but a man she hadn't noticed behind her reached it first, opened it and glared at her impatiently, hands poised over the keys. Of course they would want her to tell them her password rather than risking her deleting the drive before they could see what she knew.

Beth took a deep breath and looked steadily at the Master. It was silly for her to think she could make him believe she wasn't scared out of her mind. He could certainly hear her heart beating madly in her chest just as Luc could.

She exhaled loudly and said, "Luciano three hundred exclamation point, capital *l*, no spaces."

The man typed and then nodded to the Master. He flipped

quickly through the information in her folders, opening the image files—pictures of Luciano healing, his burned home, the karyotype and the pictures of the virus from the electron microscope. He opened the word document journal she had created for logging her experiments and documenting Luc's day-to-day improvements. He then turned the screen to the Master and let him review all.

"You have been very busy indeed. So, it is a virus. I suspected as much. The Vampyre packaged it with all the details needed to create a monster. And you would do what with this information?"

"I believe we could learn much about human healing and regeneration. The medical benefits of that information could change medicine as we know it. Ultimately, I would hope there would be a way to remove the less desirable effects of the virus and give those who are infected a more normal life in the sun without the need to consume human blood."

"I see. So, you would experiment with this virus as the Vampyre did; infect a few and see what happens?"

"No, of course not. It would need to be very carefully studied in a laboratory, perhaps with animal testing. Any exposure to humans would be after extensive research to be sure it was safe to use."

"Safe; that's the problem now, isn't it? What makes you think the virus the Vampyre created could ever be safe? Imagine what could be done if the military knew of our existence and decided to make an army of super soldiers? Do you really believe they would wait to be sure it was 'safe' before testing it on their 'volunteers?'"

Beth believed science was pure and that fellow scientists would share her desires to use the discoveries to help human kind. She hadn't seriously considered it falling into the wrong hands apart from those of the Master. But she had to admit he was right. "Anything could become a weapon in the wrong hands."

A quick snort was his response. He drummed his fingertips against one another, glancing down at them as he did. "And what would become of us vampires when the public discovers we are living among them and aren't just movie screen monsters? They will hunt us down, even your precious Luciano, and exterminate us if they can. Experiment on us at the very least."

Beth couldn't really argue with this. She had worried about the same. It was why she had chosen to treat Luciano herself in her own home rather than making her medical colleagues aware that he existed.

Beth held the Master's gaze, not backing down rather than respond.

"I will take your silence as agreement. So, what is to be done with you?" Here was the real question.

"You have all of my research. Let Luciano and me go and I will never pursue it again. We will leave and stay out of your way."

The Master chuckled and leaned back in his desk chair, a half-smile on his thin lips. "I think we both know that Luciano cannot go free. But that doesn't mean you have to die as well." He paused as if to let him sparing her life sink in, believing Beth would forget about Luc and his life to save her own. "I have use for a woman in your position. Forget about Luciano and your research. Work for me and I can promise that you will have all you want."

"Work for you, as in provide a cover for your murders?"

The half-smile was now gone. "I have power and resources you cannot imagine. I could make you a very successful woman. Don't let a silly thing like love deprive you of your future. Luciano is a monster just as I am. Were he to live, he would tire of you quickly. When one is immortal, relationships with humans are brief and have little value. Serve me well and perhaps I could make you immortal one day as well."

The half-smile was back again. The urge to wipe it off was almost more than Beth could take. Serve him? She was a modern American woman; the idea of serving anyone was like swallowing acid. Her fear had turned to anger, and her hands clenched into fists. "That's not going to happen. If you kill me, I will fail to make one very important phone call, a call I make every week. If I don't make that call, my research gets released to the world. If you kill me, the secrets will come out; *your* secret will come out."

That half-smile was gone again. The Master placed his hands on the chair arms and leaned forward, looking Beth directly in the eye. "Last chance. Work for me and live, or refuse and die. I will kill you and clean up whatever messes you might leave behind. I have been alive for a very long time and I will be here long after anyone with a memory of you is gone. Accept my generosity or don't. It changes nothing for me either way."

Beth thought of the day she received her MD and recited the Hippocratic oath, the face of her colleague who the Master had certainly killed to give Peter a job, Luc's charred body after the Master's attempt on his life had almost succeeded and her revulsion toward Peter when she had discovered his falsified reports to cover the Master's murders of innocent young women. But her mind stopped on something her father had said to her not long before he died.

They had been talking about her high school freshman chemistry class. The teacher had given the exam to the office to copy. Beth had served as the seventh hour office aid and had seen questions on the test while copying it before realizing what it was. She had stopped looking after seeing the first page but was still feeling guilty about having seen that. She was trying to decide if she should go and tell the teacher, which she later did, or pretend nothing had happened. Her father had said, "Ultimately, Beth, you have to decide what you can live with and what decision will allow you to sleep at night."

If she served the Master, she would have to cover up his crimes and allow him to kill innocent people. Beth would have to ignore the insight she had gained and give up on any hope of ever helping anyone with that knowledge. And she would have to live knowing that Luc was gone. Beth was pretty certain she would never be able to sleep again.

"My answer is no," she said. "It's the only answer I can live with... even if it's not for very long." She exhaled. She felt more at peace than she had in weeks.

"As you wish." With this he pressed a button on his desk, an intercom Beth presumed, and said, "Peter, come and escort Doctor Ramsey downstairs. We are finished here."

CHAPTER 68

BETH

"YOU'RE MAKING THE WRONG decision, Beth," Peter said.

"Perhaps being a slave to the Master works for you, but it won't work for me."

Peter chuckled. "Better to be a servant to the king than his enemy. And it isn't like that. The Master supported me financially through medical school. Now I'm on my way to being a very rich man."

"By covering up his crimes? By murdering for him? He has you right where he wants you. One slip and your career is over, or worse yet, you're convicted and imprisoned. And what makes you think that the Master won't tell the authorities about what you're doing the minute you are no longer useful?"

"He wouldn't do that; but I am useful. I have his favor because I do what he asks. He trusts me in handling his affairs because he knows I will do what has to be done. And one day soon, he will turn me to share in the empire he has built for himself."

It was Beth's turn to chuckle. "Maybe he will, maybe he won't, but whatever he does will be in his interest alone. Do you really think he cares for you? I don't know exactly how old he is, but I know he has lived for many centuries. The lifespan of a human is nothing to him. You will be gone in the blink of his eye. Giving you these small things to get what he wants is like a man giving table scraps to a dog." Beth couldn't think about her life when compared with Luc's either. She knew that Luc would live many lives long after she was gone unless she could unravel the effects of the virus and give him back his humanity.

While Peter maintained his composure, Beth could see she hit a nerve.

As they walked, they passed several of the Master's thugs. They nodded to Peter as they passed. Clearly, he was in a position of authority to them, but the glances didn't meet his eyes. She assumed the acknowledgement of Peter was out of duty and respect for or perhaps just fear of the Master and not for Peter himself. Nonetheless, they would serve the Master and not allow her to leave. Fighting was futile.

"Speaking of 'scraps,' I thought you might be getting hungry, so I've arranged for you to have some food and water."

"Why would you or the Master feed me when you're planning to kill me soon anyway?"

"The Master may wish to kill you, but I do not. In fact, I think we could make a great team."

"A team?" That wasn't going to happen.

"Yes, a team. You don't need to die, Beth. There is nothing you can do now about Luciano, but you can still have the rest of your life. It's not like Luciano has never killed."

Her heart tightened at the sound of Luc's name.

"Yes, but out of necessity, not for pleasure."

"But why shouldn't they? The vampires are superior beings, Beth. No one gets mad at lions and tigers for eating deer and zebra. Just like deer and zebra, humans are the vampire's food source."

"So, what are you? The Master's favorite zebra? What happens when he gets hungry and there's no one else around?"

His jaw stiffened. "I could say the same of you, Beth."

With that Peter stopped at a silver metal doorway, one of many identical doorways along the hall they had been walking through. He opened the door and, with a flourish of his hand, said, "After you."

Beth thought that even if she couldn't fight or run, she could at least let Luc know she was here if he was close enough to hear her.

"Luc, I'm here!" she screamed as Peter slammed the door in her face.

"Enjoy your last supper," Peter said through clenched teeth.

CHAPTER 69

LUCIANO

LUCIANO NO LONGER HAD a sense of time. He didn't know how long he'd been in the cell. He was certain it had been days since he'd heard Beth call out to him, or at least he thought he had heard her. He was so consumed by his thirst he was no longer certain if it had been real. He prayed not. He tried to imagine that she had eluded the Master, that she had run instead of coming here to try and save him.

He wondered how long it'd be before all reason left him and the monster inside him took over completely. He could feel the drain of the daylight hours, and with that and the thirst combined, he could scarcely move his limbs.

He heard the footsteps of several people approaching his cell before the small window to his prison again slid open.

"Luciano, doing well I see." It was the Master, the last voice Luciano wished to hear. But even in his pain he felt rage building.

"Your young Doctor Ramsey, completely predictable, came to bargain for your release. Of course, you and I both know that was never really an option. But dangling that little carrot brought her right in."

Luciano's hands clenched into fists, nails digging in and drawing blood from his palms.

The Master chuckled. "Don't worry, we'll be reuniting the two of you shortly. I thought since you had your last night together in the train car you would enjoy meeting her there. I am quite curious to see how long you make it before you feed on her."

Luc tried to raise himself, but his strength failed and he fell back onto the cot.

"It seems she is as fond of you as you clearly are of her. Pity. Women who fall in love with you don't seem to live very long," he said, a smug grin across his lips.

He turned to what must be his men behind him. "Take him."

CHAPTER 70

BETH

BETH HAD BEEN IN the small silver-walled room for three days. She had lain on the small cot and tried to sleep, but every time she closed her eyes and drifted off, she saw Luc. He would reach toward her to take her hand and burst into flames.

She had finally given up. She had seen no one since Peter had left her the day she arrived. She drank water from the sink to stay hydrated but was beginning to get a little shaky from the lack of food.

Beth used her nervous fingers to coax her hair back into a ponytail. There was no mirror in the small cell, so she couldn't check to see how straight it was. The fact that she even thought about checking it now seemed absurd. She went to the sink, turned on the faucet and drank from her cupped palm. She splashed some water on her face and hoped that would help her stay focused.

There was a knock at the door and then the sound of keys in the lock. Beth's heart jumped. Perhaps this was it. They had come for her. It was time to die and no one would ever care what her hair looked like.

When the door swung open, her heart sank. She recognized the man at the door as one who had come to pick her up from her house what now seemed so long ago. His muscles had muscles, and he was large enough to fill the entire opening. She knew there was no use fighting. He had a hood in his hand. She looked from it back to him.

"Where are you taking me?"

"It's a surprise," he said. His eyes looked Beth over from her toes back to her eyes. "Shame."

It made Beth's skin crawl, but she was determined not to show him he'd rattled her.

He placed the hood over her head and grabbed her arm roughly to lead her out the door.

Chapter 71

Luciano

"Luc, are you alright? Luc?" Beth asked.

The Master's men pushed Beth through the door of the boxcar much as they had done with him only a few hours before. Luc smelled her blood and heard her rapidly beating heart begin to slow slightly when she saw him. For a moment he could barely think, struggling against the raw need of his thirst, holding his breath to avoid the scent. He trembled from the effort, balling his fists and squeezing them with all his might as he slumped against the wall of the boxcar. At first, he could only focus on controlling his thirst, and it took some time before her words sunk in. But he would need to draw in breath to speak and that meant more of the tempting scent of her blood, so he remained silent.

He was vaguely aware of her searching the boxcar with her eyes, looking for anything that could help them. He saw her eyes linger on the camera the Master's men had mounted in one of the upper corners. He knew she would realize as he had that the Master was watching.

As he became marginally more tolerant of her scent, his mind flashed back to their time together in the boxcar. He remembered watching her face as she slept, longing to hold her and the joy of their first kiss. But with the memory of their kiss also came the memory of her warm lips on his, her body pressed tightly to him, and the memory of her scent, just as arousing to him as her kiss. Immersed in the memory, he didn't register Beth's approach until he felt her hand on his shoulder.

"Don't touch me!" Luc yelled and jerked away.

"Luc, it's okay."

"No, no it is n-not...o-kay. I haven't fed in... days. Do you know... what... what that means?" He didn't wait for her response. "Soon I will lose control and... and kill you... just like I killed my wife... my wife." His voice was near a whisper, shaky and on the verge of incoherent as he struggled to maintain his thin grasp on control.

"But you won't, Luc. I *know* you won't. I trust you," Beth soothed.

Luc tried to convince himself. He tried to believe she was right and that his love for her would keep him from harming her, but he had killed before in a moment of blinding hunger. At some point he believed it would no longer be a matter of will.

BETH

Hours had passed in silence. The sunlight had faded and then vanished altogether from the space between the door panels. Beth had considered their options and needed to talk to Luc. She had given him space while thinking through their situation and now dared draw close to him.

He sat with his arms tightly clasped around his shins, rocking.

"Luc, you have to listen to me," Beth said as she approached with her back to the camera. The Master could not know her plan.

Luc shuddered in response to her drawing near but didn't speak.

"Luc, the way I see it, this can end in one of only three ways. First, you wait to feed on me, you lose control and take my life, and then have to live with the consequences." The wince on his face in response was clear. "Second, you resist until you are so weak that you can't even feed to save yourself, let alone save the two of us, and we both die here together. And let me say, I have no intention of starving to death here in this boxcar, never to be found. Third, you feed on me but stop before I'm dead. It will give you the strength to break through the door and free us both. Then you can feed me your blood to turn me before my heart stops beating." With this she sat silently, waiting for his response, each second seemingly drawn out into minutes.

"I can't, Beth," Luc whispered, every word labored and spoken with painful slowness. "I am so drained, I'll need nearly every drop to regain enough strength to break free. And once I start feeding on you... if I feed on you... I won't be able to stop. It will be like my wife all over again. I will kill you. I would rather us both die here than to bear that pain again."

"But you won't kill me, Luc. That was a very long time ago. You have more control now. You can stop and turn me. I trust you, Luc. Don't you understand that? I trust you with my life." And she realized in that moment, she meant it. She would have laid down her life to save the lives of others without hesitating but, since her father, she had never trusted another in that way. She had never found someone else that she believed would give their life for hers, never trusted enough to let down her guard for them to see her true feelings, never trusted that another would not leave her or hurt her... until now.

"If I feed you my blood and you survive the change, you will lose everything. Surviving, we would be on the run forever. *Forever.* You may never discover your cure and be human again. You may never be able to practice medicine again."

Beth reached for Luc's shoulder, and this time he let her. "Some things are more important than science." These were words she never imagined she would say, but they were true. Luc was more important, and their love for one another was too.

With this, a slight smile crossed Beth's lips. She tried to tell him all the things she didn't have time to put into words with her eyes. And she made certain that they contained no fear.

LUCIANO

Luc had listened to Beth's words. He knew feeding on her and changing her was their only chance to survive, but the weight of the decision was immense. Luc knew that taking the life of another person he cared for so deeply was more than he could bear. If he took her blood and she didn't survive the change, or if he fed on her and couldn't stop before he had taken her life, he knew he would then take his own.

The hunger gnawed at him, and over the last hours he had battled every moment not to feed on Beth. Was he hearing her words now only because it would allow him to slake his thirst? Because it would take away the pain that wracked his body each time he inhaled the scent of her blood? Was he about to give in to this because he truly believed he could control the thirst and keep her alive to change her, or because he just couldn't take the agony of the hunger a moment more?

Luc had never created another vampire. What if he wasn't capable? Perhaps only those much older than he, like the Master, could complete such a task. What if there was something more than he and Beth had discovered that was required to make the change and avoid her death in the process? Beth was so full of life. She loved her career and thrived on science. Even if he was successful, this would very likely mean that she could never return to mainstream medicine. If they escaped, they would be hiding from the Master for the remainder of their existence. While she knew this, her concept of a lifetime was far shorter than that of a vampire. As the years passed, would Beth come to resent him for turning her?

As Beth said, their other choices meant certain death for her. And allowing her to die by doing nothing was also not something he could live with. As Beth had spoken, he remembered how she had cared for him, telling him about her life as he healed. It had touched him in ways he had no longer thought possible and awakened feelings in him that he had believed had died with his wife. He wasn't ready to let that go having only just found it.

He looked again into Beth's eyes. He saw love. He saw trust. And he saw hope. He wanted... no, he *needed* more time with her, whatever it looked like. No matter the pain, no matter the hunger, he would find a way to stop. He would find a way to save her.

Luc spoke nothing but stared back, calmer now, and gave a single, nearly indiscernible nod. With that, Beth laid her head on his shoulder.

Luc pulled her arm to his lips, her back to the camera, and fed.

The taste of her blood in his mouth was all-consuming. He was lost in it. The warmth filled his mouth and caught fire in his veins, sending shudders through his body. He drew deeply over and over, soaring in the pleasure that slaking his thirst provided and the sweet, sweet flavor of her. He felt his strength once again surging within him.

But he forced his eyes open and saw Beth's head resting on his shoulder. He slowly became aware of the rhythm of her heart as it slowed, becoming more erratic. He wanted more, he wanted every drop, but most of all, he wanted Beth.

Stop! he thought.

STOP! he screamed.

And with her heart still beating, he pulled her wrist from his lips.

MASTER

As the Master looked on from his monitor, Beth leaned in close to Luc. The smug smile was once again on his lips. She was foolish and tempting fate. He waited for Luc to lose control and feed.

His chin jutting forward, he looked down his nose at the monitor.

And moving so quickly the camera couldn't record the motion, the doors on the boxcar burst open, swinging wildly on their hinges. Luc leaped from the boxcar, Beth in his arms, and disappeared into the darkness.

CHAPTER 72

BETH

BETH TASTED THE BLOOD on her lips, cold and thick like syrup. She gulped at it, ravenous, nearly tearing through the bag that held it. She didn't pause to wipe the dark crimson rivulets that dripped down her chin. While the blood was cold on her lips, when it hit her tongue it turned to liquid fire, warming her from within. She felt the heat as it spread down her neck, to her chest and then out to her limbs. The sensation was exquisite, and she nearly moaned at the sheer pleasure of it.

Having drained the entire unit, she reached for a second and downed it nearly as quickly, oblivious to anything else around her. She closed her eyes, beginning to feel the hunger subside.

Beth barely paused from drinking until she had finished the fourth unit. It wasn't until then that she noticed the empty blood bags on the ground surrounded by bits of hay and dirt. She looked at her hands, slick and red with blood. She looked down further to see her blood-stained shirt. Then finally, she looked up at Luc, standing before her.

She had been so consumed with feeding that she hadn't even seen him until now.

A slow smile spread across Beth's blood-covered face. "It worked. We made it."

Luc nodded, his face moving from one emotion to the next, struggling to maintain his composure, tears threatening in his eyes. But he didn't speak. He held out his hand to help her up.

Beth felt the stickiness of the blood on her chin and used her shirt to wipe it away. She took Luc's hand and stood, marveling at the sensation of his touch. It was as though every nerve in her hand, and even some she had never had before, had awakened and fired at the same time. She could feel every crease in her skin and the bones and tendons beneath.

She reached for him, wrapping her arms around his neck and pulling him close. His body against hers was an overload of sensation, every cell rejoicing in the touch. She could hear her heart and his, now beating at the same fast pace. His scent engulfed her, but it was more than that. She could smell her blood within him, the field he had run through to get here, the boxcar where they had been. She didn't know how, but she could also smell that he was much older than she, almost as though each decade had left its own scent beneath his skin. And she could smell tears.

She pulled back to look up at him, and saw the tears glistening on his cheeks. She kissed each of them as they fell, tasting the salt, and then met his lips.

There was no longer a difference between them, and he held nothing back.

They kissed as though they had waited for lifetimes and would never have the chance again. She opened her mouth to his tongue and wound her fingers into his hair. She felt his hand cup her backside and press her even more tightly against him. She ran her hands over his shoulders and down his back, feeling the twitch of every muscle fiber her fingers passed over. At his waist, she lifted his shirt and ran her hands up his back. While the sensation through his shirt had been exquisite, skin-on-skin was like fireworks igniting her fingertips with each stroke.

A small gasp escaped her, and she had an overwhelming urge to bite him, feeling her fangs elongate.

Momentarily shaken by the urge, she broke off the kiss and ran her tongue over the tips of her fangs, eyes wide, looking up into Luc's face. His eyes were heavy with desire, but as he watched her, a slow smile spread across his lips, revealing his fangs as well.

"Now I get it," Beth said, eyes wide. A shy smile spreading across her face, she understood fully now that Luc's fangs the first time they had kissed had revealed his physical desire for her far more than any intent to feed on her. "This is going to take a little getting used to."

Luc chuckled, pulling her into another embrace, nestling his chin against the top of her head, her head tucked against his chest.

Beth could feel the sun had set and the night calling to her, full of promise. Forever, Luciano had said. And forever meant time for everything.

Even if anyone had been watching, the two figures moved hand-in-hand through the darkness and to the back of the cabin at the lake too fast for human eyes to see. The lock was carded in record time and the door swung open.

"I'll only be a second," Beth said and ducked inside. She went directly to the bathroom. No need for lights now; her night vision was perfect. She upended the trash can and, with a smile, stuck the small flash drive taped there into the pocket of her favorite jeans. In a second, she was with Luc again, intertwining her fingers in his.

"Where would you like to go?"

"Well, I've always wanted to visit New Orleans. And now that I'm a vampire, I can't think of anywhere that would seem easier to blend in, except maybe Las Vegas."

Luc laughed and smiled down at her. "Then New Orleans it is. Should we call a car?" he said, teasing, knowing what her answer would be.

Beth considered it for only a moment and then, almost giggling with excitement as she thought about her new abilities, said, "No, let's run!"

EPILOGUE

THE FOLLOWING FRIDAY MORNING, at 9 a.m. sharp, eight identical packages were delivered to eight scientists in three countries; a package each to two scientists in Chicago; New Orleans; Rome, Italy; and Victoria, Australia. In each location, one virologist and one geneticist. The letters they received were identical save for the location of the tissue banks. The first read:

May 4th, 2023

Dear Dr. Giffard:

My name is Dr. Elizabeth Ramsey. I am a forensic pathologist and until just recently, worked with Heartland Forensic Specialists in Kansas City, KS. We have not met, but I have studied your work. I am enclosing a record of my recent observations on a most unusual patient. I have discovered that his DNA has been modified through the use of a novel retrovirus causing numerous chromosomal alterations. Some of the alterations have resulted in unique abilities such as increased strength and rapid healing, as well as negative side effects such as extreme sensitivity to UV light. I have sent this same information to seven additional virologists and geneticists.

I must tell you that if you are receiving this information, I am likely dead for knowing what I now share with you. Those who would have kept the information silent are powerful and resourceful. Study this material and make your own decision about whether or not to proceed. Should you choose to pursue it, I have stored tissue and blood samples in your name at Precision Biological Services (see attached account information).

I believed, and still do, that the knowledge to be gained is worth the risk.

Sincerely,

Elizabeth Ramsey, MD

Acknowledgements

Special thanks to my immediate family, Kyle, Orion, Zoey and Max, who always believed I could write this book and to Kyle for agreeing to invest in me to make it happen.

Thanks to my good friends, Holly, Jackie, Trish and Mike, who not only encouraged me but also were beta readers and offered invaluable advice on how to make this book better.

A heartfelt thank you to my friend Lori, who may never read my book because it is scary, but who never ceased to build me up and cheer me on.

Thank you to all of the SelfPublishing.com team for guiding me along my writing journey, especially my SPS coach Ramy Vance for the excellent advice and encouragement to move forward. To my editors, Zac Tighe of Copysmyths (developmental editing—www.copysmyths.com), and the team at Motif Edits (line and proofreading—www.motifedits.com), thank you for helping me take my writing up a notch to be all it could be.

selfpublishing.com

Now It's Your Turn
Discover the EXACT 3-step blueprint you need to
become a bestselling author in as little as 3 months.

Self-Publishing School helped me, and now I want them to help
you with this Free resource to begin outlining your book!
Even if you're busy, bad at writing, or don't know where to start,
you CAN write a bestseller and build your best life.
With tools and experience across a variety of niches and professions,
Self-Publishing School is the <u>only</u> resource you need to
take your book to the finish line!
DON'T WAIT
Say "YES" to becoming a bestseller:
https://self-publishingschool.com/friend/
Follow the steps on the page to get a FREE resource to get started on
your book and unlock a discount to get started with Self-Publishing
School

About the Author

Hello! And welcome to my world. Bring your imagination and pull up a chair.

During the daylight hours I am a doctor, a pathologist to be specific, who enjoys looking at what makes all living things tick from the inside out. I grew up in Kansas next door to Toto and Dorothy, where I raised 3 children (all human) with my high school sweetheart. I have recently retired from 20-plus years of mainstream medicine, to explore what my imagination believes it could be.

When night falls and the moon rises, I can't help but imagine and write about the science that would make what others believe to be mythical, well...real. Just because current science can't explain them doesn't mean they can't exist.

So, look below the surface with me, indulge my inner mad scientist, and let's have a little fun.

I hope we have the chance to chat soon.

Email: tammy@friendswithmonsters.com

Facebook

Newsletter

CAN YOU HELP?

Did you know? Reader reviews are very important to an indie author's success? They validate our work and help others find our stories. If you enjoyed Vampyre Hypothesis, please leave a review filled with stars at the link below.

http://www.amazon.com/review/create-review?&asin=B0D4W1SDVK

Thanks so much!

Tammy Battaglia

www.ingramcontent.com/pod-product-compliance
Lightning Source LLC
Chambersburg PA
CBHW030353130626
46549CB00004B/1479